Play today in the primary school playground

Play today in the primary school playground
Life, learning and creativity

edited by
Julia C. Bishop and Mavis Curtis

with a Foreword by Iona Opie

Open University Press
Buckingham · Philadelphia

Open University Press
Celtic Court
22 Ballmoor
Buckingham
MK18 1XW

email: enquiries@openup.co.uk
world wide web: www.openup.co.uk

and
325 Chestnut Street
Philadelphia, PA 19106, USA

First Published 2001

A catalogue record of this book is available from the British Library

ISBN   0 335 20715 4 (pb)   0 335 20716 2 (hb)

Library of Congress Cataloging-in-Publication Data
Play today in the primary school playground : life, learning, and creativity /
edited by Julia C. Bishop and Mavis Curtis.
     p.   cm.
   Includes bibliographical references and index.
   ISBN 0-335-20716-2 – ISBN 0-335-20715-4 (pbk.)
   1. Play–Great Britain–History.   2. Games–Great Britain–History.
   3. Recesses–Social aspects–Great Britain.   4. Playgrounds–Social aspects–Great
Britain.   5. Children–Great Britain–Folklore.   I. Bishop, Julia C., 1960–
II. Curtis, Mavis, 1936–
   GV1200 P42   2001
   306.4'81–dc21   00-044120

Typeset by Graphicraft Limited, Hong Kong
Printed in Great Britain by Biddles Ltd, Guildford and King's Lynn

Contents

List of contributors

Andy Arleo is a senior lecturer of English at the Institut Universitaire de Technologie de Saint-Nazaire, Université de Nantes, and a member of the research laboratory Langues et Civilisations à Tradition Orale, Centre National de Recherche Scientifique, in Paris. His research interests include children's folklore, the relationship between music and language, and the use of music and song in foreign language teaching. He has published many articles on these subjects in folklore and linguistics journals, and has also co-authored a book on European children's songs, *Chants enfantins d'Europe* (Editions L'Harmattan, 1997). He is a former president of the Association des Professeurs de Langues des Instituts Universitaires de Technologie.

Marc Armitage is an independent children's play consultant with the play education and research partnership, Playpeople. His background is that of a practising playworker and teacher in children's play and childhood. His specialist areas of work are play within the school environment, and participation and involvement of children in research and development work. He is currently researching the relationship between public playgrounds and children's use of space in the UK and Sweden, and also the role of fear and 'spooky characters' in children's pretend play on school playgrounds around the world.

Julia C. Bishop gained her PhD in folklore from the Memorial University of Newfoundland, Canada, in 1992, specializing in traditional song. She has published articles on folksong, folklore fieldwork and the use of folklore in education, and was the editor of *Folk Music Journal* from 1993 to 1995. She currently teaches at the University of Sheffield, UK, and is conducting research into the James M. Carpenter Collection of folksong and folk drama.

Carole H. Carpenter is a professor in the Division of Humanities at York University in Toronto, Canada, where she teaches children's literature and culture, childhood culture studies and Canadian studies. A folklorist (PhD, University of Pennsylvania, 1975), she has done considerable research on identity, folklore and multiculturalism in Canada as well as on Canadian children's culture. She has published extensively, including three major resources in Canadian folklore studies. Currently she is involved in a comparative study of the role of children's literature (and specifically folklore therein) in reconstructing identity after the adoption of multicultural policies in Canada, Australia and South Africa.

Mavis Curtis has worked for many years with both adults and children in education and social services. She gained her PhD in 1998 with a study of children's oral tradition. She has published articles on children's play and is currently researching into the relationship between oral tradition and change in a school's physical environment.

Dr June Factor, a senior research fellow at the Australian Centre, University of Melbourne, is a writer and folklorist. Among her many publications is a series of popular books of playground lore for children, beginning with *Far Out Brussel Sprout!*, first published by Oxford University Press in 1983. She was awarded the Opie Prize for her social and cultural history, *Captain Cook Chased a Chook: Children's Folklore in Australia* (Penguin, 1988). Her latest book, *Kidspeak: A Dictionary of Australian Children's Words, Expressions and Games*, was published by Melbourne University Press in November 2000.

Elizabeth Grugeon is a senior lecturer in English in Primary Education in the School of Education, De Montfort University, Bedford, where she teaches undergraduate courses in curriculum English, children's literature and language. She has co-authored *Teaching, Speaking and Listening in the Primary School* (David Fulton Publishers, 1998) and *The Art of Storytelling for Teachers and Pupils* (David Fulton Publishers, 2000). She continues to look at and write about how children's language experience out of the classroom contributes to their developing literacy and learning.

Simon Lichman is the director of the Centre for Creativity in Education and Cultural Heritage, Jerusalem, Israel. He has a PhD in folklore and has worked in the fields of folklore and education for 24 years, in England, the USA and Israel. He teaches courses in the use of folklore in multi-cultural education and coexistence work in teacher training and enrichment programmes. He has published articles on folklore, ethnography and multicultural education.

Dr Kathryn Marsh is a lecturer in music education at the Sydney Conservatorium of Music, University of Sydney, Australia, where she teaches subjects relating to primary school music, multicultural music education and research methodology. She has had many years' experience as a primary school teacher, teacher inservice trainer and state consultant for music and multicultural education. She has written many publications both for teachers and for scholarly journals.

J.D.A. Widdowson is Professor of English Language and Cultural Tradition at the University of Sheffield, where he is also Director of the National Centre for English Cultural Tradition (NATCECT). His many publications include *Learning about Linguistics* (Hutchinson, 1974), *If You Don't Be Good: Verbal Social Control in Newfoundland* (Memorial University of Newfoundland, 1977), *Dictionary of Newfoundland English* (University of Toronto Press, 1982), *Folktales of Newfoundland* (Garland, 1996) and *Lexical Erosion in English Regional Dialects* (University of Sheffield, 1999). He is currently preparing an edition of *Everybody Gather Round*, the N.G.N. Kelsey Collection of London children's games and rhymes.

Foreword

Iona Opie

When, in 1951, my husband Peter and I had finished *The Oxford Dictionary of Nursery Rhymes*, we began our quest for schoolchildren's lore. We ourselves were poorly educated in the traditions of the schoolyard, having been to private schools, though this had the advantage that most traditional childlore was new to us, and vitally interesting. As it was generally assumed at the time that such lore was on the wane, the purpose of our first survey was to find out how much of it still existed, if any, and whether it varied from place to place, either in quantity or in local association. We began by writing to *The Sunday Times*, in November 1951, saying what we wanted to do, and asking for help in doing it. It seemed there was already a lot of interest, especially among schoolteachers. We had 151 offers of help from teachers who were willing to get information from their own schools, and to get in touch with friends who were teaching in other parts of the country. Our aim was to obtain material from places as evenly distributed as possible throughout Britain, and from the children who were most in possession of the lore – that is, the age range between 7 and 11, with the emphasis on the 8- and 9-year-olds. We knew it was important to enquire from as many children and in as many schools as possible. In one school very little lore may be found; in another, only a few miles away, the tradition is rich and vibrant. It depends on the school itself, the geography of the playground and the restrictions put upon play. Small country schools, with rural playgrounds that may include a hazel copse and a stream, foster ancient imaginative games of bandits and mothers-and-fathers. Large city schools, with barrack-like buildings and crowded asphalt playgrounds, are nevertheless seething with traditional lore. The children live in a social pressure-pot. The constant change of population brings a constant influx of new games, witticisms, stories and jokes. The only full version of the evocative old singing game 'Here Comes a Jew, a Jew from Spain' that I found was in the depths of Salford in 1975.

These valiant teachers became personal friends, although we met few of them face to face. They set the children writing about the games, rhymes, legislation and language of their own out-of-school lives and, although this was done mostly during English lessons, we emphasized that spelling and punctuation did not matter. The approach was as informal as possible. If we could not understand exactly how a game was played, we wrote to the child who had described it and asked for more details. They were always most obliging. Indeed, it is flattering to be the one dispensing knowledge, rather than the other way about. Soon we were being asked for guidelines on the sort of material we needed, for children's memories need to be jogged as much as adults' do. We kept the questions as open-ended as possible. They might be 'any game played with a ball', or 'any names for people you don't like', or 'any game involving running to a certain place'. It is restricting to ask children if they play Hide and Seek when the local name may be Block, or to ask Scottish children about Hopscotch when in Scotland the game is called Peever. In our later surveys, the suggested topics were often as wide as 'What do you think is the most stupid game you have ever played?', which produced some marvellously splenetic replies.

The 1950s survey yielded more material than we could have dreamed of. Instead of one book, we saw that we would need to write several. After *The Lore and Language of Schoolchildren* came out to unexpected acclaim in 1959, we ran another survey, chiefly asking for games; and after *Children's Games in Street and Playground* was published in 1969, a third survey was needed to acquire updated material for the next volume, *The Singing Game* (1985). The skipping games and other games using equipment, such as balls, fivestones, and Marbles, had to be left for a further volume because there were so many of them, and that volume appeared as *Children's Games with Things* in 1997. (The original schoolchildren's contributions are now in the Bodleian Library, Oxford, along with the other Opie files and papers. The recordings I made in the school playgrounds and on housing estates during the 1970s are now in the British Library National Sound Archive, London.) We were, over the years, in direct touch with 20,000 of the children who were currently using this lore; yet, in spite of all the questioning and interviewing, I doubt we found out everything there was to know. Our main informants were 8- to 10-year-olds in British state schools, but in 1960, our midway date, there were 2,002,000 schoolchildren in that age group. We found out, perhaps, what was most common and most typical, but we also found some exciting rarities, such as Knifie (Mumble-the-Peg) in the Isle of Lewis, and the old hide-and-seek game of Smuggle the Geg, known as Hunt the Keg in St Andrews and Smooglie Gigglie in Golspie.

As we gathered this considerable mass of material we began to appreciate its wider implications. Children are but younger adults. Their behaviour is fundamental human behaviour, not yet obscured by a veneer of civilization. Behind the verbal traditions of the playground can be heard age-old prejudices, beliefs, hates, resentments and ambitions. Amidst the bustle and noise of the playground can be seen remarkable skills of organization, quick agreements and decisions, and instant adaptability. The basic games demonstrate pleasures of strategy and movement that probably predate language itself. We can begin to understand what constitutes fun, what humour is thought cleverest, what noises are most satisfactory to make, what prowess is admired. Simply by examining which songs and rhymes are the most popular, we can see that the mental attitude found most useful when making one's way in an uncaring world is insouciant, defiant, offhand, pretending not to care. The important thing in a playground or other gathering is to protect one's ego.

The charm of the lore is that it is voluntary. Children are not made to recite 'I Went to a Chinese Restaurant', they choose to do so. It is easy to guess why the choice is made. There is still a lingering feeling, among British schoolchildren anyway, that anything Chinese, being unfamiliar, is funny. Wrapping a loaf of bread in a five-pound note is nicely comic. The nonsense rigmarole that the Chinese people say in the rhyme ('My name is Alli alli, Chickerlye, chickerlye, Om pom poodle, Walla walla whiskers, Chinese chopsticks, Indian chief says "How!"') is an achievement to learn, and a triumph to recite, especially when performing a complicated clapping routine at the same time. An enterprising child can become famous by introducing a new ending – instead of 'Indian chief says "How!"', for instance, they might say 'Indian chief – corn beef, "How!"'. One of the aims of collecting school lore is to assemble enough data to see into the minds of the children of a particular era, their preferences and the reasons for those preferences. The reasons may be as much to do with the sound of a verse as with its subject matter. The undefinable appeal of sounds, even if the sense is not evident, is also the reason that the old singing games, shaped by time, are so beloved of poets and readers of poetry. When *The Singing Game* came out, I was not surprised to hear that it was being bought by connoisseurs of surrealist poetry.

The historical aspect of children's lore is, to my mind, vital. The history of a game like 'Thread the Needle' can be followed down through centuries. We know its twentieth-century manifestations, but what then? The structure of a game changes over the years to suit the social climate. Nubile maidens played ring or line singing games in the fifteenth century as part of the process of wooing a young man; in the twentieth century, younger girls played those games for their entertainment value, especially when, as in 'The Dukes a-Riding', they were given a chance to be rude about their friends. The words, too, change over time; it is a long evolutionary process, which incidentally obviates many of the so-called 'historical origins'. 'Here We Go Round the Mulberry Bush' was, in its first wording, 'Nettles Grow on an Angry Bush' (and what *that* is a corruption of, I cannot imagine). It is for people with patience and the spirit of enquiry and, yes, love, to notice and make a note of what children have chosen to preserve from the past. A local postman wrote to me not long ago to thank me for a copy of *The Lore and Language of Schoolchildren*, recently out of print. He said, 'I already know its companion works, so rich in children's exemplary inspirations, which are yet a truly still-living, shared tradition. And of course, so enjoyable. Only this morning, on my round, I saw some children singing "The Spanish Lady", and how it has stayed with me since!'

Neither should we ignore the ephemeral amusements, and the crazes that come and go within weeks or months. Opportunists, children exploit their environment. In bright sunlight they masquerade with their own shadows, and burn holes in their clothes with the aid of magnifying glasses. In rain, they experiment with the possibilities of puddles. Sticks, stones, holes and pavements inspire fleeting games which may last only minutes. Crazes are easier to notice. I remember especially the fluff-gathering craze of the early 1960s, when children pulled wisps of wool off each others' jerseys, trying to make the largest ball, and the 'Spons', triangular creatures of unknown origin or meaning, home-made from scraps of cloth, which invaded the schools later in the decade.

The most compelling reason for recording children's lore, for me, was to leave a picture, for future generations, of how the children of today amuse themselves in their own free time. This certainly was in my mind when, from January 1970 to November 1983, I made a weekly visit to the playground of Liss Junior School, Hampshire, observing the social scene and the interactions between the children, listening to their opinions of each other, describing what they were doing and writing down their jokes and stories. I wished there had been a similar account of life in a British playground during the 1870s. Quite apart from the sensation of being there, I would so much have liked to compare the past with the present. William Hone was of a like mind. Chronicling Shrovetide games in *The Every-Day Book* for 15 February 1825, he says:

> this information may seem trifling to some, but it will interest many. We all look back with complacency on the amusements of our childhood; and 'some future [Joseph] *Strutt*' a century or so hence, may find this page, and glean from it the important difference between the sports of boys now, and those of our grandchildren's great grandchildren.

The authors of the chapters in this book, based on papers originally presented at the immensely successful and enjoyable conference entitled 'The State of Play: Perspectives on Children's Oral Culture', at the University of Sheffield, Easter 1998, are all expert observers, recorders and interpreters of contemporary children's play. They provide a worldwide view of the lore, in many different facets. Needless to say, they, and the other speakers at the conference, all discounted that long-lived and lusty meme, nowadays fuelled by newspaper articles in the tabloid press, 'children don't play their own games any more' (or even, 'children don't know how to play any more'). It is truly a privilege to have been asked to write the foreword to this book.

Iona Opie

Acknowledgements

We gratefully acknowledge the financial support of the British Academy in connection with the conference from which the chapters in this book derive. The National Centre for English Cultural Tradition, University of Sheffield, and the Folklore Society also played an important role in supporting the conference and contributing to its organization. The publication of this book could not, of course, have taken place without the cooperation and hard work of all the contributors and we thank them for their patience while the volume was in preparation. Facilities for the editing work were generously provided courtesy of the director and staff at the National Centre for English Cultural Tradition. Our colleagues and friends helped with various editorial tasks, particularly Michael Heaney, Steve Roud, Tecwyn Vaughan Jones and members of the 'State of Play' discussion list. For helpful suggestions and comments on the draft of parts of the book, we are grateful to Philip Hiscock and the readers of the original proposal. Finally, we would like to express our gratitude to our families for their support, discussion and tolerance while we were busy working on the book.

Photographic acknowledgements

Chapter 2: all photographs © Marc Armitage
Chapter 4: photograph © Kathryn Marsh
Chapter 8: Figure 8.1 © Simon Lichman;
Figures 8.2–8.6 © Rivanna Miller
Cover: all photographs © Mavis Curtis

Introduction

Julia C. Bishop and Mavis Curtis

The decline of play in today's world?

In Britain, the popular perceptions that 'children don't know how to play any more' and that 'the traditional games are disappearing' seem never to have been so widespread as in the early twenty-first century. Writing in 1980, Alasdair Roberts (1980: xi) declared that the main purpose of his book, *Out to Play*, was 'to remove children's games from the realm of nostalgia and demonstrate that they are as lively and varied now as they ever were'. Iona Opie discusses the spate of press coverage in the early 1990s given to British teachers' fears that ' "children appeared to have lost the art of playing games", claiming that they simply sat around bored, or played solitary games on their computers' (Opie and Opie 1997: 9). The research of Peter Blatchford in England supports the notion that these perceptions are widespread among school staff. His interviews with teachers and headteachers in primary schools in south-east England in 1987–8 reveal widespread concerns about children's school playground behaviour, including aggression, desultory behaviour, the decline of traditional games, the marginalization of girls and the likelihood of problems arising during the long lunchtime break rather than morning or afternoon playtimes (Blatchford 1989: 9–30).

Parallels to these views are found in other parts of the western world. Ruth Brinton's research into play traditions in southern France quotes the views of adults, including a primary school headteacher, that, in the words of one, 'Aujourd'hui les enfants ne jouent plus; ils ne savent que se battre' ('Nowadays children do not play any more; they only know how to fight') (Rodriguez 1980: 44, quoted in Brinton 1985: 1).[1] As several contributors to this book note (see Chapters 1, 2 and 9), such views are also prevalent in North America and Australia.

As folklorists and others have been at pains to point out, these concerns are not new and in their tenacity have acquired the status of traditional beliefs in themselves (Opie and Opie 1969: 14). Iona and Peter Opie, for example, document examples stretching back at least 350 years (1997: 8; cf. Parry-Jones 1964: 240; Brinton 1985: 1–2). The reasons often cited today for the decline of play are also remarkably similar to those of the past. In the nineteenth century, commentators blamed national schools and the coming of the railway; in the twentieth century, first cinema, radio and gramophone, and now comics, television and video games, are the common scapegoats.[2]

The background to the book

It was against the backdrop of these concerns that the editors of the present volume convened an international conference entitled 'The State of Play: Perspectives on Children's Oral Culture' in 1998, hosted at the University of Sheffield by the National Centre for English Cultural Tradition, in association with the Folklore Society. Since, at this time, it was also the centenary of the publication of Alice Bertha Gomme's groundbreaking children's folklore collection, *The Traditional Games of England, Scotland, and Ireland* ([1894, 1898] 1984), and 40 years since Iona and Peter Opies' seminal publication, *The Lore and Language of Schoolchildren* (1959), it was an opportune moment to review the present state of children's oral culture, especially as it related to current concerns about children's play.

Play Today in the Primary School Playground contains a selection of the papers presented at the conference, now in revised form and with one subsequently written contribution. The research described dates almost entirely from the 1980s and 1990s and so corresponds to this period of particularly intense concern regarding the decline of children's play traditions. Yet, the picture of children's free play activities which emerges is predominantly one of vibrancy, creativity, continuity and variety, not one of decline. For this reason, it seemed important to make the authors' findings available to a wider audience, including not only academic colleagues interested in children's play, but adults such as teachers and playground supervisors directly concerned with it on a day-to-day basis. The focus is on 'middle childhood', the period between early childhood and adolescence (Stone and Church 1957; Roberts 1980), with much of the research centring on traditions in the primary school playground. In general, the approach is more descriptive than prescriptive, but the authors' findings challenge us by implication to examine our adult assumptions about children's contemporary play activities, and the effect of our personal experience on our perceptions of them. They urge us to take a longer, closer look at the reality and the complexities of what happens on today's primary school playground and other places where children play together. The overriding message is that we should be reserving judgement on much of what children choose to do while playing together, allowing children the space, in physical, temporal and psychological terms, to take responsibility for their play. This is, after all, an area of their lives in which they are truly the experts and it is only from them that we can gain an informed understanding of what constitutes 'play for today' and how adults might best support it.

The authors of the chapters in this book come from a variety of backgrounds, including folklore studies, playwork, ethnomusicology and education. Since each mentions to some degree the work of folklorists in the study of children's play, this introduction will introduce some of the relevant folklore scholarship in this area and briefly elucidate the terminology, concepts and methods employed in contemporary children's folklore research. It is necessary to do this since such research seems to be largely absent from the current debate about the supposed decline of children's play. In Britain especially, folklore studies has struggled to establish itself as an academic discipline in higher education institutions, despite acceptance and expansion in many other countries (Widdowson 1987), and academically trained scholars struggle to disentangle themselves and their work from popular misconceptions concerning what folklore is and how it is studied (cf. Smith 1981; Buckland 1993).

Having surveyed folklore studies and its contribution to the study of children's play, we will present a classification system of children's play traditions. The classification system demonstrates the breadth of play traditions and at the same time offers a preliminary framework by which adults can organize their observations of what, at first glance, appears to be a noisy mêlée of activities on the playground. We conclude the introduction with a look ahead to the concerns of the chapters within each section of the book.

The development of children's play research within folklore studies

The term *'folklore'* (initially hyphenated as *'folk-lore'*) was coined by William Thoms, writing under the pseudonym Ambrose Merton, in 1846. He glossed the new term 'the Lore of the People' and proposed that it be used to replace such designations as 'popular antiquities' and 'popular literature' (the precursors of what is known today as folklore studies). He did not define who 'the People' were that he had in mind (although see Nicolaisen 1995: 72, who argues convincingly that Thoms was thinking of a rural audience), but it is clear that childhood traditions formed part of the definition from the start, since the principal example given by Thoms is that of a children's custom in Yorkshire. In this custom the children were formerly (and may be still) accustomed to sing round a cherry-tree the following invocation:–

Cuckoo, cherry-tree,
Come down and tell me
How many years I have to live.

Each child then shook the tree, – and the number of cherries which fell betokened the years of its future life.

(Quoted in Dundes 1965: 6)

Dictionary definitions of the term '*lore*' give 'a body of traditions and knowledge on a subject', or 'accumulated wisdom, learning', but Thoms is content to exemplify his usage with a list, including 'manners, customs, observances, superstitions, ballads, proverbs, etc., of the olden time' (quoted in Dundes 1965: 5). The emphasis is clearly on cultural products – forms of behaviour, such as observances, and genres, such as ballads – especially in the areas of traditional custom and belief, and traditional language and song.

Just over 30 years after Thoms' proposal, in 1878, the Folklore Society was formed. Among its founders was Lady Alice Bertha Gomme, wife of George Laurence Gomme, an influential folklorist of the time and president of the Society in the years 1890–4 (see Dorson 1968: 220–9). Alice Gomme's monumental publication, *The Traditional Games of England, Scotland, and Ireland*, published in two volumes in 1894 and 1898 respectively (Gomme [1894, 1898] 1984), was intended as the first part of a dictionary of British folklore, planned, but never completed, by her husband. It contains detailed descriptions of around 800 games and their variants, based on data from 76 correspondents and relating to 112 locations (Boyes 1990: 199). Although sometimes criticized for relying too much on the memories of adult middle class correspondents, the book does draw to some extent on the observation and testimony of children themselves, including working class children, as Boyes has pointed out (1990: 202). The Gommes were strong proponents of the latest theoretical approach of the time, based on the theory of unilinear cultural evolution and the idea that many contemporary manifestations of folklore could be interpreted as relics of adults' customs and beliefs from former times. The games of Victorian children could therefore, they believed, shed light on the way of life of our ancestors. Thus, Alice Gomme traced a link between children's games of chance and skill and ancient harvest and funeral rites, for example. Although now superseded as a theoretical approach, the value of Alice Gomme's game descriptions remains, focusing attention, as they do, on the game traditions of girls, as distinct from those of boys, for the first time. Indeed, Gomme's work did much to establish the study of children's folklore as a valid field of investigation in its own right, especially the 'singing game', a term which Gomme herself established in the discipline (Opie and Opie 1985: 23; cf. Gomme 1894).

Elsewhere, folklorists and others were pioneering the study of children's oral traditions in their own countries, notably William Wells Newell, who published *Games and Songs of American Children* ([1883] 1963), and Henry C. Bolton (1888) in America, and Franz Magnus Böhme in Germany (1897). Such pioneering publications were a major impetus to further collecting in the twentieth century. In Wales, for example, William George initiated a competition at the National Eisteddfod in 1911 'to do for Wales what the Alice Gomme collection has done for England' (Jones 1986),[3] while Maclagan considered his *Games & Diversions of Argyleshire* (1901: vi) an appendix to Gomme's *Traditional Games*. These were followed, in the English-speaking world, by the work of researchers such as Halpert (1946), Brewster (1952, 1953), Mary and Herbert Knapp (1976), and Jones and Hawes (1987) in America; Howard in America and Australia (1938, 1965, 1971); Sutton-Smith in New Zealand (1981b); Fowke in Canada (1969, 1988); Norah and William Montgomerie (1985; see also Bennett 1998) and Ritchie (1964, 1965) in Scotland; James Carpenter (1972) and McCosh (1976) in Britain and America; and Douglas (1931) and the Opies in Britain (Opie and Opie 1959, 1969, 1985, 1997; Opie 1993).[4]

The focus of these collections has been cultural products – 'childlore' such as 'games, riddles, rhymes, jokes, pranks, superstitions, magical practices, wit, lyrics, guile, epithets, nicknames, torments, parody, oral legislation, seasonal customs, tortures, obscenities, codes, gang lore, etc.' (Sutton-Smith 1970: 1; cf. Halpert 1971 – see Chapter 7, p. 139). Such items were regarded as folkloric because they were passed on by word of mouth (oral transmission) and informal watching, listening and copying of others (customary example). These most basic means of human communication are so commonplace as to be often overlooked or unremarked by adults, especially in literate societies where the supremacy of the written and especially the printed word is taken for granted (cf. Finnegan 1992). Yet, as discussed by Widdowson in Chapter 7, it is through oral transmission and customary example, principally in the family situation, that very young children first learn language and socially acceptable behaviour. As children grow older and begin formal schooling, their informal interaction becomes more peer-group dominated, resulting in the transmission of traditions from one child to another (horizontal transmission).

Of major importance in the twentieth century was the transition from collecting the memories of adults about their childhood traditions to collecting directly from the observation and interviewing of children themselves. Establishing the interest and worthiness of children's own traditions – removed from the realm of adult recollection and possible nostalgia – and children's commentary on those traditions, was achieved in Britain by the work of Iona and Peter Opie, whose books have been widely read by the general public as well as teachers and academics. They too were members of the Folklore Society, Peter Opie being president during 1963–4 (see Simpson 1982), but they eschewed the 'survivals in culture' theory of the Gommes in favour of a survey of children's traditions with comparative and historical observations. What the Opies collected were the games, lore and language known by contemporary children. As they stated in *The Lore and Language of Schoolchildren* (1959), their collection from the 1950s and 1960s 'is made up of what will be the childhood recollections of the older generation after AD 2000' (p. 9). As a result of their in-depth research, which relied (as Iona Opie's Foreword to this book describes) principally on written correspondence with children, they were able, in *The Lore and Language of Schoolchildren* to propound a 'revolutionary new view of children's culture . . . that the rhymes children made for themselves were "more than playthings", their verses were vivid, constantly renewed art forms, which also functioned as vital social supports amid the jostling life of the school yard' (Boyes 1995: 131).

The recognition that these forms are specific to children as a group serves to underline an important development in the interpretation of the term 'folklore', a century or so after Thoms' coinage. Alan Dundes' formulation (1965: 2) that 'the term "folk" can refer *to any group of people whatsoever* who share at least one common factor' (original emphasis), such as 'a common occupation, language, or religion', sought to emphasize that 'everyone has folklore', not just the unlettered, uneducated, rural, elderly and marginalized, as some of our academic forebears believed. This idea has now become accepted as a central tenet of the discipline.[5] Nowhere is this more obvious than in childlore, since everyone has been a child, although their experience of childhood may vary widely. An important corollary of this shift has been the consideration of folklore as an expression of group identity (see, for example, Jansen 1965; Mechling 1986).

At the same time, there has been a reconceptualization of the term 'lore', especially among folklorists in North America, who recognized that the emphasis on cultural products, items or texts tended to abstract them from their social and cultural context. Drawing on anthropological theory, items of folklore began to be documented in relation to their broader social and cultural milieux, and in the context of their actual performance and use. Analysis stressed the relationships between the forms of folklore and their function, and between the individual and their folkloric repertoire (Bascom 1965; Pentikäinen 1976; cf. Van Peer 1988).

The challenge to the dominant concern with the verbal, behavioural and cognitive categories of cultural tradition, emanating from the discipline's strong leaning towards the humanities, was not complete, however. During the 1970s, and particularly under the influence of linguistic theory, a conception of folklore as a process of communication rather than a set of products or texts was introduced. This approach stressed that 'lore' was not just a form of knowledge but involved the active realization of that knowledge in a 'performance', be it of a traditional story, song, proverb or action. Thus, the performance of folklore emerged from the stream of everyday interaction and involved varying degrees of artistry and aesthetic judgement in order to be effective (Ben-Amos and Goldstein 1975; Bauman 1984). This involved the formulation of perhaps the most influential new definition of the term 'folklore' as 'artistic communication in small groups' (Ben-Amos 1971: 13). Such a definition thus moved away from concepts of folklore as rooted in time and emphasized folklore as a communicative process within the context of face-to-face performance. Although tending to emphasize verbal folklore, this definition has been widely drawn on by folklorists in North America and beyond. Nevertheless, debate continues as to the usefulness of the term *'folklore'* itself due to its popular but outmoded connotations (see, for example, the articles in the Summer 1998 issue of the *Journal of American Folklore*, 111).

In the field of childlore, the conceptualization of folklore as performance and communication has led to a focus not only on the social, developmental and educational, but also on the cultural, expressive and aesthetic (see, for example, Kirshenblatt-Gimblett 1976; McDowell 1979; Goodwin 1985; Beresin 1995; Roemer 1995). It is perhaps this which distinguishes more recent folkloristic research from much contemporary sociological and psychological work in the field of children's play. In particular, folklorists have tended to concern themselves less with child development and socialization (that is, stressing 'time future' in representations of childhood, as discussed by James and Prout 1997: 239–41), and more with what Sutton-Smith baldly stated as 'the nonserious things of life' (1970: 2). Since the 1970s these 'nonserious things' have been dignified with the term 'expressive culture'. This may have no obvious survival value or adult-oriented benefit, but nevertheless forms a significant part of children's experience of childhood. For adults to appreciate this, they have to surmount what Sutton-Smith refers to as 'the triviality barrier', in which the 'nonserious' is not necessarily deemed the unimportant:

> The infant appears to babble for the joy of hearing himself. The child plays for the fun of it. The adults return addictively to their games for the enjoyments they find contained within them. We are saying, that is, that childlore deals not only with a definite series of *expressive forms* that can be traced throughout human development, but that these forms are normally, in some sense, self-motivating structures. Which is after all only what generations of humanists have been saying when they have claimed that poetry, drama, and other forms of human expression have their own intrinsic vocabulary and system of internal dynamics which must be understood in their own right before it is possible to study how they can be put to the service of this or that functional end.
>
> It is true, then, that childlore deals with behaviour that has traditionally been regarded as nonserious, but as this behavior appears to be a systematic part of the human repertoire, to think, therefore, it is unimportant might be a mistake.
>
> (Sutton-Smith 1970: 4, original emphasis)

As stressed by Factor in Chapter 1, and demonstrated by a number of contributors to this book, children's play traditions often reveal dimensions of creativity, artistry and complexity in their own right, including carnivalesque, subversive and parodic elements as well as normative ones. It is the paradoxical nature of children's lore which forms the focus of much discussion here, especially the central section of the book, and the way in which, as Factor highlights, 'children's play traditions unify conventional opposites' (see p. 25). This results, in this book specifically and more widely in this field, in a concern with the children's point of view concerning their own traditions, and a methodology which tends towards the accumulation of empirical data drawn from detailed micro-studies, based largely on ethnographic observation and interview, prior to broad generalization (see, for example, Dargan and Zeitlin 1990; Hughes 1993; Beresin 1995; articles contributed to *Children's Folklore Review* 1977–, the Australian *Children's Folklore Newsletter*, and the British Folklore Society's *Children's Folklore Newsletter*). While one cannot speak for all folklorists and those in affiliated disciplines who study childlore, Boyes (1995: 138–9), with reference to children's verbal traditions, perhaps encapsulates the premise on which much of this research into children's play traditions as a whole is based:

> children's traditional culture is an expression of their own beliefs and values, not isolated from contact with the adult world, but specific to themselves. Rhymes and other linguistic play are created and reproduced for children's own purposes, not those of folklorists, the educational system or publishers . . . Children create and pass on their rhymes for their own enjoyment as they play. They are a living, active art, made by children for their own purposes, their content to be taken in at the children's own level, and that is how they are best understood.

Such detailed studies as those mentioned above are timely. So often, children's playlore is overlooked by adults because it is seen as unimportant. Indeed, as seems to be the case at the present time, adults only tend to notice play when it becomes a problem. In Britain, North America and Australia, for example, this has led to the reduction of the amount of time allowed for free play within the school day, with such substitutes as organized sports, extra lessons and an earlier end to the school day encroaching on children's own 'time out' (see Chapters 1, 5 and 9).

Defining 'traditional games'

This brings us full circle to the complex of ideas popularly associated with the 'problem' view of playtime (see Blatchford 1994) – namely, that children indulge in desultory behaviour in the playground, that traditional games are no longer played and, therefore, that children do not know 'how' to play any more (which sometimes leads to the teaching of traditional games to children by lunchtime supervisors, teachers, parents and grandparents). One of the keywords here is 'traditional', and yet what is so often missing in this debate is a critical consideration of what we mean by 'traditional games' and 'children's traditions'.

There is, of course, a recurrent perception of traditions generally as dying out (and this was a powerful motivation to fieldwork and documentation of traditions for many of the early folklorists, including Thoms; see Dundes 1979). This perception relates to the way in which the meaning of the word *'tradition'* is often constructed – as fixed, immutable and resistant to change, and therefore, by definition, as ancient and with origins lost in the mists of time. As Raymond Williams has so perceptively pointed out, 'it is sometimes observed, by those who have looked into particular traditions, that it only takes two generations to make anything traditional: naturally enough, since that is the sense of tradition as active process. But the word tends to move towards age-old and towards ceremony, duty and respect' (1983: 319). Here, then, is a notion of tradition as rooted in time and, in particular, as a passive process of handing down matter unchanged over a long historical period. Could it be, then, that the phrase 'traditional games' in popular parlance tends to connote a repertoire of play activities known to have a long history (and some of them certainly do)? Or is it more a matter of us adults being familiar with certain games from our own childhoods which come to form for us what 'traditional games' must be? But even so, why does it matter so much to adults that we do not always see these games to the same degree, or in the same form, or at all, in contemporary playgrounds?

This appears to relate to the additional element which Williams (1983: 319) highlights – of *reverence* for tradition:

> tradition survives in English as a description of a general process of handing down, but there is a very strong and often predominant sense of this entailing respect and duty. When we look at the detailed processes of any of these traditions, indeed when we realize that there are traditions (real plural . . .) and that only some of them or parts of them have been selected for our respect and duty, we can see how difficult Tradition really is, in an abstract or exhortatory or, as so often, ratifying use.

Somehow what we perceive to be the older games, the play activities with a longer history, must be of value precisely because they have been passed on from one generation to the next. Hidden in this line of thought is the assumption that tradition is, by definition, 'good', 'positive', 'valuable' and 'desirable'. Yet, as Williams points out, the process by which certain things are deemed traditional and accorded respect is a highly selective one. There seems to be something of a popular consensus that 'traditional games' denotes such activities as Hopscotch, Marbles, group skipping, and singing games. We need to keep in mind, however, that play activities, such as practical jokes, initiation rites, games involving forceful physical contact, racist and sexist joking, nicknaming and taunting, are equally as traditional, in the sense that they have a long and documentable history. Yet, it is clearly not these traditions which are seen as declining and whose passing is so lamented in the playground today.

By contrast, contemporary folklorists have tried to construct a notion of tradition as a dialectical process within culture (cf. Toelken 1979) – in other words, a process of both continuity and change, stability and variation, dynamism and conservatism, both through time and across space. This leads to the perception that, rather than such-and-such a tradition dying out, traditions have often been modified and altered. By allowing change, creativity and resurgence as part of our understanding of traditions, and emphasizing that traditions are not passed on by some superorganic process but one which is actively shaped by human agency, we avoid the fallacy that traditions are necessarily continuous, and allow that they can be stopped and restarted at any point. The fascination is then with how traditions are altered and renewed, how older elements are combined with newer ones within culture, and how traditions can be added to with new words, new behaviours, new beliefs and new compositions. Tradition is seen as an ongoing process which does not die out but whose manifestations in forms, beliefs and activities (such as children's rhymes and games) wax and wane and transform, making perceivable lineages and setting in motion new ones through time and across geographical space.

Thus, play traditions are not necessarily old or even passed on between two generations. They may be brand-new and enjoying lively and swift transmission among contemporary children of the same age group. This allows the children to recreate almost instantaneously the latest mass media influences in their own performances. The reader will therefore encounter a wide-ranging definition of what constitutes children's play traditions in this book. The definition includes imaginative play, games made up on the model of music videos, and parodic rhymes and chants with a highly contemporary frame of reference. It also includes the skills and artistry needed to successfully learn, adapt and perform these items. Given the perhaps bewildering variety of these activities, we now present a classification of childlore. This is designed to introduce the reader to the basic categories referred to in the ensuing chapters of the book. It also suggests some of the general characteristics of the different categories, allowing adults to refine and structure their own observations of children at play.

Classifying children's play traditions

Approaches to classification

Children have a play repertoire which they dip into according to the circumstances in which they find themselves, varying their games according to the weather, the physical surroundings, the number of playmates and the length of time available. If adults want to study what children do in free play, then it is also useful for them to have a structure which will help them make observations which are meaningful to others. In other words, there is a need for a classification system which would be acceptable to everyone in order to aid communication. A classification system which includes all the different kinds of play will also help demonstrate the range and variety of children's play traditions.

We have only to consider the use of the term 'singing game' in this volume alone to realize that a universally accepted classification would be helpful. Marsh (see Chapter 4), for example, following the usage of Iona and Peter Opie, includes clapping games under the label of singing games. Curtis (see Chapter 3), on the other hand, uses the term in the same way as Hinkson in the monograph *Victorian Singing Games* (1991) – a song which accompanies a dance and where the text, or part of it, often provides the instructions for the dance, as in 'Here We Go Round the Mulberry Bush'. Dundes suggests that a game set to music could be called a 'folk dance' (1979: 343). He has a point. The movement in singing games such as 'Here We Go Round the Mulberry Bush' is indeed dance, a factor which is ignored in the present terminology. And what do we term the song and dance routines which children perform copied from S Club Seven and other pop groups? Where would they fit into a classification?

Adults come to children's lore with their own agenda. As we have already seen, the theoretical basis of Alice Gomme's work was the belief that children's folklore was the repository of ancient customs which had almost disappeared (Gomme [1894, 1898] 1984). Her work, being intended as the first part of a dictionary, is in alphabetical order. The difficulty with Gomme's system is that games have a variety of names, depending on the locality where they have been collected, and because Gomme failed to carefully cross-reference each game, it is often difficult to discover whether or not her book contains a particular game. Her American predecessor, Newell, arranged many of the games in his *Games and Songs of American Children* according to their category of use ([1883] 1963). His categories included love games, playing at work, humour and satire, and the pleasures of motion. Drawing on the observations of Halpert, Withers, in his introduction to Newell, characterizes this as 'a remarkable and imaginative pioneer thrust toward what was later to be called "functionalism"' (Newell [1883] 1963: vi).

The Opies themselves divided their material into four parts. Their first book is concerned mainly with language: satirical and nonsense rhymes, wit and repartee, verbal tricks, riddles, truce terms, nicknames and so on (1959). Their second book deals with games in street and playground: 'the games that children, aged 6–12, play of their own accord when out of doors, and usually out of sight' (1969: v). It contains an enormous number of games and, recognizing the shortcomings of the Gomme alphabetical system of recording, the Opies went out of their way to make sure games were identifiable by their form rather than their name, which varies from place to place. As they say in the Preface, 'we have . . . given thought to the order in which the games appear, arrangement being by the basic motif of the game' (1969: vi). This, along with the contents and analysis, provides a tool for locating a game description, even if the regional name is different from the alternatives recorded in the book. The Opies were able to do this because they had large amounts of material which could be broken down into very finely delineated categories. They therefore have 'catching games' (broken down into five subsections), 'seeking games', 'hunting games' and so on. The book also contains 'pretend' play. Their third book is concerned with singing games in which they include clapping rhymes (1985), and the fourth with play with things (1997), which is organized according to the play object used.

The difficulty with this approach for most people is that they are unlikely to have the quantity of games which the Opies had, and writers on children's lore now have the Opie books to refer to, so the need to identify a game or a variation can often be fulfilled by referring to their work. For adults needing to organize a smaller amount of data, the Opies' categories are very refined and what may be more useful is a system where the categories are broader, so allowing researchers to see a wider sweep of childlore.

In the 1960s and 1970s Roberts and Sutton-Smith posited the conflict/enculturation hypothesis that child training induces conflict which can be resolved in games and that the structure of a game will reflect the child's upbringing and role in society (1971). The three groups of games they suggested were games of physical skill, which would be dominant in cultures where achievement was encouraged, games of strategy, where cultures stressed obedience training, and games of chance, correlated with training in routine responsibilities and a belief in benevolent gods. Eifermann investigated this theory and suggested that this was an over-simplification, that there was at least another category, which she labelled 'memory-attention', and that there was often a mixture of attributes (1971). It is also possible, of course, for children to change the category by the way they play the game. Goldstein, for instance, watched how children perform a counting-out routine, as distinct from how they *say* they perform it. He found that children could be seen to change what purports to be a game of chance to a game of strategy by manipulating the count (1971b: 167–78).

Halpert (1971) provides a comprehensive list of genres in children's verbal folklore, using the content of the rhymes to distinguish one category from another (see Chapter 7) while Alan Dundes has made some very interesting observations concerning the structure of games which are, he says, paralleled in folktales (1964). The themes which occur in many folktales, he argues, also find physical expression in games. Certainly some games, such as the Grandma games of Punjabi-speaking girls, where a dialogue between grandma and children precedes a chase (Curtis 1998), and which are almost identical to such British games as Old Mother Grey (Opie and Opie 1969: 307), appear to replicate folktales. But Dundes has also shown that games such as Tig (also called Tag or He) have the same component parts as folktales. Dundes points to one type of folktale, the cumulative tale – an example of which would be 'The Enormous Turnip'. Here, first the farmer tries to pull up the turnip but fails, then successive people and animals are called upon to help until eventually there is a long line of creatures all pulling at the turnip, the weight of the mouse being the factor which tips the balance and results in the turnip being uprooted. Dundes likens stories of this kind to Chain Tig in which, when a person is touched, they must join hands with whoever is 'on' and help catch the others. A singing game example of this cumulative motif would be 'In and Out the Winding Bluebells' in which one person weaves in and out of the ring, collecting people as they go. One can certainly see that children are exploring the same emotions when, for instance, they hide in a game of Hide and Seek and when they listen to the story of Jack hiding from the giant in the giant's oven in 'Jack and the Beanstalk', but, while a comparison of games and folktales aids insight into how the games are experienced, it is not helpful in constructing a classification.

Roberts and Enerstvedt conducted an interesting study in Norway where they asked children themselves to categorize their own play activities, though the categories themselves were devised by adults. The only difference they could find in the 58 games sorted was that girls categorized Marbles and a coin game as ball games whereas boys thought of them as war games (1986: 5–28).

More recently Blatchford has tackled the problem of classification by simplifying the basic structure devised by the Opies, and categorizing the games described under 24 headings. As Blatchford comments, 'there are enormous difficulties involved in documenting and categorising children's games' (Blatchford *et al.* 1990: 169). Nevertheless, undeterred by the difficulties, we have attempted our own classification, which includes verbal, physical and imaginative play. It is based on the function of the specific kind of play and is a development of the system devised by the Opies, with certain additions and, we hope, clarifications (see Table 1).

Some explanations

The material is divided into three sections: play with a high verbal content, play with a high imaginative content and play with a high physical content. The classification moves from the purely verbal to the purely physical, so verbal play such as epithets, jeers, narratives, riddles, jokes and entertainment rhymes heads the list followed by verbal play which accompanies movement. We then move on to imaginative play which

Table 1 Classification of play traditions

High verbal content		General verbal play: jeers, epithets	
		Narratives	
		Jokes, riddles	
		Entertainment rhymes	
		Counting out	
	Singing games	Song and dance	
		Clapping rhymes	
		Skipping rhymes	
		Ball-bouncing rhymes	
High imaginative content	Role enactment		
	Acting games	Set plot and characters	
		Set plot, characters and dialogue	
High physical content	Games without playthings	Individual	
		Group	High-power It
			Low-power It
			No It
		Team	
	Games with playthings	Individual	Balls
			Ropes
			Stones
			Miscellaneous
		Group	Balls
			Ropes
			Stones
			Miscellaneous
		Team	Balls
			Ropes
			Stones
			Miscellaneous
	Making things		
	Collecting things		

may contain either or both high verbal and high physical content. The third section, games high in physical content, includes not only physical games but also collecting and making things such as bows and arrows or paper fortune-telling squares.

The three main sections of the classification are subdivided according to the way the material is used by the children. Therefore, a rhyme which accompanies skipping will be designated 'a skipping rhyme' and so on. There are some games which may be included in more than one category, skipping games regulated by a rhyme being a prime example. In such cases as these, the rhyme is treated separately from the physical activity.

The problem with assigning material according to its function is that children sometimes use material for different purposes. A rhyme such as:

Mary Jane went to Spain
In a chocolate aeroplane

which was used in Leeds, West Yorkshire, in the 1920s as a ball-bouncing rhyme (Kellett n.d.) has changed its form slightly and is now:

The Queen of Spain
Went up in a chocolate aeroplane

and is used for clapping (Curtis 1998). However, the fact that a rhyme may shift from one category to another only serves to highlight the flexibility of oral tradition and demonstrates how a classification system can illustrate both continuity and change.

Entertainment rhymes

The term 'entertainment rhyme' may need some explanation. There are a number of rhymes which do not accompany any activity. They are often scatalogical or sexual in nature, or subversive, and publishers in the past have often been reluctant to publish them because of the fear of shocking adults. Parodies of nursery rhymes come into this category, an example taken from Curtis (1998) being:

Mary had a little lamb.
She fed it on cream crackers,
And every time it dropped a crumb
She kicked it in the knackers.

Singing games

It seems sensible to extend the definition of singing games so that the term includes games which have movement where the movement is accompanied by singing or chanting. The term will then include clapping and skipping games, as well as the older kinds of singing game, such as 'Oranges and Lemons' or 'Farmer's in His Den'. There should also be some recognition of the dance element in these games. The term 'singing games' is therefore subdivided into song and dance, clapping rhymes and skipping rhymes. Song and dance includes both the older traditional games such as 'Oranges and Lemons' and the new traditions – for example, song and dance routines such as those copying the Spice Girls. Many of these are ephemeral, so it is a category which is likely to demonstrate change and reflect media influence. Dance is defined, after Royce, as patterned movement in time and space performed as an end in itself (see Royce 1980: 3–8).

The term 'singing', as anyone who has recorded songs in a playground can vouchsafe, is not to be thought of as pure-toned, accurately pitched melody. Sometimes a tune will be pitched and sung accurately but this will be rare and often rhymes will be chanted, in a sort of heightened speech. Speech and song have much in common: rhythm, pitch, tempo, timbre and expression. Schafer (1970), asserting that verbal sense must become less important as sound changes from speech to song, plots the changes. He sees the stages (as listed in Hall 1984: 61) from maximum sense to maximum sound as:

1 Stage speech
2 Domestic speech
3 *Parlando* (recitative)
4 *Sprechstimme* or *Sprechgesang* (vocalization between speaking and singing as in the music of Schoenberg)
5 Syllabic song
6 Melismatic song (one syllable sung to several notes)
7 Vocables (pure sound)
8 Electronically manipulated vocal sounds.

In versions of songs and rhymes recorded in Victoria, Australia, Hall (1984) states that the majority of performances from children of junior school age lies somewhere between Stages 3 and 5 above. She defines *parlando* as speech with emphasized paralinguistic features, especially amplified intonation and intensity of expression. Its features are that it is often performed in dramatic context: jokes, tale-telling, role-playing in the playground. The voice is projected with an increase in volume and higher pitch. *Sprechstimme* is defined by Hall as maximum amplification of heightened speech intonation on a scanned poetic text with dramatic connotations. Most adult forms of *Sprechstimme* are contrived art forms such as Chinese opera, but some children perform in a mode similar to this. Speech intonation is exaggerated to the maximum manageable level but, in song terms, the notes are 'out of tune' because the performer is still intoning partly in spoken mode. Hall adds a further category between heightened speech and *Sprechstimme* – recitation. This she defines as the repetition of scanned and unscanned poetic texts on a base note of limited intonation with regular but restricted ornamental pitches and strong, even metre. It is found in spoken playlore and the recitation of multiplication tables (Hall 1984: 116).

Imaginative play

These games call on a combination of verbal and organizational skills which fall between the categories of high verbal and high physical content. Some will be highly verbal while others will be full of physical action, but among their characteristics, according to Smilansky (1968), are rôle-playing and make-believe transformation. Sarbin (1954) distinguishes between role-enactment (being someone else) and role-taking (seeing something from someone else's point of view because one is interested in another's motivation). This is a useful distinction pursued by Flavell who defines role-enactment as 'the general ability and disposition to "take the role" of another person in the cognitive sense, i.e. to assess his/her response capacities and tendencies in a given situation' (Flavell 1975: 5). The second aspect he identifies as the more specific ability to use this understanding of the other person's role as a tool in communicating effectively with them. He defines the essential element of role-taking as an ability to grasp the attributes of another person which are not immediately perceptible – for example, the other person's needs, intentions, opinions and beliefs. The role-taker's estimate of these attributes is the synthesis of information from two sources: the knowledge of people and their behaviour in certain situations, and the perceptual input from the overt behaviour of the other or from cues in the immediate situation. It is the first of these definitions, role-enactment, which concerns us here. In a hierarchy of skills, role-enactment is obviously at a simpler level than role-taking, since the second involves an ability not only to enact the role of the other, but to analyse the motivation of the person being imitated (Flavell 1975).

When role-enactment games are examined closely, they can be seen to fall into two groups: those where the characters are set by the overall idea of the game, with teacher and pupils in a game of School, for instance, where characters, plot and dialogue, if it exists, are improvised, and those where the characters and plot are fixed by the game, but the dialogue is improvised. In Curtis' 1998 study, for instance, one group of children was found to be playing the imaginative game of Neighbours, in which the children used the plot and characters of the Australian television soap opera to construct an ongoing acting game. These have been called 'acting games' in the classification.

There is a further group of games which really falls between the two categories. In Curtis' 1998 study there were several games played only by Punjabi-speaking girls and called by them Grandma games, mentioned earlier. These had set characters and a dialogue which usually culminated in a chase. They have a great deal in common with high-power It games, such as What Time Is It, Mr Wolf?, where there is an 'It' and players who exchange dialogue. In the Grandma games, however, the dialogue is much more protracted and does have scope for some improvisation, however minimal. They therefore form a sub-category of the acting games.

Games high in physical content

Moving on to the section of games high in physical content, these are divided into those with and without playthings, with a distinction being made between individual, group and team games, a group being defined as more than one person. The difference between group play and team play is as follows: in group play, each person is acting individually but needs other players to take part for the game to be complete. So a skipping game will be a group game because the person skipping is performing as an individual but needs others to take part, turning the rope and joining in with the performer. Most group games can also be played individually when the player is intent on improving their performance. Performance in the group will often be competitive. In team play all the players, in theory at least, are playing for the team and not for themselves as individuals. One of the tensions in football as played in the playground is the difficulty some children have in playing for the team and not themselves.

A great deal of social learning occurs in children's unsupervised play and therefore a distinction is made between games according to the role of the 'It'. In a chasing game such as Tig/Tag/He, the role of the 'It' is to chase and try to catch one of the other players. When another player has been caught, that person becomes the chaser. The role of the 'It' is simple, and this, following Gump and Sutton-Smith's definition (1971: 390–9), is called 'low-power It'. There are games, however, where the role of the 'It' is much more complicated. If we consider a game such as Grandmother's Footsteps (also known as Black Pudding, Hot Chocolate, Peep behind the Curtain and no doubt many other variants), the role of the 'It' is to stand alone with their back to the other players, to turn round from time to time, to try to detect movement in the players creeping up behind and to send those players who have been seen to move back to the beginning. The 'It' here is therefore controlling the game and has the power to control the movements of the other players. This entails a responsible use of the power invested in the role, which in its turn results in the practice of sophisticated social skills. The role of the 'It' is therefore described as being high power. For those adults interested in the social learning which occurs among children, the group of games where the 'It' has a great deal of power is an important one. The distinction between 'low' and 'high' power in games with playthings does not apply.

Setting out the full extent of children's verbal, imaginative and physical play in this way shows the variety of experiences available to children during their free play activities, and demonstrates the potential for learning and enjoyment which a rich and fulfilling playtime can generate.

The scope and structure of the book

This book focuses specifically on children's play traditions – verbal, physical and imaginative – as distinct from other aspects of children's folklore, such as customs, beliefs and narrative traditions, although the reader will find reference to research in these other aspects in the bibliography. The book is not, however, an attempt to document systematically whether traditional games are in decline or not. Rather, it consists of two orientating chapters, in Part 1, which present the contrasting perceptions of adults and children in today's world regarding play, with particular reference to the school playground. These are followed in Part 2 by a series of in-depth empirical studies of specific schools, playgrounds and current play traditions in Australia, Britain, Continental Europe and North America. These illustrate the kind of diachronic, synchronic and cross-cultural perspectives needed in order to undertake a holistic study of cultural tradition, and underline not only the continuity of many contemporary children's play traditions, but also their creativity, renewal and variety. Part 3 broadens out to demonstrate the possibilities and importance of play traditions in a number of different contexts, namely the relevance of children's traditional verbal creativity to formal language learning, the potential of the sharing of play traditions between generations and between members of different cultural groups in order to foster understanding and respect, and the role of children's free play in promoting their spiritual and psychological well-being. The book concludes by considering what constitutes 'play for today' and the role of adults in relation to it.

All the participants at the 'State of Play' conference, from which all but Chapter 5 derive, were privileged to have the presence of Iona Opie and hear her opening address. It is likewise a privilege that she has agreed to write the Foreword to the present volume. No one who researches into children's play traditions can do so without, at some point, drawing on the work of Iona and Peter Opie. With this in mind, we very much hope that Boyes' tribute to their achievements might be extended to contemporary research on children's play traditions, verbal, cognitive and behavioural, including the contributions to this book: 'The Opies' legacy allows us to see beyond unsubstantiated generalisations about the wholesale destruction of children's games to recognise the value of their ability to make creative change and give customary shape to innovation' (Boyes 1995: 145).

Notes

1 We are grateful to Andy Arleo for drawing our attention to these references.
2 See Blatchford (1989: 15, 23, 29; Opie and Opie 1997: 8; cf. Parry-Jones 1964: 238; Webb 1984: 15; Arleo *et al.* 1997: 20). Some have also pointed to changes in the school environment itself. Damian Webb, for example, blames the introduction of mixed-sex schooling (1984: 15), and Parry-Jones the abolition of the eleven-plus exam and the concreting of playground surfaces (1964: 237–8).
3 Despite George's attempts to publish this collection, it remains unpublished and is now in the archive of the Museum of Welsh Life (MWLMSS 1970). We are grateful to Tecwyn Vaughan Jones for this information.
4 For further studies of children's folklore, see Grider (1980), Halpert (1982) and Sutton-Smith *et al.* (1995).
5 Nevertheless, Dundes' formulation has been subjected to criticism and refinement (for example, Oring 1986: 1).

▰▰ Part 1 ▰▰

Today's play: adult and child perspectives

▰▰▰▰▰▰▰▰▰▰▰▰▰▰▰▰▰▰▰▰▰▰▰▰

The introduction to this book highlights that there have been, and continue to be, widespread concerns among adults regarding the quality of children's play in middle childhood. This raises the question of whether children themselves share the same perceptions and concerns. The limited amount of research in this area of which we are aware suggests that children's experiences of school playtime differ markedly from those of adults (for a review of this research, see Blatchford 1998: 11–20). In one study, conducted in London, children were overwhelmingly in favour of playtime and the opportunity it provided for self-directed play activities. A minority expressed concerns as well, such as disruptive behaviour and having to play outdoors in bad weather (Blatchford *et al.* 1990). Lack of games did not seem to be a problem for the majority of children in this particular study, although 15 per cent of them were reported as disliking playtime because 'they said they had nothing to do or no one to play with' (Blatchford *et al.* 1990: 167). This emphasizes the mutual influence of friendship groups and play activities and points to an extremely significant factor in the dynamics of the playground (see, for example, Sluckin 1981; Marsh 1997; Blatchford 1998). Another finding of this study was that some children disliked playtime because of 'frustrations that arose out of specific games or activities, for example, trying to play football in a confined space, being knocked over when running, getting a football in the face [and] losing balls over fences' (Blatchford *et al.* 1990: 167).

The following chapters by Factor and Armitage focus on these broad themes and issues expressed by adults and children and explore them in more detail. In Chapter 1, Factor provides an important orientation to the whole topic of children, childhood and play. Her characterization of children's subcultures as stemming from the tension between children's desire for independence from adults and their simultaneous dependence upon them is fundamental to an understanding of their play. Hence, children's play activities manifest a number of apparently opposing features, including conservatism and innovation, inheritance and improvisation, universality and localness, and conventionality and subversiveness. These qualities are vividly and recurrently illustrated in the in-depth studies which form Part 2 of this book.

June Factor goes on to explore adults' perspectives on children, childhood and children's culture, and specifically the traps which adults tend to fall into when considering these topics. In particular, she focuses on three common perceptions: first, that 'today's children aren't as well-behaved, innocent and sensitive as they used to be' and that 'they don't play like they used to'; second, that childhood itself is nothing but a social construct, inseparable from contemporary ideas about childhood and childrearing; and third, that children's play is trivial and unimportant and can be ignored or replaced by more constructive activities, such as organized sport or formal lessons. Despite their long history and widespread currency in contemporary Britain, Australia and the USA, Factor effectively counters each perception with evidence to the contrary.

Chapter 2, by Marc Armitage, both follows on from and complements Factor's chapter. In order to re-examine the adult idea that children's play is in some way lacking today and therefore in need of adult intervention, Armitage concentrates on building up a picture of the primary school playground from the point of view of the children who play there. His observations are based on a considerable amount of evidence, drawn from observation of playgrounds and interviews with schoolchildren carried out over a ten-year period in a large area of northern England. His central finding is that, despite many modern playgrounds not being conducive in their layout and topography to the children's needs, children are remarkably creative and ingenious in the ways that they adapt the playground environment for their play.

In plotting the relationship between the different kinds of space afforded by the playground and the kinds of play which take place in each, Armitage demonstrates how the frustrations noted in the study mentioned above by Blatchford *et al.* (1990) can arise. The effect of the shape of the playground and its relationship with the school buildings emerges as a crucial factor in the degree of success with which children can find a conducive place to play their preferred game. A key point which arises from these examples is that adult knowledge of and sensitivity to the children's perceptions of the playground space is crucial to fostering free play activities. This should also be informing policy with regard to the design of new playgrounds and the modification of existing ones.

Together these two chapters introduce the broad characteristics of play in middle childhood, especially its paradoxical nature, as well as one of the principal sites of contemporary children's play (the playground) and the way in which the topography of the site influences what children play. They also illustrate children's and adults' very different 'ways of seeing' (Berger 1972) play activities and the play environment. This sets the scene for the fieldwork-based studies which follow in Part 2, which focus largely on the school playground and the many and varied forms of play to be found there.

1

Three myths about children's folklore

June Factor

The French poet Paul Valéry was the author of many fine pieces of literary and cultural criticism. In one essay, he wrote: 'I apologize for thus revealing myself to you; but in my opinion it is more useful to speak of what one has experienced than to pretend to a knowledge that is entirely impersonal, an observation with no observer. In fact there is no theory that is not a fragment, carefully prepared, of some autobiography' (1958: 58). I recall Valéry's words because it is more than 25 years since I began, quite without forethought or intimation of what lay ahead, to explore an area of human activity now generally known as children's folklore. This chapter is certainly as much a fragment of autobiography as, in the words of another Frenchman, a 'so-called "objective" mode of historical discourse' (Barthes 1970: 148). I want to avoid that particular kind of fiction, to make clear that it is *my* experience that shapes and colours these reflections on certain contemporary notions about childhood.

A quarter of a century ago, almost by accident, I found myself knee-deep in collections of school playground lore gathered by my students – young adults at an Australian teachers' college. Without design, or any notion of where it would lead, I fortuitously embarked on a journey which seems to have no end. Like someone bitten by a malarial mosquito, my crowded life remains infected by persistent curiosity about children, especially about what they do when no adult is telling them to do anything, and where, and how, and with whom, and above all, why.

The tools for this journey have been the usual scholarly apparatus: observation, questions, reading, reflection, research, debate, more reflection, more reading, more research, always more animated argument and always a continuing close scrutiny of 'the field' – commonly called children.

Like many a journey, this one has been sparked by curiosity and fuelled by pleasure – but also by indignation. There is pleasure in observing, recording, analysing and sometimes celebrating the extraordinary richness and diversity of children's folklore. Compared with adults, the young are small, weak, ignorant and powerless. They are also full of energy, passion, curiosity and imagination. Bruno Schulz was remembering childhood when he wrote that 'there is no dead matter . . . lifelessness is only a disguise behind which hide unknown forms of life' (1989: 31). 'The consistent aversion of the child to carefully established reality is universal', according to the Russian poet Kornei Chukovsky – and he knew of what he spoke (1963: 93).

Cultural differences notwithstanding, the relationship between growing children and their adult community manifests tensions. These are inherent in children's limited capacities and limitless imaginations, their dependence on adults and their intermittent but inexorable striving for emancipation from dependency. It is likely that this dialectic provides the impetus for children's subcultures of verbal and kinetic play. It may also help explain the paradoxical nature of children's lore. Like the arts, which also create their own virtual worlds, children's play traditions unify conventional opposites. They are at once conservative and innovative, inherited and improvised, rule-bound and adaptive, collaborative and competitive, ritualistic and creative, universal and minutely local, secure and challenging, self-regulatory and group-orientated, stylized in form and boundless in content, conventional and subversive – the poetry of hard truths expressed through symbol, rhythm, rhyme, repetition and a generous dollop of recalcitrant humour.

There is no danger of being bored when you are a student of children's folklore, and that is no small pleasure. Sutton-Smith was right when he said that 'as we enter a culture through one tiny vantage point, one tiny peep-hole, much else comes into view' (1986: 253). Children's folklore provides a means of examining age-old questions about human growth and change, and casts some light on the various nature–nurture debates. But this peep-hole is not for the romantic, the timid, or the straight-laced.

Ever since the first of my for-children collections of Australian children's verbal lore, *Far Out Brussel Sprout*,[1] was published in 1983, another kind of peep-hole, my letter-box, has bulged with correspondence from the young, who have sent me their favourite rhymes, riddles and other playlore. Not long ago, a young boy sent the following joke:

> One day there was a little boy and a little girl. The boy said to the girl, 'If you climb up the flag-pole I'll give you 10 cents.'
> The girl said yes, and she climbed up the flag-pole.
> The boy said, 'I tricked ya, I tricked ya, I just wanted to see ya knickers!'
> And the girl said, 'I tricked ya, I tricked ya, I haven't got any on!'

There are at least a dozen variants of this old chestnut in the Australian Children's Folklore Collection, the largest public archive of children's folklore in Australia.[2] But another joke, which arrived in a letter from a 10-year-old girl, was less familiar:

There was Pants and Dick, and they were trying to hide from the teacher. Pants jumped up on top of the cupboard and Dick jumped inside the cupboard. The teacher came into the room and said, 'All right – Pants down and Dick out!'

Which brings me to the indignation. Not about childhood vulgarity, a universal phenomenon and one which provides children with a seeming air of 'knowing', of maturity, through forms of comic subversion. Rather, my concern centres on the myths which encumber all the modalities of children's folklore – the ridicule, the taboo-breaking, the games and riddles and rhymes. These myths are the unsubstantiated but widely accepted beliefs about childhood and children's subcultures which flourish despite significant evidence to the contrary.

A common myth is at the core of that well-used phrase, 'the good old days'. Such times, according to the speaker or writer, still existed when they were young. Then, children were – depending on the bent of the narrator – more polite, more cooperative, certainly more innocent; they played Marbles and Jacks and hopped and skipped and sang songs and generally had a lovely time. In contrast, today's youngsters are seen as worldly, attracted to crude humour and instant gratification, their imaginations desensitized by an over-abundance of flashy toys provided by mass-produced technology. They have only a vestigial repertoire of the old play traditions; soon these too will be gone.

For the nineteenth-century children's folklorists in Britain and the USA, this myth was part of a larger fiction. William Newell wrote in his introduction to the 1883 publication of *Games and Songs of American Children*: 'this collection represents an expiring custom. The vine of oral tradition, of popular poetry . . . is perishing at the roots; its prouder branches have long since been blasted, and children's song, its humble but longest-flowering offshoot, will soon have shared their fate' (Newell [1883] 1963: 1).

Newell was expressing a conviction popularized by Wordsworth, Ruskin and other Romantics – influential writers and thinkers who lamented the loss of the traditions of rural life. Industrialization, the growth of cities and the spread of book-learning were destroying, they believed, the old folk ways grounded in the countryside, including, ultimately, the playlore of children.

Beyond that elegiac vision (which had elements of historical truth) lay the fiction of the primitive. Nineteenth-century Social Darwinism conveniently separated the 'advanced', 'civilized' societies (white, educated and of European origin) from those – supposedly of earlier evolution and hence less civilized – called 'primitive' or 'exotic'. Anthropologists jumped on boats and travelled long distances to document the strange traditions of foreign 'primitives'. Folklorists, perhaps less adventurous or more impecunious, stayed at home and found their own primitives: peasants and children.

Some argued an ingenuous equivalence between early cultures and early life. 'Children of civilized or so-called civilized parents are simply small savages writhing in the bonds of petticoats or knickerbockers', declared an Australian with an interest in children's song games in 1898 (Daley 1898). Others, like Lady Alice Gomme, believed that among children and peasants one could find relics discarded by the cultivated. She collected children's games in England, Scotland and Ireland in the 1890s, she said, because they were 'some of the oldest historical documents belonging to our race . . . monuments of man's progress from savagery to civilisation' ([1894, 1898] 1984: 531). It was thought that the folklore of children existed as the fossilized remains of earlier adult traditions.

Such views began to fade as both folklorists and anthropologists documented the existence of comparable children's playlore in very different societies as well as the general coexistence of adult and child traditions. As Caillois remarked, 'we are not at all certain that prehistoric children might not have been playing with bows, slingshots, and peashooters "for fun" at the same time that father used them "for real"' (1961: 61).

Yet elements of this myth have persisted in contemporary thinking, long after the decline of Social Darwinism and the notion of children as the primitives of the race. That other folk memory – Blake's green and pleasant land engulfed by dark satanic mills[3] – is embedded in imagery still more potent, it seems, than all the wonders of modern technology. Distrust of the processes and products of machine culture continues, at some level of consciousness, more than 200 years after the cataclysm called the Industrial Revolution.

When English educator David Holbrook wrote so passionately about the imminent disappearance of British children's traditional games and rhymes, he blamed 'recent developments in television, in the mass-production of toys, in family life, and the tone of our ways of living' (1957: 12). That was in 1957, two years before Iona and Peter Opies' first book, *The Lore and Language of Schoolchildren* (1959), exploded the children-don't-do-that-any-more myth in the UK. Since then, folklorists around the world have published an array of compilations of children's playlore, and there are now journals, theses and conferences dedicated to a lively and flourishing childhood tradition.

It is therefore difficult to excuse reputable writers such as Neil Postman and Marie Winn, who sometimes sound like Holbrook with an American accent. Their books, published in the early 1980s, ignore more than two decades of accumulated data. By insisting that in the USA at least, 'children's games . . . are an endangered species' (Postman 1982: 4), such writers betray a disturbing ignorance at odds with their considerable public reputation. Yet few reviewers challenged these assertions, and there has been no shortage of readers and admirers.

Postman (1982) and Winn (1983) have given a popular gloss to the notion that children's play traditions are in decline by attaching to it the old fear of technology. Television is Postman's particular bête noir, a machine which he asserts destroys 'information hierarchy' and hence an essential differentiation of knowledge between adults and children (1982: 77).

Despite evidence to the contrary, it is now a truism among many educators and social reformers that children's playlore is in decline, and that this, like the canary in the mine, portends danger to our collective (social) health.[4] In 1998, following the shooting by two young boys of four fellow students and a teacher at a school in Arkansas, I heard an American psychologist speaking authoritatively on Australian radio. Dr Dennis Embry, who was introduced as chief executive officer of Heartsprings Foundation Inc., which develops strategies for working with violent youth, asserted that children in the USA no longer play as they once did, and that much school culture is primitive and negative. Embry might well have quoted Postman's poignant litany: 'that technology itself has been deified, that the political process has been degraded, that the adult mind has been diminished, and that childhood is waning are woeful signs' (1982: 146).

'Childhood is waning'. That is Postman's thesis, possible, he says, because 'childhood is a social artifact ... like all social artifacts, its continued existence is not inevitable' (1982: xi, xii). Welcome to myth number two.

Unlike the first myth, the concept of childhood, beyond infancy, as essentially a social artefact, a construct of culture and ideology, is comparatively recent. This is probably to its advantage. Its identification with theories of cultural relativism, and latterly its use in challenging long-held assumptions about how children should be reared, has given it a cachet of importance, even truth, in some academic circles.[5] To argue that childhood and children's subcultures exist as a phenomenon of human development in every society – not outside culture but more than a cultural construct – is to risk pejorative labels such as biologism, essentialism and a-historicism. But what is the evidence?

That the adult culture provides the framework of children's lives and much of its detail, and that the culture is of course a historical creation, differing from place to place, from time to time, is not in dispute. What we eat (once we have teeth), what we wear, where we live, the language we speak, even the ways we are likely to view the natural world, other people and ourselves – these are all shaped by the accident of the society and culture into which we are born. Nationality, class, gender, religion – a host of historically created and changing economic, social and cultural influences mark every child's life.

Views about the nature of children and the appropriate ways in which they should be reared – what we now call ideologies of childhood – also vary, both within and between cultures. Officially, the Romans saw children as empty vessels to be filled with adult learning; yet Roman literature contains ample evidence of reciprocated affection between parents and children not compatible with such a mechanistic approach, and who knows what slaves and servants in Rome and the empire's far-flung outposts thought about childrearing? Puritans caught a glimmer of mischief in a child's eye and knew that Satan's imp must be birched to goodness; the number of times such precepts were commanded from pulpits suggests a population not entirely in accord with the prevailing ideology. Rousseau's imaginary children partook of the qualities of the noble savage, and the founding father of the kindergarten, Frederick Froebel, saw the child as a tender plant who would flower into loveliness and goodness with appropriate, kindly adult attention.[6] We have had kindergartens for many years now, but western societies continue to direct, manipulate and regulate children's lives.

We must distinguish between the actual lives of children and the ideologies about childhood. Linda Pollock puts its neatly: 'The concepts of childhood and adolescence may have changed, but this does not indicate that the actual experience of the young has altered' (1983: 65).

Children's dependence on adults is almost total in infancy, which is no doubt why even the most convinced childhood-is-a-social-construct theorist exempts the earliest years of human life from the debate. As children grow, become mobile and play together, Anthony Burton (1978: 59, 61) has observed:

> they begin to develop thoughts, feelings and behaviors which are particular to themselves . . . They are economically dependent for food, clothing and shelter on some source beyond themselves; and they are also dependent in the sense that their ability to understand the world is developing and not yet what it will become . . . At the same time they do have scope for many cultural activities which are peculiarly their own.

Children do not merely take in adult culture. They are not passive sponges. Even toddlers subvert direction with giggles, seeming deafness and other useful stratagems. According to Nicholas Tucker (1977: 22), 'In a crude sense, children are likely to show certain childhood traits in some broad areas *whatever* the culture. To ignore this and treat children simply as products of adult social expectations is bound eventually to lead to oversimplifications'.

By what Alasdair Roberts (1980) calls 'middle childhood', the period between early childhood and adolescence, youngsters are masters of an array of cultural forms and modes of social interaction overlapping but often quite distinct from the adult culture. These subcultures create what I have called a double helix, 'one strand representing the universal, ubiquitous features of childlore, the other the particular manifestations of children's play lives which result from specific circumstances' (Factor 1988: xiv).

Play is at the core of middle childhood. It is a means of integrating the child's outer and inner worlds. It is a medium of friendship, and a protection against enemies; the language and rituals of play provide a form of collaborative discourse which distinguishes 'us' from 'them' through a shared aesthetic of performance. Secure in the arena of play and make-believe, children can safely explore and experiment. Play's disengagement from everyday reality gives children a sense of control over the messy fluidity of life; play both distances and patterns experience, and gives it shape and meaning through form. Of course, as life cannot be controlled, the effort is endless; both children and adults continue to invent and reinvent forms of order and beauty.

Although we go on pretending all our lives that we are princes or princesses disguised as ugly frogs, it is in childhood, as Bruner *et al.* (1976) have remarked, that play holds a centrality which is channelled among adults into more specialized imaginative activities: religious rituals, drama, song, dance, poetry, painting.[7] The characteristics and qualities I have ascribed to childhood are not necessarily exclusive to the young, but they are dominant in childhood.

The commonality of playlore in childhood makes it possible for us to recognize the game of Knucklebones depicted on a piece of terracotta dated about 800 BC (Lovett 1901: 280), the clay breasts and mud dolls of Aboriginal girls playing Mothers and Babies in Arnhem Land in the 1930s (Thomson 1983: 38) and the mocking ribaldry of village children in West Java in the 1970s as they hopped around, scratching their backsides and singing a song about the dire effects of the jengkol fruit on adult bowels (Romet 1980: 34). It is why the activities depicted in Brueghel's 1560 painting of children's games are still paralleled in thousands of contemporary school playgrounds, in dusty streets, on sandhills and in mountain villages. Of Brueghel's more than 80 games, only one has disappeared in Australia: Whipping Tops. But then Brueghel did not know about Elastics.

When I was writing *Captain Cook Chased a Chook: Children's Folklore in Australia* (Factor 1988), I was struck by the extraordinarily resilient and adaptive nature of children's play. So powerful is the urge to play, to move outside the limitations of the immediate moment, the here and now, that children even in the most terrible circumstances insist on playing. George Eisen has documented, in a book of great significance for the understanding of childhood, the play lives of youngsters in the ghettos and concentration camps of Nazi-occupied Europe. Amidst the most appalling misery, fear, hunger and cruelty, children played as long as there was breath and strength in their bodies. A nurse in one of the children's blocks in the Auschwitz/Birkenau concentration camp remembers some of the bigger boys playing Roll Call:

> They took on the roles of the sick who fainted during roll call and were beaten for it, or they played 'Doctor' – a doctor who would take away food rations from the sick and refuse them all help if they had nothing to bribe him with . . . Once they even played 'Gas Chamber'. They made a hole in the ground and threw in stones one after

the other. Those were supposed to be people put in the crematoria, and they imitated their screams. They wanted me to show them how to set up the chimney.

(Eisen 1988: 80–1)

Eisen writes: 'A child's mind had a formidable ability to lift him or her above the ruined houses . . . the corpses, and the ever-present hunger . . . [The] play activities made life's continuation possible for a little while longer by making the camps, ghettos, and the cramped hideouts somewhat more bearable' (pp. 75, 61).

It is this 'formidable ability' to transform reality through play which is the reason the onslaught of manufactured playthings is not catastrophic: children recast and transfigure the new material for their own purposes. At a conference on play held in Paris a few years ago, a Greek researcher described how a group of young girls from a Peloponnesian village, proud owners of Barbie dolls, happily treated their playthings like village infants – to be baptized, taken to weddings, and generally mothered (Gougoulis 1992).

In Australia, television programmes are remorselessly parodied:

The Adams Family started
When Uncle Festa farted
They thought it very funny
When he blew up the dunny
And landed in the sewer
A drain of raw manure.

Television is also adapted to older forms of play. A Sydney 12-year-old explained the way she and her friends played a variant of the Who Knows the Right Answer? game: 'We have to tell . . . the time and the channels . . . and the person got to tell what program is it, like if I ask 7.30 Sunday night on Channel 7, they got to tell what is it . . . then they got to run to the other side and to their side' (Palmer 1986: 108).

It is misguided to assume that the intent of manufacturers, or parents, will entirely determine children's play. Cultural imperialism, the endless onslaught of American commercial culture, is resisted, even undermined, through the imagination, innovation and traditional play practices of the young.

For historians, the most influential exponent of the notion that childhood is an adult-created social category was Philippe Ariès. His remarkable 1960 foray into the history of childhood (translated into English as *Centuries of Childhood* in 1962), generally is credited as the first promulgation of the thesis of 'the invention of childhood' – in Ariès' view, a development which occurred in the seventeenth century.

At first, nobody paid much attention. Richard Vann, who has mapped the reception of Ariès' book, notes that scholarly reviews were in short supply for half a dozen years on either side of the Atlantic and in all relevant disciplines (1982: 281–3). Yet, by 1968, according to Vann, 'writers of sociological textbooks were writing their potted history introductory sections with heavy reliance on Ariès' (1982: 283). These days, Ariès' proposition (albeit in an often oversimplified and sometimes distorted form) is alive and well, and not just among sociologists. He has acquired classic status.

A recent book, *Australian Childhood: A History* (1997), by an academic historian, Jan Kociumbas, provides a useful illustration of Ariès' continuing influence. The assumption that childhood is an adult creation – an assumption central to the book – is acknowledged by the writer and sourced to Ariès as well as some later 'authorities'.

Since attention to childhood by historians in Australia has been minuscule, a book with such a title is welcome, and it certainly provides valuable information about Australian children's lives in a variety of social settings. The book is clearly written, not lacking in passion, and richly detailed. However, it is not a history of Australian childhoods but a chronicle of the subjugation and manipulation of children and their parents, especially their mothers, by the capitalist state and its organs of control.

Kociumbas' history suffers from the fault noted in 1978 by Burton when writing of the work of earlier anthropologists: 'The young have been studied with something else in mind' (1978: 55) – in this case, the desire to expose the cruelty, exploitation and injustice of Australian capitalism as it impinged on women and children.

How is it possible for a contemporary historian to write about children with little more than token reference to the lives of the young with each other: playing games, repeating and amending rhymes, riddles and jokes, imagining, pretending, making and unmaking friendships – that part of childhood experience during which, in Robert Louis Stevenson's (1882) felicitous phrase, the young change 'the atmosphere and tenor' of their lives? How can children's very particular ways of seeing the world be ignored?

The myth of determinist social causation, now deeply entrenched, makes it possible. And the consequence, in Kociumbas' case, is an oddly old-fashioned history, despite her radical tone. She appears unaware of, or uninterested in, the considerable critical literature directed at Ariès' arguments since the early 1970s.

Ariès misreads historical evidence, such as medieval children being dressed in clothing similar to adults, to assert childhood's absence before the seventeenth century. Postman notes changes in the pattern and content of contemporary adult organization of children's lives, leaps to the conclusion that reading has given way to television viewing among the young, and determines that this marks childhood's decline (1982). Kociumbas takes all that for granted; she no longer has to 'prove' the artificiality of the notion of childhood, only to document its particular social conditioning in Australia.

Those of us who study children's folklore, who observe the commonality of this phenomenon as we carefully note its differences and variations across time, place and cultures – what influence have *we* had on the development of the mythic, widely accepted theory of childhood as a social construct?

None. Which is not surprising in the case of Ariès, whose book first appeared 40 years ago, when children's folklore research and publication was not extensive. In the 1980s, Postman acknowledges the significance of children's playlore as a marker of childhood, but insists that, in contemporary American society, 'children's play has become an adult preoccupation, it has become professionalized, it is no longer a world separate from the world of adults' (1982: 130). He indicates no knowledge of the work of American scholars in this field. Nor, in the 1990s, does Kociumbas refer to any Australian or overseas folkloristic studies.

Folklorists need to attend to this myth because its exponents, largely unintentionally, help feed a view endemic in so-called developed societies – that what children do in their free time is unimportant, or worse, useless and therefore in need of adult intervention. And so to myth number three.

For hundreds of years, perhaps for much longer, many adults have viewed children at play as engaged in harmless high-jinks, games in which everyone argues over the rules or their application, with lots of running around, giggles, squeals and shouts – a bit like puppies or kittens, all young things play. Just a way of socializing and exercising, good for the muscles and the lungs, and it gives fidgety, restless children an opportunity to let off steam.

Since the invention of mass education, most teachers regard recess and lunch breaks as an opportunity for tea, chat and recuperation away from the classroom. Those teachers rostered on school playground duty ensure a minimum of mayhem among the boisterous young, and the picking up of rubbish. Few adults in school playgrounds or other places where children are free to play show much interest in the games and other playlore of their charges. After all, children do not know enough to be doing anything important.

For youngsters, a useful consequence of this myth of playlore's insignificance has been the comparative lack of adult interference in their play. This has permitted children to organize themselves as they wish, free of the imposition of current adult notions of how and what to play. It has also protected the young from cries of outrage and worse when they sing and chant their mantras of insult and abuse: 'Shove off, square eyes!'; 'Drop dead, pizza head!'; and

Girls are weak
Chuck 'em in the creek
Boys are weaker
Chuck 'em in deeper.

Boys are weak
Chuck 'em in the creek
Girls are stronger
They live longer!

However, the increasing professionalizing of sport, together with concern in many developed countries about people's weight and its relationship to lack of physical exercise, has led to accelerated attempts to regulate
children's free playtime. In countries like Australia, physical education
teachers and other well-meaning adults organize mini-athletics and
diverse sports-oriented activities. In schools, teachers hand out basket-
balls and footballs and other adult-focused game equipment at recess
and lunchtimes, encouraging their students to practise the skills needed
for highly competitive adult team games. A mother's encounter with just
such a teacher catches both the child's pleasure in traditional play, and
the attitude of the 'professional' who knows what is really important:

> My little daughter, aged five, is playing hopscotch with a friend. With
> great care and deliberation she looks for a pebble, and in a moment
> of luck finds the Perfect Stone . . . [The children] begin hopping,
> wobbly, not exactly landing on the required squares, but who cares.
> My daughter has a look of deep flushed pleasure as she tosses the
> stone and does some inexpert hops . . . A teacher comes beside me
> and watches. 'So good for their gross motor development,' she coos
> approvingly. 'You would be amazed how these apparently useless
> childhood games prepare them to play competitive sport.'
>
> (Manne 1998)

The mother's reflection is interesting:

> What, a moment before, was innocent fun has been instantly recast
> as sound investment in future success. Children nowadays live in a
> landscape of childhood where clearly defined paths of development,
> laid down by adults, carve up the terrain. Not even an inch of that
> turf may lie fallow.
>
> (Manne 1998)

There is nothing unusual about this teacher. No one has encouraged
her to observe the subtle, textured learning initiated and enhanced by
children's playlore. She has no notion of why the young play collaboratively more than competitively, nor why they assign skill a lower priority
than friendly communication and interaction. Her adult culture values
sport, and somewhere in her teacher training she has imbibed a kind of
Whig theory of child development – the young have one purpose, to
grow more and more mature. That growth is what one should encourage, so pastimes such as Hopscotch are viewed as merely training for the
important, mature activity of competitive sport. A narrow concept of
usefulness prevails.

If children's folklore for so many adults is trivial, even frivolous, then it is not surprising that they should attempt to substitute activities of a more valued kind. And if some adults regard sport as more commendable than Hopscotch and hand-clapping, there are others who would replace such profitless play with something serious and important – academic work.

This is the logic behind the 1998 decision of the Atlanta public school districts in the USA to 'eliminate recess in elementary schools as a waste of time that would be better spent' on school work. According to the superintendent of schools in Atlanta, 'we are intent on improving academic performance. You don't do that by having kids hanging on the monkey bars' (Johnson 1998). The newspaper article in which this educational insight was quoted notes other American schools where play is curtailed, or turned into ' "socialized recess", where children are required to take part in structured, monitored activities' (Johnson 1998).

Oh brave new world, that has such experts in it . . .

A similar philosophy is now increasingly permeating after-school and holiday programmes in Australia, some of which consist of little more than sport and crafts, plus homework. This is depressing, and certainly needs to be challenged. But we should not forget the resilience and resourcefulness of children who want and need to play. The USA, currently home of the abolish-recess tendency, also provides an effective illustration of the enduring nature of children's playlore.

In 1980, an elementary school in Georgia introduced a policy very similar to that currently operating in Atlanta. According to a study undertaken that year, at Alps Road Elementary School:

> recess is short and often given over to a physical education lesson or a supervised kickball game; the lunchroom is strictly supervised; and in-class break times are sometimes forfeited as penalties for bad behavior. Unstructured time for students has been shrunk to a minimum for the sake of discipline and academic progress.
>
> (Tobin 1982: 4)

While the researcher recorded a decline in the more elaborate time- and equipment-based games at school, such as skipping and ball-bouncing, many survived in the home environment. During school hours, children found opportunities for verbal play and a variety of hand games in the cracks and crevices of the carefully organized adult timetable:

> the children are able to spread the dreaded cooties [imaginary infection] around the dinner table, divine futures whilst standing in line, exchange hand-slaps and finger tricks in corridors, chant rhymed insults to each other on the kick-ball field, perform intricate hand-claps on the school bus, pass slam books around during class, and share non-verbal riddles and construct folk toys with the aid of school notepaper.
>
> (Tobin 1982: 10)

This is not an argument for accepting the foolish, narrow and often counter-productive precepts of those in positions of authority who blunder and trespass on children's playtime. But we can take some comfort from the knowledge that the traditional lore of childhood appears stronger and more enduring than the most authoritarian school superintendents and their ilk.

It is a long time since I first began to journey among what the historian Peter Laslett called 'the crowds and crowds of little children ... strangely absent from the written record' (1971: 109–10). In that time I have had the privilege of learning a good deal from children themselves, and from the memories of adults, about the power and the passion of the young at play.

This work has also given rise to controversy, to anxious mutterings and calls for censorship from those who cannot bear too much reality, who recognize children only when they are dressed in the deceptive veils of innocence and purity.

Of this I am certain: children's folklore is not something that can be sanctioned and certified; it is not a pleasing attachment or adornment to the lives of children. It is a central element of human social, psychological and cognitive evolution. To study the cultures and traditions of childhood is one way of seeking to understand the complexity of human growth and change. In doing so, we would be wise to take note of the Opies' warning: 'folklore is not young; and it is as wily as a serpent' (Opie and Opie 1980: 68).

Notes

1 The series now consists of seven books, published by Hodder Headline and Allen & Unwin. An earlier collection, *Cinderella Dressed in Yella*, co-edited with Ian Turner and Wendy Lowenstein (1978), was considered by the publisher and many reviewers to be a book for adults.
2 The Australian Children's Folklore Collection is now housed in the Museum of Victoria.
3 William Blake, English poet, artist and visionary (1757–1827). These phrases, which have entered the language, come from a famous poem, sung in churches and by choirs under the title *Jerusalem*.
4 Examples of books influenced by a similar perspective include Somerville (1982) and Packard (1983).
5 A recent sociological, sometimes critical re-examination of the notion of the 'construction' of childhood can be found in the collection edited by Allison James and Alan Prout (1997).
6 Discussion of early attitudes to childhood and pedagogy can be found in Cubberley (1920) and Rusk (1962).
7 See, for example, Bruner *et al.* (1976), Schwartzman (1978), Winnicott (1971), Einon (1985), Kleiber and Roberts (1983).

2

The ins and outs of school playground play: children's use of 'play places'

Marc Armitage

At first glance the typical UK primary school playground at the start of the twenty-first century seems to be a mass of confusion, movement and noise – little organization or structure seems evident as is often reported by teachers and midday supervisors who point to an absence of traditional games and activities and a distinct lack of play.[1] This common view leads many adult members of the school community to the same conclusions as Brian Sutton-Smith that 'the older view that we need only leave children alone and their spontaneity will do the rest no longer holds' (1981b: 289). Direct interaction with children and intervention in their play is seen as necessary to regain some value in the experiences that children gain from the time they spend on the playground.

This negative perception is, however, just that, a perception, and one that on closer investigation is found to be false. Iona and Peter Opie have drawn attention to the fact that:

> It is remarkable how much guesswork has been expended on classical, medieval, and Tudor pastimes, simply because the learned commentators in the eighteenth and nineteenth centuries, closeted in their studies, lacked knowledge of the games that their own children were playing in the sunshine outside their windows. And this in itself is an illustration of the gap there always is between the generations.
>
> (Opie and Opie 1969: viii)

In this they could easily have been writing about the modern primary school playground and the staff room that sits beside it, as even a brief period of structured observation reveals a very different picture. It reveals a primary school playground that is full of imagination, fantasy and mystery; friendship groups; organized and highly structured games; quiet, reflective play; and noise and movement. Perhaps even more remarkably it reveals a playground divided into distinct and widely accepted places, each reserved for a specific game or form of play unique to that place, and often unique to a specific group within the school's child population.

Peter Blatchford has observed that 'adults face particular difficulties in understanding much of what goes on in the playground. Sometimes when in a school playground an observer can record individual behaviours, but remain unclear how they fit together' (1994: 19). However, by reviewing the information found in around 90 case studies of what actually happens on primary school playgrounds across a large geographical area of the North of England it is possible to begin to make sense of what one sees.

This chapter, based on fieldwork carried out on primary school playgrounds across Yorkshire, Lincolnshire and Nottinghamshire throughout the 1990s, draws in particular on the results of 90 play audits (a list of those referred to in the chapter is included in the appendix). These audits, which are carried out in cooperation with children at each school, are aimed at learning what happens (in terms of play) within the school grounds, where it happens, who does it, and what it is called. This is done through a combination of observations, interviews, mapping exercises and general conversations with children and adults during playtimes and lunchtimes.[2] The chapter will explore the relationship between what children do on the playground and where they do it, and conclude with the implications this has for the design of school playgrounds.

A place to play

The typical UK primary school provides for its children a place to play – the school playground. As early as 1660 the educationalist Charles Hoole stated, 'there should be a paved court around the school, part of which should be "shedded or cloistered" over to enable scholars to play outside in wet weather' (quoted in Seabourne 1971: 65). Under the continuing influence of nineteenth-century British educationalists such as Wilderspin, Stow and Froebel, the provision of a playground, or schoolyard, in elementary schools of England and Wales had become 'normal' by the mid-1850s and it is rare in the UK at the start of the twenty-first century to find a primary school that does not have a playground.[3]

However, as Colin Ward remarks, just because one particular area has been designated by adults as a playspace, this is no guarantee that it will be used as such by children (1990: 180), whereas other features and areas around the school grounds which are definitely *not* provided for play will be used. This is a phenomenon that often perplexes and annoys the adult members of the school but occurs simply because 'contemporary designs (or absence of design) for the play space around school buildings ignore the needs of the games which children actually play' (Moore 1986: 76).

In many areas of providing play provision for children, designers have been guilty of basing that provision on the needs of adults or on what adults feel children could and should be able to do, rather than the needs of children or what children actually do. This is especially so in providing a place to play at school where the design of the modern school playground may provide even fewer play opportunities than those of the past. J.S. Reynolds, in his book *Hints on School Building* (1863 – see Seabourne 1971), recommended that 'more than half the total site area [of a school should be] occupied by the playground, which was equipped with swings, parallel bars, etc., and partly covered over for use in wet weather' (quoted in Seabourne 1971: 224). An inspection of the drawings of new schools built in the towns and villages of England and Wales right up to the inter-war years of the mid-twentieth century shows that advice of this sort was taken, but from the early 1950s onwards school design began to take on a new model.

It is very evident walking around schools designed during this period that the priority given to the provision of a playground as both a place to play and an integral part of the school was beginning to change and even the provision of play equipment in the yard was becoming an exception and not the rule. Throughout the next two decades the process continued and by the mid-1980s the transformation seemed complete – it is now a rare sight indeed to see play equipment in the grounds of a primary school.[4]

Even the proportion of the site given over to a hard surface playground seems to have gradually reduced to the extent that the most recent primary school built in my own home county has a total playground area that is very small in comparison to the area of the school buildings, even smaller than those playgrounds provided at local schools built during the 1980s. At least most primary schools of today have the benefit of a playing field. Unfortunately, this is a part of the school that cannot effectively be used for a significant part of the year due to wet weather and to which access is sometimes actively restricted during playtimes. It is interesting to note that the school field typically receives few mentions by children when completing a play audit at their school and, although the field and other grassed areas are mentioned, the most significant parts of the school to children themselves tend to be on or very close to the playground surface.

These general design changes to the playground, coupled with more recent reductions in the time made available for playtime in UK primary schools, demonstrates that neither the freely chosen, self-directed play of playtimes, nor the playground itself, are afforded the same priority in the overall education of the child as they were in the days of Wilderspin, Stow and Froebel.

It is possible that these changes have contributed to the current perception of this apparent 'lack of play' held among the adult community in our schools, even without these adults realizing that these physical and

Figure 2.1 Typical modern primary school playground: a flat, featureless square or rectangle, set away from the school buildings and producing no easily definable areas that children can use to keep distance between different types of play.

administrative changes have actually taken place (for example, some express genuine surprise at learning that the provision of play equipment was once the norm), but it is important to remember that, as the Opies have remarked, such perceptions have existed over many generations of adults – even throughout the more enlightened times noted above. Despite this, the result of the school play audits seems to be that the present generation of children still manages to satisfy the basic developmental needs that their bodies unconsciously tell them they require, without the direct involvement of adults and in a play environment that can be unattractive, barren and seemingly devoid of play value (see Figure 2.1).

The play audits have also demonstrated that different age groups within the primary school use their school grounds in very different ways and that there is surprisingly little variation between what happens at one school within a particular age group and another. What might be even more surprising is that there is also little variation in *where* various forms of play take place within the school grounds, to such an extent that it is possible, with a little practice, to walk around a school site without the presence of children and still identify places that are used for specific forms of play. These places could be further defined as 'playspaces' and 'play features'.

Play and spaces

Adults at a school will sometimes designate a particular space on the playground as being for one activity, or more often for one particular group, but children themselves define the whole of their available playspace into a number of accepted spaces, some of which are at odds with those that have been adult-designated. Perhaps the most obvious example of an accepted and/or designated space is that set aside for football. It is certainly the one space and activity that generates the most frequently reported complaints and conflicts among both adult and child members of the primary school.

On a modern school site, where the playground is either square or rectangular and set away from the school buildings, football tends to dominate the playground, often with more than one game happening in the same space at the same time.[5] Typically, more than half the hard surface area of a school site will be occupied by football, which is generally played by less than a quarter of the school population, often boys only (see Figure 2.2). This figure is remarkably consistent from school to school: for example, at one school in Immingham, North Lincolnshire (February 1997),[6] there are two rectangular playgrounds of similar size at right angles to each other. Of these one is exclusively taken over by boys playing football. In addition, younger children will often escape the hustle and bustle of the accepted football space and

Figure 2.2 Rectangular playground dominated by boys playing football. Typically, more than half the available hard surface will be taken over by boys playing football with sometimes, as in the example here, more than one game in the same space at the same time.

use part of the second playground for football too, increasing the amount of space taken up with this one activity to more than half the space available.

A second example can be found at a primary school in the city of Hull (September 1997) which has a single large, wide-open playground and no school field. Here, the older year groups within the school each have their own definable and accepted space around the centre of the playground for football. This results in something like four large spaces being occupied by this one fast-moving activity which can make access from one part of the playground to another hazardous to say the least. Not surprisingly, problems of moving around the playground were the most frequently recorded 'worst thing about your playground' among children at this school. This example may be an extreme one, but even where a school has two separate square or rectangular playgrounds, one designated for infants and one for juniors, this does not seem to ease the situation as each playground becomes dominated by football players, in effect doubling the potential for conflict.

There are occasions when, recognizing the conflict that domination of large amounts of space creates, an attempt is made by adults at a school to demarcate a space for football. Painting boundary lines, designating an existing painted netball court or using a line of plastic cones are common methods which schools use to do this. However, all fail as these boundaries do not stop the ball, and wherever the ball goes, the game goes. Even at those schools where the children themselves define a netball court as being 'the football place', if it is painted onto a wide-open playground that extends beyond the court lines, again the game spreads to take over all the available space.

Nor does banning football seem to work. At one East Yorkshire school, for example (April 1994), the popularity of bringing rolled-up pairs of gloves to school, even during summer, was found to be a method of escaping the 'no using footballs on the playground' ban. I have also regularly observed stones, plastic bottles and smaller-sized balls, among other things, being used to defy similar bans at a number of schools. Attempting to ban the playing of football seems generally unsuccessful.

Where the space in use for football also coincides with the accepted space for other forms of play, conflict in the form of minor accidents and squabbles increases. What Iona and Peter Opie call 'play with things' (Opie and Opie 1997) – hoops, beanbags and, in particular, skipping ropes, and so on – does not mix well with football; nor does football and chase play, or what children around the study area variously refer to as Tig, Tigs, Tiggy or Dobby games, as these different forms of play often occupy the same space. At those schools with a single rectangular playground this can be a considerable cause of conflict and often results in groups of children, particularly girls, being squeezed into corners and along the edges in a desperate attempt to get some distance between different forms of play (see Figure 2.3).

Figure 2.3 Football often squeezes play with things (such as hoops, beanbags and, in particular, skipping ropes) into corners and along edges of the playground. Girls especially lose out in the use of open spaces at schools with wide-open playgrounds.

Adults can sometimes add to this conflict. For example, at one primary school in Hull (January 1998) the children were unable to play football in the customary accepted space due to building work. Seeing this, the deputy headteacher pointed to another part of the playground and said, 'Go and play football over there'. The children were visibly reluctant to do so until prompted further by the adult. The space which the deputy head was pointing out was that accepted as being the space for skipping; however, the children did go and play football there, which then of course displaced a number of girls skipping because 'Mrs __ told us to play here'. This one seemingly innocuous act went on to cause a great deal of resentment among a significant number of children at the school for some time – resentment that went largely unnoticed among the adults at the school.

Noticeably, the situation differs greatly when the school playground is either U- or L-shaped, or wraps around the school buildings (also producing U- and L-shapes). Complaints by children about movement from one part of the playground to another are fewer and football is not said by children to cause as many conflicts as it does on square or rectangular playgrounds. It seems that the boundaries provided by the very shape of the playground and/or the presence of walls contains the movement of the game within a more defined space which, unlike designated spaces using painted lines or cones, has a boundary which actually stops the ball. In schools with playgrounds like this the space taken up by football is often much less than half the available playground area yet still typically involves the same proportion of players.

Playgrounds that wrap around the school buildings, especially where outbuildings produce lots of nooks and crannies, also show an increase in the number of accepted spaces for other forms of play. For example, at one small primary school on the Yorkshire Wolds (February 1994), the south arm of a U-shaped playground is used almost exclusively by infant years' children even though it has not been designated as such by adults. Football and chase games are played along the west arm only, and skipping and hiding games around the north arm. Very rarely do infant years' children venture into this latter area, even though it is less than 40 metres from their accepted space.

In addition, a number of outbuildings along the north arm of the school produce three defined spaces. The biggest of the three is used exclusively for skipping and people skip nowhere else but here. A second is used exclusively for what I refer to as parallel games, in other words games played between one parallel line and another. Games such as Hot Chocolate, Ice Cream, Grandmother's Footsteps, Peep behind the Curtain, Polo, TV Polo and May I?, which are essentially all the same game, are played exclusively here and again nowhere else on the site.[7] It is a common finding of the play audits that where there exist these easily defined spaces, specific games and activities tend to be played in a very limited number of places, and more often than not in one exclusive place only (see Figure 2.4).

Other physical differences to the school site also seem to be accepted as definable boundaries between accepted spaces. At the Hull school mentioned earlier (January 1998), where the deputy head inadvertently moved football players into the area used for skipping, this latter space is at one extreme end of a rectangular playground and has no three-dimensional boundary to mark it as 'different'. However, this small area has a completely different surface material from the rest of the playground, one that not only looks different but also feels different underfoot.[8] When mapping the site during this school's play audit, this particular space was consistently recorded by children as being a 'different' place from the rest of the playground.

This division of playspace based on physical boundaries is not peculiar to children within school grounds only. Robin Moore has noted in children's use of the built-up environment in general that 'a strong sense of enclosure and physical differentiation can stimulate the use of a small portion of an otherwise large, underused, open space' (1986: 146).

Of the example forms of play mentioned so far, football and chase games require a large amount of open space and play with things (skipping in

Figure 2.4 A National School building built in the first half of the nineteenth century. The playground wraps around the building, creating a U-shape, and the existence of outbuildings creates nooks and crannies which are informally accepted as being reserved for one particular type of play.

particular) also requires open space, but perhaps less so than football and chase games. Parallel games also require space but in a slightly different way as not only is the space needed much less than the other examples, but this space also needs the greater definition of two easily identifiable facing lines. Together, these four very different forms of play have been recorded as being common to all 90 schools covered by the play audits. Also common to all those schools studied have been similarities in where these forms of play take place.

If the school has a square or rectangular playground set away from the school buildings then the main area of the playground tends to be dominated by those activities requiring open space, with play with things and parallel games sometimes being squeezed into the corners and edges. Where the playground is either U- or L-shaped, these activities dominate less space, but can still be a point of conflict, in particular at the point where the various arms of the playground meet. Where the proximity of the playground to the school buildings, and the existence of nooks and crannies or other physical elements of the site act as easily identified boundaries, then children create accepted spaces for specific forms of play, gaining distance between one form and another. Where this happens, different forms of play do not come into close contact and as a result conflict across the whole of the general playspace seems reduced.

Play and features

During a play audit carried out at a primary school near Doncaster in West Yorkshire (October 1996) a structured game that was popular among the infant years' children was recorded which they called Tiggy Round the Tortoise. This was a chase game centred on a roughly 1-metre wide, domed feature made of small stone blocks that did indeed look like a tortoise shell. This feature was generally referred to among the child population of the school as 'the tortoise' and was not only used for this one specific game but also acted as a geographical pointer, or reference point, that children used during their everyday conversations about the playground. This forms an example of a unique 'feature', rather than a space, acting as the centre of a specific game or form of play.

The example of the tortoise is one which is unique to that one school but, in a similar way to the relationship between play and spaces, there are some forms of play that are consistently centred around easily identifiable and accepted features in the school grounds. At a Hull primary school (July 1998), for example, junior years' children play Marbles exclusively on one of any number of square, metal drain covers dotted around the site (although those that are close to the shelter of nearby walls prove the most popular). These drain covers do not have a smooth surface but are full of raised metal studs that make the movement of the Marbles a little unpredictable. In the centre of the drain cover is a raised circle in which the manufacturer's name is written in raised letters. The aim of the game in this case is said to be to get your marble in this centre area within a given number of moves while your opponents do the same (see Figure 2.5).

Although the playing of Marbles has not been recorded at all schools in the study group, where it has been recorded (about 65 per cent of all cases) there have been only two examples where the most popular spot for playing Marbles has not been on a metal drain or sink cover.[9] This is sometimes complicated even further when children clearly see a difference in features that might appear to adults to be the same or at least similar. An example of this can be seen at one Hull school (February 1994, January 1998) where junior years only play on square drain covers, and the one and only example of a round drain cover is used exclusively by infants. This was, I was told, because 'the round one is easier'.

At the same school there is a long aluminium drainage cover running almost the full length of one playground, a distance of about 30 metres. During the accepted Marbles season (which starts any time between February and May at this school), the whole feature disappears under a crowd of people playing Marbles along the metal slots that run across its length (see Figure 2.6). The playing of Marbles becomes so popular here that the headteacher has introduced a method of drawing the season to a close – she opens her diary during an assembly and exclaims, 'I see from my diary that Marble season ends a week on Friday!' And sure enough, it does.

Figure 2.5 Marbles being played exclusively on a metal drain cover. Some drain covers are considered more difficult than others.

Figure 2.6 A long aluminium drain, the whole length of which is filled with Marbles players during the Marbles season.

Figure 2.7 A short length of metal fencing used as the 'jail'. Almost all the junior years' children at the school referred to this as the 'jail' and used it as the place where those caught during Cops and Robbers are locked up.

The use of drain covers for Marbles is not the only example of a specific feature being used for a specific form of play. In the corner of one playground of a primary school in Lincolnshire (December 1996), there stands the only example of a piece of metal fencing anywhere on the site. It is approximately 2 metres long by about 1 metre high and when questioned no members of the adult community of the school could recall why this odd piece of fencing had been put there, or even when. When questioning the children at the school, though, this feature was consistently referred to as the 'jail' and was said to be the place where the 'robbers are taken to and locked up' during chase games such as Cops and Robbers (see Figure 2.7).

At the school the existence of this feature and its use as a jail was well-known among all but the very youngest children, despite the fact that only junior years' boys were ever observed using it as a jail. The existence of some form of team-based chase game that involves capture and imprisonment at a specific and well-known feature within the school grounds is, however, another common form of play that has been recorded at all schools covered by the play audits. Contrary to what might be thought by adults, though, a game like Cops and Robbers does not simply 'begin', but rather the 'robbers' go to a given point on the playground, which is generally said to be a bank, or shops (in one school in Lincolnshire this was said to be the 'pub', October 1996). The robbers then proceed to rob this place, at which point the 'coppers' appear, having left their starting place, chase the robbers, catch them and take them back to their starting point, which is the jail.

There are a number of interesting consistencies in the way this type of imprisonment play is carried out. First, this form of play has been recorded at all schools so far surveyed. Second, the start of the game is very similar from place to place, as is the fact that the place where the robbers are taken to and locked up is referred to as the jail, prison, cells or dungeon. However, the most interesting consistency is that in more than 80 per cent of cases the specific feature accepted as being the jail is something which has vertical metal bars.

For example, at one Hull primary school built in the 1880s (September 1997), the jail is a set of strong vertical metal bars covering the floor-level windows to the caretaker's basement (see Figure 2.8). At another, more modern school in Hull, built in the late 1970s, the jail is a high black metal fence around the school's nursery unit, and at one East Yorkshire primary (March 1996) a raised concrete platform in front of one

Figure 2.8   The 'jail' at a school built in the 1880s, showing use of yet another feature with vertical metal bars. The pattern of wear and tear marks on the paintwork of this feature is typical of those in use as a jail and shows that the feature has been used in this way for many years.

Figure 2.9 A school built in the 1960s showing another jail using vertical metal bars. The children at this school call this the 'dungeon' and include the steps as part of the feature.

particular doorway flanked by a set of blue metal railings is called the 'dungeon' and is used as a place to 'lock the robbers up' (see Figure 2.9). Once again the audits reveal that there is generally only one such accepted feature within the school grounds and very rarely more than two.

There are school sites, though, that are nearly or completely surrounded by metal fencing. At one school (July 1996) which has high metal fencing on three sides of a large rectangular playground, I could not work out by observation where the equivalent feature might be. Signs of physical evidence also proved fruitless on the non-painted fencing. When questioning children about how they played Cops and Robbers, though, the jail was revealed. At this school the place where the robbers were taken to and locked up is called the 'coppers' gate', and it was actually an easily overlooked padlocked and unused gate in one corner of the fencing (see Figure 2.10).

It seems that when there is simply too much metal fencing to easily identify a place of imprisonment, a more defined feature, usually a gate, is used. There are, however, school sites on which there are no metal features which could act as a realistic jail, and in these cases other features are pressed into use. A particular inward corner of a building might be used,

Figure 2.10 Sometimes a school playground is surrounded by metal fencing. In this case a more defined feature, the 'coppers' gate', is used as the playground jail.

as well as groups or single examples of fixed benches, and the narrow space between two drainpipes has also been recorded. But the most common alternative feature, accounting for more than 10 per cent of examples, is very surprising.

During the play audit at a primary school in Hull (November 1996), a group of children were observed standing against a wall of the school buildings, each with their hands held behind their back. On closer inspection, each child was found to be holding onto a black metal over-flow pipe leading from the toilet cisterns on the other side of this wall. This, they said, was the jail and they had been caught and locked up by the cops. These small pipes, which are sometimes made of metal and sometimes plastic, are at just the right height for many children to be 'locked up' to.

The existence of one, or at most two, accepted and well-known features in use as a jail has also been recorded at all schools in the study group without exception, but knowledge of these features is often limited among infant years' children and usually non-existent among adults.

However, infant years' children do seem to use these jail features too, or sometimes have their own equivalent, but they use them in a very different way. Whereas juniors will concentrate on chasing and capture, infants use them as a focal point for more fantasy-based pretend play which results in imprisonment. The use of a place of imprisonment, which is often the same as, or within a few metres of, that used by the older children is still important but it is not referred to in the same way, and there is one additional feature associated with this latter form of play that has equal significance.

For example, at one East Yorkshire primary school (February 1998) there is a set of benches arranged in a U-shape within a few metres of a line of plastic overflow taps used by older children as the playground jail. These benches act as a focal point for much pretend play among the infants who use these benches as the house of a monster figure, such as a ghost or witch. During one observation session a group of about four or five infant years' girls and boys, with their coats fastened around throats like capes, were observed playing a game around this 'house'. The group was tempting a monster (one of the boys) to leave the safety of his house and chase them. This finally happened and after the monster succeeded in capturing all the other players they were brought back to his house where he announced:

Monster: My bite's poisonous. [*Throws his arms up and growls. One person runs away screaming*]
2nd Person [*to the monster*]: Do it again. [*He growls again, then the 2nd person leaps onto the floor and shouts out*] 'Eat me!' [*All the others scream loudly*].

This form of play, which has also been recorded at all schools in the play audits, almost always has a violent storyline that follows the same structure – that is, as Iona and Peter Opie note, 'in some places the evil one is a wizard, a wolf, or a ghost, but the fate of those caught is the same, to be boiled in a stewpot and eaten' (1969: 343).

Very noticeably, at the base of one of the bench supports around the monster's house is a small, dug hole, about 20 centimetres across, which regularly has combinations of small twigs, stones, grass and small flowers (such as daisies) placed in it. This is said to be the place where the 'witch makes potions'. The same was said of a smaller hole in the bench itself which also had small stones and grass placed in it (see Figure 2.11). Compare this with an infant school in East Yorkshire (March 1997) where the area inside a large bush at the edge of the playground is said to be the 'witch's house' or 'cottage' and proves to be the focal point for similar play to the above. On the main branch of a small tree alongside this is a circle formed from a point where a smaller branch has been cut

Figure 2.11 With added pebbles, grass and small flowers, this hole in a bench top acts as a cauldron where the 'witch makes potions'. The bench is also used by infant years' children at the school as a centre of pretend games involving monsters and witches.

off. This is called the 'cauldron' by children at the school and is the place where the 'witch makes spells'.

In fact, the existence of at least one cauldron or stewpot which can be found near to or in the area used as the witch's house, cottage or castle has been recorded in nearly all examples of this type of play found in the play audits, and it is often this accepted feature that defines where this form of play is carried out more than the feature used as the place of imprisonment. Almost always these features are either holes in the ground specially dug for the purpose, or are holes in bench tops, tables or tree logs. There have also been a number of occasions when more artificial things have been identified as the main feature. On four occasions, for example, the small metal door on an outward wall that covers the school's heating oil supply point has been said to be the 'furnace' (with at one school children saying they could look through the keyhole and see the bones of the 'bad children being burnt', April 1994) (see Figure 2.12). One more example of this is a small painted square on the surface at one edge of a primary school playground in Hull (January 1993, November

Figure 2.12　Some cauldrons on the playground are places where spells and potions are made but others have a more sinister use. This is the 'furnace' where, looking through the keyhole the children could see the bones of the 'bad children being burnt' who had been put there by the 'witch'.

1996) that children said they called the 'witch's dungeon'. Just to the north of this was a line of painted floor circles, one group of which were referred to as the 'pots', and another as the 'plates'.

Identifying the feature in use as a jail has usually been easy – junior years' children seem to have no fears about passing on this information and excitedly explain how the feature is used. With the witch's house and cauldron, on the other hand, identifying the feature in use has sometimes proved problematic. The problem does not seem to be one of younger children having difficulties expressing themselves about this form of play, but more of a reluctance to discuss it. Possibly as a result of this there have been a few examples where locating such a feature has proved impossible or, more often, where the feature has been observed in use but not verbally confirmed by the children. However, in almost all cases one or more specific feature has been found to be widely known and accepted as being a witch's house and a cauldron and has acted as a centre for this form of pretend play.

Summary and conclusion

The completion of the 90 play audits has provided an opportunity to make sense of what takes place on the typical primary school playground. What these audits reveal is a picture of an informally organized playground and surroundings that are made up of accepted spaces and features that act as the centre of particular forms of play, some of which are unique to one particular age group within the school. The observations made in this chapter on accepted spaces for football, play with things, chase games and parallel games, and on specific features used for Marbles and games of imprisonment are only a few examples of play activities and specific games that have not only been observed to be evident at all schools in the study group but have also been found to be carried out in remarkably similar places.

The work on which these observations are based is continuing. In particular, two play audits have now been made at three different primary schools, each more than five years apart. The significance of this is that between one audit and another the whole child population of the school has changed. It is revealing that the accepted spaces and features have a consistency over time as well as location, so much so that it may well be that once a particular space or feature has become accepted as the place where that particular activity is done, it remains so until we adults make significant changes to the playground. At the school with the tortoise, for example, a second visit carried out after 1996 failed to record the game Tiggy Round the Tortoise being played. The reason was simply that the feature at the centre of this game had, between visits, been removed as a possible safety hazard, despite the fact that no accidents had been recorded on this feature in more than 25 years.

Such actions may be open to question but of more general concern might be the continuous habit of designing school playgrounds as large open squares or rectangles set away from the school buildings. This environment, devoid of access to nooks and crannies or other three-dimensional features that might serve as defining boundaries, makes it difficult for children to define their own places and gain distance between different forms of play. When this results in different forms of play competing for space then conflict is bound to arise. The blame for the results of this conflict is rarely laid at the door of those who designed this overall space in the first instance, but rather on the children themselves who valiantly battle to make the best of a bad job. As Robin Moore observes, 'we have no business making policy and spending money on facilities for children until we have an understanding about what parts of the environment children actually use, and why' (1986: xvi).

The primary schoolchildren of today can quite easily be left alone on the playground and their spontaneity will do the rest. This is in fact what already happens. But for them to be able to make use of this spontaneity to the best of their ability, and do so without the need for direct adult intervention in their play, the environment provided for them as a place to play must respect the finding that children themselves are informally organizing their available spaces and features to meet their own needs. As adults, our role should be to support this and provide an environment that caters for what children actually play as opposed to what they should or could play, or even what we think they play.

Appendix: unpublished play audits

January 1993, Hull Primary School
February 1994, Hull Primary School
February 1994, East Yorkshire Primary School (Yorkshire Wolds)
April 1994, East Yorkshire Infant School (Hull Valley)
December 1994, Hull Primary School
July 1995, Hull Primary School
January 1996, Hull Primary School
March 1996, East Yorkshire Primary School
July 1996, Hull Primary School
October 1996, North Lincolnshire Primary School (Axholme)
October 1996, Doncaster Primary School
November 1996, Hull Primary School
December 1996, Lincolnshire Primary School
February 1997, North Lincolnshire Junior School
March 1997, East Yorkshire Infant School (Holderness)
September 1997, Hull Primary School
January 1998, Hull Primary School
February 1998, East Yorkshire Primary School (Bridlington)
July 1998, Hull Primary School

Acknowledgement

The author wishes to thank all the children and schools involved in this research.

Notes

1 In the current education system in England and Wales, a primary school is one which caters for children aged between 5 and about 11 years. This age group is sometimes further divided into infant years (5 to around 8 years) and junior years (9 years plus).
2 There are times when a fifth objective is added to the remit of these play audits: 'How long is each type of play/game played for?'.
3 The government's own Committee of Council on Education, for example, produced designs for model schools from the mid-1840s that included the provision of a schoolyard as a standard element of the design.
4 Although there have been various periods of interest in reintroducing play equipment into school grounds, most recently during the mid-1980s and again

towards the end of the 1990s, the number of primary schools in the UK with some form of play equipment within the grounds is still low. Of the schools covered by the play audits only 6 per cent have some kind of manufactured play equipment with modern, fairly recently added equipment being the most common. Even covered play space, as advocated by the early educationalists, is uncommon with just under 4 per cent of schools in the audits having sheltered outdoor space. However, in a number of other schools it was possible to see where there had been covered areas that had subsequently been dismantled or built under.

5 It is not always the exact centre of the playground that football dominates. Sometimes the space used is on the main playground but off-centre, or is along one edge. The reasons for this are almost always environmental. For example, at one school where football was played exclusively along one edge of the playground, the reason was reported to be because after rain large puddles would form in the centre and along the opposite edge. Even in this example, though, the game still spread to take over adjacent playground space.

6 All the references to schools in this chapter have used the audit reference number rather than the name of the school. (See Appendix.)

7 For a more detailed description of these and other games mentioned in the text, see Opie and Opie (1969).

8 The surface material for the main part of the playground is a very dark tarmac, whereas this small area is made up of large, square concrete sections that are actually part of an older playground surface.

9 This is not to say that children do not play Marbles in other parts of the school, just that in the schools covered by the play audits the most popular Marbles playing place was on drain and sink covers. In the two examples where this was not the case, both in Hull (July 1995 and January 1996), the most popular spots were in holes dug in the ground (see also Opie and Opie 1997).

Part 2

Creativity, continuity and variety in contemporary play traditions

To conduct fieldwork among children and investigate their play is not the simple matter that it might first appear. It takes skill, sensitivity and rapport to win the trust of the children and to be allowed, as an adult, to enter their culture. How this is done, including issues of how the fieldworker presents him- or herself and how she or he explains the research and gains the informed consent of the children, are just some of the many ethical issues fieldwork with children raises (Alderson 2000). In addition, the fieldworker has to decide on the most appropriate ways of obtaining information, such as the use of structured interviews and more casual conversations with the children, the photographing or audio- and videotaping of play activities, and participant observation in the playground (for a discussion of some of the methodological and ethical issues in conducting fieldwork with children, see Fine 1995). Indeed, fieldwork often requires the use of several of these techniques in combination, thus enabling a process of 'triangulation' in the research process (Fine 1995: 139).

In the following chapters, the authors have gained such privileged access to the play culture of children. Drawing on many of the above methods, they each present a detailed picture of children's play, principally as it takes place in specific school playgrounds in the North and South of England, France and Australia. In each case, the results of the fieldwork provide evidence of a flourishing culture of play among the children studied, a culture which exhibits all of the complexities outlined by Factor in Chapter 1 and the dynamics of creativity, continuity and variety associated with a tradition which is very much alive.

Chapter 3, by Mavis Curtis, investigates important questions regarding the sources of play activities, how they are transmitted, and the extent of children's game repertoires. While it has long been known that the games and rhymes of boys and girls are often sharply differentiated in middle childhood, Curtis presents data which challenges adults' a priori assumptions that children in the same town or school or even class will share the same repertoire. She suggests that some of this variety may be accounted for by the fact that small divergences in how a game is played or in the precise words of a rhyme constitute important markers of difference to children. Another factor may be that the transmission of tradition largely takes place within friendship groups and among family members. Thus, the knowledge is valued because it comes from a valued source, a significant other – one reason, perhaps, why out-of-school activities were not an extensive source of playlore for many of the children in Curtis' study.

Many similar processes of transmission and variation are found by Kathryn Marsh in a primary school playground on the other side of the world (Chapter 4). Her examples of singing games illustrate the way in which games and game elements are mixed and remixed in a creative process by the children in order to produce new games. Marsh also introduces discussion of another very important source or tributary of childlore, namely the mass media. Far from being dominated by media imagery and icons, however, the children select and recreate from them in a process which simultaneously emulates and mocks adult culture. The highly multicultural make up of the school studied allows Marsh to witness the interethnic and multilingual transmission of play traditions. This process is facilitated by the teachers' active recognition of cultural difference, and also by the use of formulaic and nonsense language in the children's own playtexts, fostering acceptance and integration into friendship groups for children of varying cultural backgrounds.

Elizabeth Grugeon's chapter illustrates the range and variety of girls' play traditions as observed in the space of just one playtime. Here is further evidence that new traditions of media-inspired play activities may be performed side by side with older game forms, with no sense of incongruity for the children. Grugeon's comparative comments document previous occurrences of the games. This demonstrates that many have been perpetuated over time and space and shows the ways in which the children have varied them to suit their immediate needs.

The girls quoted by Grugeon also convey a sense of what continuity and variation means in the children's terms. On the one hand, they acknowledge the immediate source of games (particular friends and relatives) which fosters a sense of a shared special culture, a culture which 'we never tell the teachers. We never do'. On the other, they may see themselves as making up new play activities, which encourages a strong sense of ownership and creativity, and allows them to 'update' their culture in ways they see as relevant to their contemporary lives. Grugeon argues that this empowering and reassuring play is under threat from adults' incursions on children's playtime, a point developed by Carole Carpenter in Part 3 of this book (see Chapter 9).

Continuing the theme of girls' games, in Chapter 6 Andy Arleo concentrates on the internationally disseminated handclapping game 'When Susie Was a Baby'. He explores in detail the kind of linguistic, musical and physical skills, highlighted by Grugeon and Marsh, which the game requires, and extends the comparative and multicultural perspectives they introduce to a cross-linguistic and cross-cultural study covering five continents. Arleo suggests that the widespread currency of the game can be accounted for in terms of its simultaneously conventional and subversive content, which deals with the life cycle of the central female character as portrayed through conventional categories of human development and time. He also argues that the game's popularity is attributable to the close but complex fit between its text, tune and movements, a fit which has been preserved, with the appropriate changes, as the game has crossed linguistic and cultural boundaries.

3

Counting in and counting out: who knows what in the playground

Mavis Curtis

Children's oral tradition is a private world controlled by children with its own rules and ways of dealing with problems. As such it provides experience of social behaviour and the possibility of practising social, physical and verbal skills which increase children's ability to function in a complicated and ever-changing world. James *et al.* (1998: 88) consider that 'the "culture of childhood" can be characterised by fluidity and movement'. They also note, however, that 'as one group of children is poised to enter the "cultural world of childhood", older children may be beginning to relinquish membership of the category "child". But united in their marginality from central social (adult) institutions, all these children share temporarily a common generational culture' (p. 88). An important part of 'the cultural world of childhood' is the games and rhymes children use, and these too demonstrate fluidity and movement. They are also deeply conservative, by which I mean that they show continuity over time and space.

In Chapter 1, June Factor discussed three myths about children's folk-lore. In this chapter I would like to tackle two assumptions which adults commonly make, one which springs from knowledge of the conservative nature of children's play but is ignorant of the 'fluidity and movement' of oral tradition – namely, the assumption that there is a fixed body of knowledge which most children possess and which constitutes 'children's oral tradition'. Having read Chapter 2 by Armitage, we know that in all the schools he has visited children play, among other things, prison games, Hide and Seek, ball games and skipping. A reading of Iona and Peter Opies' four books on games and lore (1959, 1969, 1985, 1997) confirms that, at least when they were doing their research in the 1950s, 1960s and 1970s, there was a vast body of lore, a lake rather than a pool of knowledge, which covered not only the British Isles but was widespread throughout continental Europe and the English-speaking world.

The second assumption is that the playground is the all-important place for the transmission of oral tradition between children. The playground has been described by Roberts (1980: 139) as the forum and focus of play, Sutton-Smith (1972: 11) states that after the institution of schooling in the 1870s in New Zealand, the school playground became the most important centre for children's play, and Sluckin observes that 'what the playground offers is an enormous scope to initiate, discuss, influence and change rules' (1981: 119). So they are all agreed that the school playground is a lively place where the oral tradition thrives and where games are passed on from one generation of children to the next. Yet, it seems to be a common perception among teachers and lunchtime supervisors that nothing is happening in the playground, except for fights, football and whinging, and that children are bored (Curtis 1998: 19).

Curious to know whether all children had access to the same information or whether there was variation in their oral repertoire, I undertook a comparative study of 8-year-olds in nine schools in Keighley, West Yorkshire, to tap into that lake of knowledge. Eight-year-olds were selected because it is usually not until children have reached this age that they have fully mastered peer-group-generated oral tradition (Knapp and Knapp 1976; James 1993). This is because the means of transmission is by apprenticeship: watching, practising and learning by rote, all of which takes time. A second, more pragmatic reason for selecting 8-year-olds was that, because of the structure of the education system in the town at the time, there were both first schools taking 5- to 9-year-olds, and primary schools taking 5- to 11-year-olds, so the 8-year-olds were the oldest children who could be sampled across a range of schools.

Social background

Keighley used to have a thriving economy based on cloth manufacturing and its associated engineering works. This pulled in migrants over the years, many of whom still retain some of their cultural identity. I wanted to explore to what extent cultural identity affected the repertoire of games and rhymes that the children might know. There was an influx of Ukrainians, Poles and Italians after the Second World War, and members of these communities have made positive attempts to maintain their cultural identity by keeping up links with the mother country or by attending clubs based on their cultural identity. There has also been an ongoing migration of Irish into the town since the potato famines of the nineteenth century. Many of these families are Catholic and their children attend the Catholic schools in the town, so there is a wider European connection in these schools, with children having links to extended families in Europe and Ireland. Since the 1960s there has been a wave of immigration from the Indian subcontinent. These people are mostly Punjabi-speaking Pakistanis from the Mirpur area – village people, as they describe themselves. The children of these families live in two main areas of the town and the intake of the schools in these areas is almost entirely Asian, with children speaking English as a second language. There is also a substantial proportion of the population which has not moved far from its roots, families who have lived in Keighley for at least three generations. Differences in social class among the schools were also represented in the research but these delineations were much less clearly defined than the other groupings. Because of the different cultural experiences of these groups, I thought differences might be detected in the culture of the playgrounds in the different schools. Discussion with 243 children took place, if possible in friendship groups, which at this age often means single sex groups (Hartup 1992; Blatchford 1998), so there would be little teasing between the sexes and control of the group dynamics could be kept to a minimum.

Who knows what

The material collected was divided into categories according to a modified version of the classification plan outlined in the Introduction to the present volume. The most striking fact about the games and rhymes collected was how little common knowledge there was between the schools. One might have perhaps expected that the schools where children were speaking English as a second language would have a different repertoire from other schools, but the differences did not apply particularly to those schools. Of all the categories of play, the entertainment rhymes present the most extreme example of this. Of the 28 rhymes collected, only one, a racist rhyme, was known at more than one school; it was known in two schools, neither of which had any Asian children among its population (see Appendix, Table 3.1).[1]

Of the 53 counting-out rhymes, one, 'Racing Car Number Nine' was known at all nine schools, 'Ickle Ockle' was known at eight, 'Eeny Meeny Miney Mo, Put the Baby on the Po' was known at seven, as was 'Ippy Dippy Dation', 'Mickey Mouse Built a House' and 'There's a Party on the Hill' (see Appendix, Table 3.2).

Of the 16 singing games collected, none was known in every school. 'London Bridge' was the most well-known, being described at six schools. Both Catholic schools had more singing games than the others, School A having 13, while School B had 8. Singing games are often taught in the nursery, so it may be that nursery classes in both Catholic schools were involved in the teaching of singing games to a greater extent than the other schools.

In skipping, no rhyme was known in every school. 'I Like Coffee' was the most popular with a mention in six schools, while 'Bluebells Cockleshells' and 'I Know Knickerboy' were known at five.

Among the 34 clapping rhymes, there was one which was known at every school: 'A Sailor Went to Sea' (see Appendix, Table 3.3).

So we can see that of the games high in verbal content, only one counting-out rhyme and one clapping rhyme was common to all nine schools.

Now let us consider the games with a high physical content. Of those without playthings in the individual category there were no games in common. Similarly, there were no team games, though in fact there was only one team game without equipment collected, and that was *Kabadi*, a Pakistani game. Of the group games without an 'It', again there was no knowledge common to every school, though Rock, Scissors, Paper was known at five schools. Of the 25 'low-power It' games, the most popular was Scarecrow Tig, known at eight schools, while Normal Tig was played at seven schools and Bob Down Tig, Place Tig and Hide and Seek were all played at six of the schools.

Of the 16 'high-power It' games, two were known and played at all nine schools. They were Bulldog's Charge and Black Pudding (see Appendix, Table 3.4).

So again we can see that among games high in physical content there is very little knowledge common to every school, only two 'high-power It' games being universally known.

Of the 12 individual games with playthings, skipping was played at all nine schools while, of the seven team games collected, football was known at eight of the schools. It had actually been banned at two schools – at one because of the proximity to the road, and here children had circumvented the prohibition by using rolled-up anorak hoods; at the other it had been banned in an attempt to divert the boys' energies into other activities. Both these schools were therefore counted as having the game, since what was being measured was not what the children were actually playing at the time, but what they knew, what their repertoire was. The school which was not counted as having football was a very small school with few children in the older age group and here the children made no mention of football.

Of the 24 group games, again no game was common to every school, but Hopscotch was played at eight schools. This may have been due to the almost ubiquitous Hopscotch patterns painted on the playgrounds (see Appendix, Table 3.5).

So again we can see that among the games high in physical content with playthings, only skipping was common to all the schools.

Of the 27 games high in imaginative content, it was not expected that there would be any overlap between schools, since imaginative games are the result of the experiences and interests of individual children. Army was a popular game at six of the nine schools, however.

We can see, therefore, that the sum total of games and rhymes shared between all nine schools was one counting-out rhyme, 'Racing Car, Number Nine', one clapping rhyme, 'A Sailor Went to Sea Sea Sea', two 'high-power It' games, Bulldog's Charge and Black Pudding, and skipping.

It is possible for there to be partial explanations for the differences. The results could conceivably have been obtained because children talk about what is important to them at the time and not what they were playing six months, or even six weeks, ago. Yet the research methods were the same for each school, the interviewer was the same, and the interviews were of sufficient duration and depth, giving children ample time to discuss the past as well as the present, and I am confident that most of the repertoire, whether active or passive,[2] of the children interviewed was recorded. The time of year differed and we know that the weather affects what is played (lunchtime supervisors at one school were keen to stress this), but research was undertaken when the weather was reasonable. No research was done in the winter months, December to February, so the bulk of the research was undertaken between March and November 1992 and between March and July 1993.

The picture we have, then, is of fragmentation rather than cohesion, of each school having its own repertoire of games and rhymes, so the idea that there is a body of knowledge which most children share does not appear to be true. It would seem at this stage of the research that there is a body of knowledge which some children have access to and others have not, and, rather than a lake of knowledge, perhaps a better analogy would be a collection of streams of information which trickle along and are tapped into haphazardly. Which aspects of oral tradition children have access to depends on a variety of factors, one of them being the school they attend.

School playgrounds as a source of knowledge

Let us now look at the second assumption, that the school playground is an important, indeed the all-important, area for the passing on of knowledge. My comments here are based on mistakes I made in the construction of my research. I assumed that there was a body of information to be tapped into and that most children would know most of it. I therefore set out to sample not the whole of a year group, but only a given number. Numbers of children interviewed depended on the circumstances pertaining at the time. Table 3.6 (see Appendix) shows the numbers and percentages involved. The percentage of children interviewed in the year group varied from only 33 per cent at one school to 100 per cent at two schools and that the 100 per cent at School A consisted of two parallel classes while at School D it was the whole of one class.

Realizing this could be construed as a weakness in the research design, I set out to demonstrate that the fluctuating numbers of children interviewed would not constitute a problem, since after having interviewed a certain number of children, one would have tapped into this lake of information and drawn off a representative sample of the knowledge they possessed. I assumed that interviewing more than about 20 children from each school would be a waste of valuable time, since the more children I interviewed, the fewer games I would collect. When I came to scrutinize the results closely, however, I discovered that the more children I interviewed, the more information I collected. At School A, where I had sampled the whole of the year group, I found children in the second class playing and knowing different games from those known and played by the first class. It seemed that the class provided a boundary which delimited the transmission of information. And if this were so for a class, perhaps there were also boundaries within the class which limited the transmission of material. It also meant that the schools where less than 100 per cent of the children had been interviewed were probably under-represented in the tables showing games and rhymes knowledge.

Follow-up research

In 1999, therefore, I went back to School G to interview both parallel classes of 8-year-olds and to try to track where information originated and how limited was the spread of that information. I shall concentrate on the two categories of clapping and counting-out rhymes for the following reasons: I have concentrated on verbal rather than physical games because this removes the added complication of the effect of the topography of the playground on the games repertoire; counting-out rhymes were studied because they are used by both girls and boys, and clapping rhymes because they are popular, so I could be sure of recording several examples, and they are used by girls, who are often described as bearers of the oral tradition.

First a description of the school: it is a first school taking in the region of 230 5–9-year-olds, with a nursery class which many of the children have attended. It is at the top of a steep hill. The suburb is about a mile and a half from the town centre and has a small hamlet as the nucleus of a swathe of modern houses at the cheaper end of the housing market. There is also a small council housing estate. Because of the steepness of the hill, there still remain a few fields too steep to build on which isolate the suburb from the town. There are also open spaces around the village as well as fields, a wood and an old quarry which were mentioned by the children as places they played. Though the Asian population of the town is approximately 20 per cent, there are no Asian children, the intake being all white. Most of the out-of-school activities, such as Brownies or youth club, are situated in the locality, and children attending the school also live locally, many of them travelling to school on foot.

The two classes interviewed, Classes 9 and 10, were small: 21 and 23 children respectively, the oldest children in the school. In the interviews

I asked them to describe their games and rhymes, and specifically asked where they had learned them. They also completed a questionnaire in which they recorded who they played with, both in their own class and in the parallel class; who they played with at home; and also what groups they attended outside school. The children were interviewed in friendship groups, which they organized themselves, which resulted in seven groups in Class 9: three groups of girls, two groups of boys and one mixed group. In Class 10 there were four groups: one of girls, one of boys and two mixed groups, one of which was chosen from people who supported Manchester United football team. This was initiated by one of the girls and vigorously supported by several boys.

This second study confirmed one of the findings of the earlier research, that there was a discontinuity of knowledge between the two classes. Table 3.7 (see Appendix) shows the amount of knowledge shared between the two classes: the clapping games and counting-out rhymes known, the groups who knew them and which school class they belonged to. It shows that both in clapping and counting out there is a common repertoire between the two classes, what one might call the school repertoire, but there is also information which is available only within the class, so there could be said to be a class repertoire. The clapping rhyme 'I Went to a Chinese Restaurant' was recorded in Class 10 as 'I Went to a Chinese Baker's Shop', which indicates that there are two separate sources of information available to each class. If we look at the information within a class, we see that much of it is limited to only one group, or even, in extreme cases, to one or two children within the group, so it could be said that each group within a class has its own repertoire, and each child has its own individual stock of oral tradition.

If we turn to a profile of each group which illustrates the different groups of games throughout the spectrum of play possibilities (see Appendix, Table 3.8) we can see that, while there are similarities, for instance in the number of counting-out rhymes known, there are also differences. One group of girls, for instance (Group 1G10) was interested in music, dancing and singing. Three of the members of this group attended dancing class and they all liked to watch line-dancing videos. They were the only group to sing a song which had been learned by the whole class for assembly, a rap, which they found very exciting. It seems probable that here is yet another boundary limiting dissemination of knowledge – material taught by adults may not easily cross the boundary into children's culture and only the group of girls interested in music had managed to incorporate into their musical and social world something taught by adults. There is also one group of boys which is recorded as knowing no counting-out rhymes (Group 2B9). From the conversation I had with them, I think they knew a swearing rhyme which was used at home but not at school, but it was not possible to record it because the sanctions against swearing imposed by the adults were severe.

How information travels

Having considered what the children know, let us now turn our attention to how information travels. First, relationships within and between classes. From the answers they gave in the questionnaire, it was obvious that all the girls in both classes had several other girls to play with. There were no loners. The same applied to the boys with three exceptions. There were two isolated boys in Class 10 who played with younger children and one in Class 9 who played with his younger brother and his brother's friends. Within the two classes, of the 12 girls in Class 9, none listed boys as playmates, though one boy listed three of the girls. Of the rest of the boys in Class 9, none said they played with girls. One girl played football with 'the boys' (unspecified). In Class 10, of the eight girls, only one named boys as playmates. She named two of the boys, and was named by three of the boys as a playmate. She was acknowledged by everyone to be very good at football and at the time of interviewing had her arm in plaster because of a fall incurred while practising karate. One other girl was named as a playmate by a boy. It is fair to say, then, that boys and girls generally played in single-sex groups.

When the links between the classes was examined, a striking feature which emerged was that the boys in the two classes played together and named each other as playmates. Of the 12 boys in Class 9, 2 had no contact with the parallel class, but the remaining 10 nominated boys in the parallel class 24 times. In Class 10, 3 appeared to have no contact with Class 9 boys, but the remaining 10 boys nominated boys in Class 9 22 times. It was not only football which surmounted the school-class barrier. One group of boys played imaginative games based on computer games: *Metal Gear Solid, Predator, Alien Resurrection* and *Tunnel Number One*. We have, then, a picture of boys who have a great many links with the parallel class, but girls who have few contacts. This is in line with the findings of Hartup (1992) and Blatchford (1998).

The children's sources for the rhymes

Table 3.9 (see Appendix) shows where the rhymes were learned.

Clapping

Among the sources identified as teachers of new rhymes were older sisters and a cousin, though one rhyme had been learned from friends at home. The more well-known rhymes had often been learned from friends at school, and even some of the boys knew 'Chinese People', which they had learned from the girls. 'I Yi Yippee' had been learned at dancing class, and the second version of 'Elvis Presley' was known by only one girl who had learned it from an older girl cousin.

These examples highlight the importance of the family as a site of learning and the influence of a child's position in the family on its ability to acquire knowledge of oral tradition. It also shows that in this particular category of game, activities outside the home and school contribute little to the pool of knowledge.

Counting out

Here we see a picture of information passed on at home and school, among friends rather than family and with no input from outside activities such as Beavers, Cubs, Brownies or dancing class. This may well reflect the nature of the rhymes, since they are used in a situation where there is no adult supervision and decisions have to be made by the group and not by someone in authority.

Discussion

Although it is probable that, because of the original research methods, the knowledge level in some schools is under-represented in the 1992–3 findings, it is nevertheless the case that knowledge within a school is fragmented. It was probably always so, but a reading of the literature often does not make this clear. The Opies were collecting on the macro level from the whole of Britain, so one could expect regional variation, but this research shows that there is a great deal of variation within a school, at the micro level. These findings appear to contradict what Armitage has to say in Chapter 2, where he stresses the continuity of experience between different schools. The contradictions are, however, more apparent than real. We are looking here at different levels of categorization. His categories are much broader. He writes of chasing games, imaginative games and 'parallel games' which, in the classification described in the Introduction, would be 'games with a high-power It'. My research focuses in at a more detailed level and shows that, while the broad category of games may be represented at each school, the detailed knowledge varies. Armitage is also dealing with activities as they are played in the playground, while this research focuses on the range of children's knowledge of the repertoire.

There is also, of course, the question of what constitutes difference. While adults may see one game, children may see a multitude. The 'low-power It' games are mostly variations of Tig: Scarecrow Tig, Bob Down Tig, Off-ground Tig and so on. When asked about their games children would often say, 'We know loads'. They would then reel off several versions of Tig and only one child commented, 'They're really only one game, aren't they?' As adults we would probably class them broadly as one game with variations and therefore perhaps see only a poverty of experience. For children each small variation constitutes a difference which makes the game separate from the others, a perception which may be paralleled by the way children endow with meaning the physical features around them, as Armitage has already shown. Adults may look around the playground and see a featureless stretch of tarmac. Children, however, may well look at the same space and see a subtle change in the surface of the play area where two stretches of tarmac meet. This slight gully will become a place to play Marbles. An adult will see steps leading up to a classroom door surrounded by parallel bars to prevent anyone falling. Children will see bars to somersault over, or an arena for playing wrestling, or a den or a farmhouse. Because of the variety of experience available to children in the playground, depending on the group to which they belong, the playground may be both a barren and a vibrant cultural experience, and both this and the differences in perception of adults and children described above may account for adult perceptions of the playground as a place where only football and boredom occur. Children engrossed in play do not present a problem in the playground and it is the others who come to the notice of the supervising adults.

An interesting question is what limits the passing on of knowledge from one child to another, from one group to another. Here it is possible only to speculate. Perhaps children see facets of their oral tradition as place specific. There are two versions of Bulldog's Charge, for instance, known to some children in Keighley. One version is the standard one, often taught in schools, where there are three parallel areas. The Bulldog stands in the middle while the players stand in a safe area to one side. The game consists of the players, when instructed by the Bulldog, running from one safe area to the other across his territory. Anyone caught must join the Bulldog and help catch the others. Children at Schools B and H described this version but then went on to explain that they sometimes played it differently at home. In the home version the Bulldog can specify how everyone must move, so an instruction could be 'Bulldog's hop', 'crawl', or 'jump', when everyone, Bulldog included, must hop, crawl or jump across the space, thus changing a game which stresses competition and speed to one of anarchy and fun.

A second possibility which restricts the passage of knowledge is children's need for time and opportunity to pass on their knowledge. A third may be the need to share their knowledge in the safety of a friendship group, who will share the responsibility and protect the individual from ridicule (which would result in loss of status), an idea discussed more fully in Chapter 4 by Kathryn Marsh. A fourth possibility is the topography of the playground which, as Armitage has described so graphically, can affect children's play possibilities. Whatever the reasons, it is clear that a great deal of information is passed on not only in the school playground but outside the playground: at home, among friends and relations. So the playground, while being an important place for the maintenance of oral tradition, is not the only environment where information is exchanged. Home and family are also important.

Conclusion

As adults the lessons we can learn from this are that we need not necessarily teach games to children whom we perceive as being bored and
needing instruction in the games we remember from our own childhood.
What limits play possibilities does not seem to be lack of knowledge in
the group as a whole but rather the inability of some children to pass on
their knowledge to a wider audience in the playground. Perhaps the role
of the adult should be to foster an environment where children believe
that the knowledge they have of their culture is valued both by adults
and by their peers. For this to happen, they need time, space and sup-
portive adults who recognize the importance of children's oral tradition.
In this way they can learn from and practise with each other the verbal,
physical and social skills which their games and rhymes engender.

Appendix

In the following tables, Schools A and B are Catholic, Schools C and D are
schools with a large percentage of children entitled to free school meals, E and F
are schools with a high percentage of children of Asian origin, G, H and I are in
more prosperous areas, while C and G have children whose families have lived in
the area for three generations. Some rhymes exist in several versions. These are
numbered in brackets.

Table 3.1 Entertainment rhymes and songs

| | School | | | | | | | | | No. of schools |
	A	B	C	D	E	F	G	H	I	where rhyme known
'Hey Pakistani'	–	–	–	–	–	–	✓	✓	–	2
'At Half Past One'	✓	–	–	–	–	–	–	–	–	1
'Baby Bumble Bee'	–	–	–	–	–	–	✓	–	–	1
'Cinderella'	–	–	–	✓	–	–	–	–	–	1
'Down in the Jungle'	–	✓	–	–	–	–	–	–	–	1
'Fatty and Skinny'	–	–	–	✓	–	–	–	–	–	1
'He's Popeye the Sailorman' (1)	✓	–	–	–	–	–	–	–	–	1
(2)	–	✓	–	–	–	–	–	–	–	1
(3)	–	✓	–	–	–	–	–	–	–	1
'Humpty Dumpty' (1)	–	–	–	–	–	–	✓	–	–	1
(2)	–	–	–	–	–	–	✓	–	–	1
'I Don't Swear'	–	–	–	–	–	✓	–	–	–	1
'I'm Getting You' (1)	–	✓	–	–	–	–	–	–	–	1
(2)	–	✓	–	–	–	–	–	–	–	1
'In 1946'	–	–	–	–	–	–	✓	–	–	1
'I was Driving'	–	–	–	–	–	–	✓	–	–	1
'I was Walking'	–	✓	–	–	–	–	–	–	–	1
'I Woke Up'	✓	–	–	–	–	–	–	–	–	1
'Jack and Jill'	–	✓	–	–	–	–	–	–	–	1
'Maggie Thatcher'	–	–	–	–	–	–	✓	–	–	1
'Mary had a Little Lamb'	–	✓	–	–	–	–	–	–	–	1
'Miss, Miss'	–	–	–	–	–	–	✓	–	–	1
'My Old Man'	✓	–	–	–	–	–	–	–	–	1
'My Uncle Billy'	✓	–	–	–	–	–	–	–	–	1
'One Bum'	✓	–	–	–	–	–	–	–	–	1
'One Fine Day'	–	✓	–	–	–	–	–	–	–	1
'Row Row Row'	–	–	–	–	–	–	✓	–	–	1
'The Ants Went Marching'	–	–	–	–	–	–	–	✓	–	1
'There Were Ten'	✓	–	–	–	–	–	–	–	–	1
'We Break Up'	–	–	–	–	–	–	✓	–	–	1

Table 3.2   Counting-out rhymes

	School									No. of schools
	A	B	C	D	E	F	G	H	I	where rhyme known
'Racing Car Number Nine'	✓	✓	✓	✓	✓	✓	✓	✓	✓	9
'Ickle Ockle'	✓	✓	✓	✓	✓	✓	✓	✓	–	8
'Eeny Miney Mo'	✓	✓	–	✓	✓	✓	✓	✓	–	7
'Ip Dip Do, the Cat's Got Flu'	✓	✓	✓	✓	–	✓	✓	✓	–	7
'Ippy Dippy Dation'	✓	✓	✓	✓	✓	✓	✓	–	–	7
'Mickey Mouse Built a House'	✓	✓	✓	✓	–	✓	✓	✓	–	7
'There's a Party'	✓	✓	✓	✓	✓	✓	✓	–	–	7
'Eeny Meeny Mackeracker'	✓	✓	✓	–	✓	✓	✓	–	–	6
'Ip Dip Dog Shit' (1)	✓	–	✓	–	✓	✓	✓	✓	–	6
'Cheeky Little Monkey'	✓	✓	–	✓	–	✓	✓	–	–	5
'Ip Dip Dog Shit' (3)	✓	✓	–	✓	✓	✓	–	–	–	5
'One, Two, Miss a Few'	–	–	–	✓	✓	✓	✓	✓	–	5
'Boy Scout Walk Out'	✓	✓	–	–	–	–	✓	✓	–	4
'If Your Initials'	✓	✓	✓	–	–	–	✓	–	–	4
'Inky Pinky Ponky'	✓	–	–	–	✓	✓	–	✓	–	4
'Ip Dip Dog Shit' (2)	✓	✓	✓	–	–	–	✓	–	–	4
'Ip Dip Sky Blue'	✓	✓	✓	–	–	–	–	–	✓	4
'One Potato'	✓	✓	–	–	–	–	✓	–	–	3
'Abba Babba'	✓	–	–	✓	✓	–	–	–	–	3
'Black Shoe'	✓	–	–	✓	✓	–	–	–	–	3
'Ip Dip Do the Girl Kiss You'	–	–	–	✓	✓	✓	–	–	–	3
'Mickey Mouse Built a House' (2)	✓	–	✓	–	–	–	–	✓	–	3
'Acka Back'	–	–	–	–	✓	✓	–	–	–	2
'Dip Dip Dip, My Blue Ship'	✓	–	–	–	–	–	–	✓	–	2
'Eesie Peesie'	–	–	–	–	✓	✓	–	–	–	2
'Egg Sugar Butter Tea'	–	–	–	–	✓	✓	–	–	–	2
'Girl Guide'	✓	–	–	–	–	–	–	–	✓	2
'Ink Pink Pen and Ink'	✓	–	–	–	–	–	–	✓	–	2
'In Pin Seventy Pin'	–	–	–	–	✓	✓	–	–	–	2
'Not Because You're Dirty'	–	–	–	–	–	–	–	✓	✓	2
'There's a German'	✓	–	–	–	–	–	✓	–	–	2
'Your Shoe is Dirty'	✓	–	–	–	–	–	✓	–	–	2

Note: A further 17 rhymes were each known at one school.

Table 3.3 Clapping rhymes

	School									No. of schools where rhyme known
	A	B	C	D	E	F	G	H	I	
'A Sailor Went to Sea'	✓	✓	✓	✓	✓	✓	✓	✓	✓	9
'Chinese Men'	✓	✓	✓	✓	–	–	✓	–	–	5
'Donny Macker'	✓	✓	✓	✓	–	–	–	✓	–	5
'My Boyfriend Gave Me'	✓	✓	–	✓	✓	–	✓	–	–	5
'Who Stole the Cookie?'	✓	–	–	✓	✓	✓	✓	–	–	5
'Under the Bramble Bushes'	✓	✓	✓	–	–	✓	–	–	–	5
'I Know a Chinese Girl'	✓	–	–	–	✓	✓	✓	–	–	4
'I Went to a Chinese Restaurant'	✓	✓	✓	–	✓	–	–	–	–	4
'Miss Mary Mack'	✓	–	–	–	✓	✓	–	–	–	3
'My Mother is a Baker'	–	–	–	–	–	–	✓	✓	✓	–	3
'See See My Playmate'	✓	–	–	–	–	✓	✓	–	–	3
'When Susie was a Baby'	–	✓	–	✓	–	✓	–	–	–	3
'My Name is Elvis Presley'	–	✓	–	✓	–	✓	–	–	–	3
'Boys Have got the Muscles'	–	–	✓	–	–	–	–	–	✓	2
'May Tithleya' (Punjabi)	–	–	–	–	✓	✓	–	–	–	2
'Om Pom Pear'	✓	✓	–	–	–	–	–	–	–	2
'Zig Zag Zoo'	–	–	–	–	✓	✓	–	–	–	2

Note: A further 17 rhymes were known each at only one school.

Table 3.4 Games with a high physical content without playthings

	Group games with 'high-power It' School									No. of schools where game known
	A	B	C	D	E	F	G	H	I	
Bulldog's Charge	✓	✓	✓	✓	✓	✓	✓	✓	✓	9
Black Pudding	✓	✓	✓	✓	✓	✓	✓	✓	✓	9
Grandfather's Chest	✓	–	✓	–	✓	✓	✓	✓	–	6
Eggs, Bacon	✓	–	–	✓	✓	✓	✓	–	–	5
Traffic Lights	✓	✓	–	✓	–	–	–	–	–	3
Truth Dare Kiss or Command	✓	✓	–	✓	–	–	–	–	–	3
Farmer Farmer	–	–	–	✓	–	–	–	✓	–	2
May I?	✓	–	–	–	–	✓	–	–	–	2
Neighbours	✓	–	–	–	–	–	✓	–	–	2

Note: A further 7 games were known each at only one school.

Table 3.5   Games with a high physical content

| | Group games with playthings School | | | | | | | | | No. of schools where game known |
	A	B	C	D	E	F	G	H	I	
Ball										
Ball Tig	✓	–	✓	✓	✓	✓	✓	–	–	6
Slam	✓	✓	✓	–	✓	–	–	–	–	4
Bingo/Donkey	–	✓	–	✓	✓	–	–	–	–	3
Kerbie	✓	✓	–	–	–	–	✓	–	–	3
Queenie	–	✓	✓	–	–	–	–	–	–	3
Rope										
Colours	✓	✓	–	–	✓	–	✓	–	–	4
Stones										
Hopscotch	✓	✓	✓	✓	✓	✓	✓	✓		8
Peetoo	–	–	–	✓	✓	✓	–	–	–	3
Fivestones	–	–	–	–	✓	✓	–	–	–	2
Miscellaneous										
Marbles	✓	✓	–	✓	✓	✓	–	✓	–	6
Conkers	✓	✓	✓	–	–	✓	–	✓	–	5
Wrestling cards	✓	–	–	✓	✓	✓	–	–	–	4
Elastics	✓	–	–	✓	–	–	–	–	–	2

Note: A further 10 games were known each at only one school.

Table 3.6   Numbers and percentages of children interviewed

School	Sample size	No. of 8-year-olds in school	Percentage sampled
A	55	55	100
B	32	64	50
C	18	60	33
D	25	25	100
E	22	72	34
F	26	52	50
G	31	46	66
H	24	50	50
I	10	10	100

Table 3.7 Knowledge of clapping and counting-out rhymes shared between parallel classes

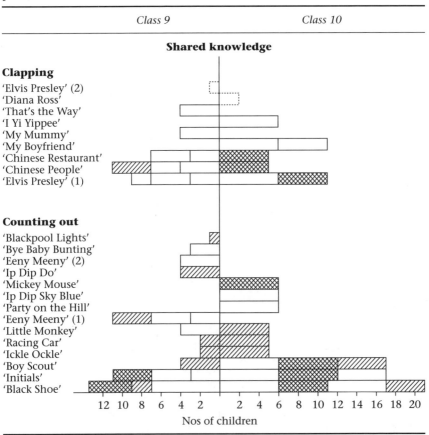

Key: ☐ Girls ▨ Boys ⊠ Mixed ⬚ Part of a group

Table 3.8 Profile of games and rhymes knowledge within groups in School G

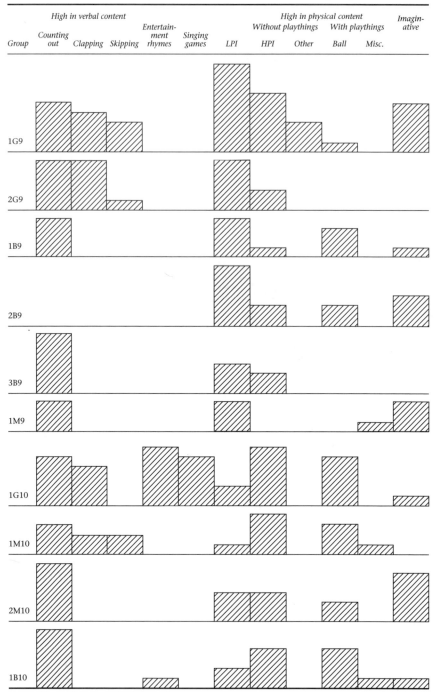

Note: LPI = Low-power It
HPI = High-power It

Table 3.8 (opposite) is labelled according to the order in which the children were interviewed. The letters B, G and M denote boys, girls or mixed, while the number following the letter denotes the class. 1G9, for instance, identifies the first group of girls interviewed in Class 9.

Table 3.9   Sources of information

Family	*Friends/Home*	*School*	*Other*
Clapping			
'Elvis Presley' (2)	'Diana Ross'	'Chinese Restaurant'	'I Yi Yippee'
'That's the Way'		'My Boyfriend'	
'Elvis Presley' (1)		'Chinese People'	
Source not identified			
'My Mummy is a Baker'			
Counting out			
	'Blackpool'		
	'Eeny Meeny' (1)		
		'Ip Dip Do'	
		'Racing Car'	
		'If Your Initials'	
		'Ip Dip Sky Blue'	
	'Mickey Mouse'	'Black Shoe'	
'Ickle Ockle'	'Boy Scout'	'There's a	
	'Little Monkey'	Party'	
Source not identified			
'Bye Baby Bunting'			
'Eeny Meeny Miney			
Mo' (2)			
'Ip Dip Do' (2)			

Notes

1 The full texts of these rhymes can be found in Curtis (1998). Some of what are termed 'entertainment rhymes' can be found in Opie and Opie (1959), many of the counting-out rhymes and 'high-power It' games in Opie and Opie (1969), many of the clapping games in Opie and Opie (1985), and descriptions of the games with playthings in Opie and Opie (1997).
2 For a discussion of active and passive repertoire, see Goldstein (1971a).

4

It's not all black or white: the influence of the media, the classroom and immigrant groups on children's playground singing games

Kathryn Marsh

This chapter addresses issues relating to children's playlore, the folkloric tradition of children's play which encompasses a range of play genres, including games and chants, insults, jokes and riddles. As the previous chapter by Curtis suggests, distinctive repertoires of playlore may be developed by single groups of children within one school. However, it is also evident from the tables of collective playlore knowledge presented by Curtis that multiple versions of playlore may also coexist at any given time.

The phenomenon of multiple variants of playlore appearing both within one school playground and, virtually simultaneously, in quite geographically separate communities of children has been widely documented by other collectors of children's folklore (Turner 1969; Knapp and Knapp 1976; Opie and Opie 1985; Factor 1988; Merrill-Mirsky 1988; Riddell 1990). My interest in this phenomenon initiated an ethnographic study of the processes through which children create, vary, teach and learn their playground singing games in a multi-ethnic inner-city primary school in Sydney (Marsh 1997). In this chapter, I will discuss ways in which the media, migration and the classroom practices of schoolteachers have influenced these processes and have contributed to the diversity of game performances in this Australian school.

My study, undertaken from 1990 to 1996, involved the audio-visual recording and analysis of more than 600 examples of children's playground singing game (predominantly clapping game) performances[1] and concurrent unstructured interviews with the children who played them. Participants in the study included 139 children aged from 5 to 12 years.

Children were informally observed and recorded playing the games in their natural context. Once initial contact had been made, some children also performed and discussed their games in a quiet area away from the noise of the playground, to facilitate recording. Where possible, children were repeatedly recorded during multiple periods of fieldwork and were asked to comment on their game practices over a number of years.

The site of this study, 'Springfield Primary School', was chosen partly because of the multicultural nature of the community which it serves.[2] It is located in an inner suburb of Sydney which, in the last decade, has undergone a process of considerable urban renewal. While some low-cost housing remains, frequently occupied by immigrant families, an increasing proportion of the area has been 'gentrified' and is occupied by the families of middle-class, predominantly Anglo-Australian, professionals. The school community is therefore variable in terms of class and ethnicity, with approximately 40 per cent of students having language backgrounds other than English. In 1995 there were 41 different language or ethnic groups represented in the student population,[3] with Cantonese and Mandarin being the principal non-English languages spoken (see Table 4.1 in Appendix). Although the arrival of Chinese-Australians in the school has been relatively recent, the school population has been multicultural for several decades.

While the extent of cultural and linguistic diversity in Australian school populations varies according to locality, an environment in which cultural pluralism is evident is more characteristic than a monocultural environment for the majority of Australian schoolchildren, Australia having been largely populated through successive waves of immigration. The ethnic and cultural diversity of the Australian population has particularly increased in the 50 years following the Second World War, with Australian immigrants being drawn from over 100 birthplace groups (Collins 1991). As discussed later in this chapter, it is my contention that the multicultural nature of the school community at Springfield Primary School has significantly influenced the processes of game variation and transmission in this school playground.

Of more pervasive significance to the transmission, creation, preservation and regeneration of playground singing games is the influence of the media environment on children in Australian playgrounds. The importance of the media in providing textual material for children's playlore has been considered by a number of researchers in this field (Opie and Opie 1959, 1985; Turner *et al.* 1982). However, as both Factor and Grugeon attest in Chapters 1 and 5, there is a widely held misconception that electronic media have contributed to a decline in children's traditional play pursuits (see, for example, Stutz 1996).

With reference to children's playground songs in the USA, Harwood (1994) has disputed this misconception. In her discussion of the interrelationship between the media and playground game performance practice, which involves the creative use by children of textual, musical and movement material derived from the media, Harwood states that 'children enter into "a dialectic with the mass media and appropriate for their own uses its materials and forms"' (Harwood 1994: 191, citing Mechling 1986: 110). Her point is that the relationship between children and the media operates in two directions, with children making choices about what to receive and what to reject. My own study supports this view that children are not victims of an all-powerful, adult-controlled media onslaught but that they utilize music, text and movements disseminated by the media in order to create new games or game variants over which they have ultimate control. Examples of this are discussed in subsequent sections of this chapter.

Influences of the media and immigrant groups on playground games

The environmental factors of migration and the media do not exist in isolation from each other. The complexity of the interaction between these contemporary influences on children's playlore in Australia might best be explored by examining a number of examples of children's playground singing games collected over a period of time in the focus school.

The first example, 'Michael Jackson', performed by a group of 7- and 8-year-olds in 1990, demonstrates the appearance of figures from popular culture (in this case, the American singers Michael Jackson and Madonna) in the texts of playground singing games, as shown in Figure 4.1. This practice has been well-documented throughout the twentieth century (Opie and Opie 1959, 1985; Turner *et al.* 1982; Riddell 1990; Harwood

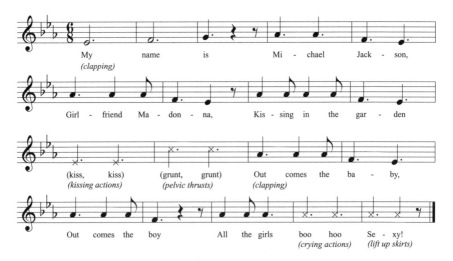

Figure 4.1 Text and melody of 'Michael Jackson' (1990).

1994). In this example, however, the sexually suggestive aspects of these singers' performances (viewed regularly on TV video clips) were also reflected in both the text and movement elements of the game. Game movements included not only clapping but emulation of kissing, pelvic thrusts and the lifting of skirts to expose underwear as a culmination of the game. Although the children strenuously denied that this game was about sexual matters, they appeared, through their movements, to be parodying adult sexuality as depicted in the media. The children maintained that the purpose of the game was to ridicule the popular music icons who had too high an opinion of themselves.

Michael Jackson also figured prominently in another singing game entitled 'Michael Jackson' performed by a different group of 7- and 8-year-old girls in 1993. The improvisatory character of this performance perhaps revealed more clearly than a well-practised performance the way in which the performers collaboratively manipulate textual, musical and movement formulae (game components) to co-construct new game performances or game variants. In this case, the majority of the formulae (for example, 'Doo-a diddy diddy dum diddy doo') have been appropriated from adult compositions and performance styles which are transmitted to the children through audio-visual media. Sources for these formulae, as reported by the performers, included a TV advertisement, the American film, *Grease*, and the Michael Jackson song, 'Black or White', from the album *Dangerous*. The game performance incorporates not only the textual and rhythmic formula repeated in the refrain of the original song ('Black or White') but also the crotch-grabbing movements and associated exclamations which accompany Michael Jackson's performance on video clips of the song, as can be seen in Figure 4.2.

There seems to be a curious balance between parody and emulation of adults in the children's performance of this game. Roseman, discussing musical outcomes of culture contact, characterizes this as the 'capture of the colonizer' (1995: 14) in which members of a colonized society (in this case, children) can take aspects of the music of the more powerful 'colonizers' (as a kind of symbol of power) and can harness the power by transforming the music into a more familiar idiom which is owned and controlled by the colonized group. In the case of children's playground games, the 'colonizer' is the adult, particularly as portrayed by the media. By utilizing and transforming adult materials into their own musical idiom, the relatively powerless children in the school playground are taking control, though fleetingly, of aspects of the powerful adult world which they simultaneously desire and dismiss. In her study of popular music in children's social lives, Minks elaborates on this point, stating that children are 'in the process of both producing and transforming received categories [of popular music] as they interacted with peers and with mass media' but that 'mass-mediated popular music cannot be understood exclusively as a tool of domination or a tool of resistance in these processes' (1999: 91).

Player 1:   This is Michael Jackson [*playing imaginary guitar*]
              Is it black or white ow ow [*holding imaginary microphone, crotch grabbing*]
              Doo diddy doo singing ow ow ow ow [*strumming 'guitar', crotch grabbing*]
              Doo diddy woo, dum diddy doo [*strumming 'guitar', dancing, bouncing on both feet*]

All: Packing my bags and walking down it too [*dancing as above*]
              Singing doo a diddy diddy dum diddy doo [*dancing as above*]
              Ow ow ow, ow ow ow [*crotch grabbing*]
              Is it black or white

Player 1:   Ow ow ow [*crotch grabbing*]

All: Black or white [*game movements as for Scissors, Paper, Rock for next five lines*]
              Black or white
              Black or white
              Black or white
              Black or white

Player 1:   And then we go 'Ow ow ow' [*flick hands from side to side*]

Player 2:   Ow ow ow [*flick hands from side to side*]

Player 1:   And then we go

Player 3:   It's Sandy time [*hands extended wide apart*]

All: It's Sandy time [*hands extended wide apart*]

(The 'Sandy' referred to in this game is a character from the film *Grease*)

Figure 4.2   Text and movements of 'Michael Jackson' (1993).

Also of interest in the 1993 version of 'Michael Jackson' is the juxtaposition of the media-derived formulae with an elimination game of apparently Asian origin, Black and White (similar to the game Scissors, Paper, Rock) which forms the centrepiece of the performance (as can be seen in Figure 4.2).[4] Presumably the component formulae have been brought together because of textual similarity, the text of the Asian game (Black *and* White) being modified to fit the text of Michael Jackson's original song ('Black *or* White') and the rhythm of Jackson's original song formula being modified to resemble the rhythm of the game chant, as seen in Figure 4.3.

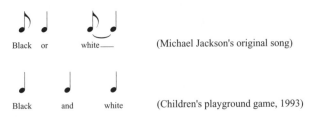

Figure 4.3   Comparison of rhythms of 'Michael Jackson' formula.

I saw no other examples of Black and White being played at the school during this time (although clearly it must have been in circulation in the playground) but was reintroduced to the game in variant form the following year. The performing group comprised two Chinese-Australian girls who had been at the school for a number of years and a Chinese-Australian girl who had initially migrated to Australia in 1993, returned for a short period to Shanghai during the Christmas holidays, and commenced at this school early in 1994. She had introduced the group to the new game, Black and White TV, which she had learned from the children in her Shanghai neighbourhood. In this case, the title initially refers to the elimination game Black and White previously discussed. The variant of the game involves stepping around pavement squares in between the elimination hand movements. The 'TV' of the title denotes the square shape of the ground on which the game is played, which is equated with the shape of a television screen. In this game the media as cultural icon is exemplified.

Black and White TV, played in Shanghai in the narrow driveways between tower blocks of flats, has easily been adapted for performance in small spaces with defined pavement squares in this school playground in Sydney. It is clear that the games Black and White and Scissors, Paper, Rock (played by many children in this school) are closely related. In the play of recent immigrants in this school, an additional adaptation has been the rendition of the text of these chants (familiar to Anglo-Australian children) in English.

In this school, however, the ethic of multiculturalism (formalized in state educational policy in 1983), in combination with the cooperative nature of game performance practice has influenced the process, as well as the outcome, of interethnic transmission of singing games. This was evident in the game 'Sei Sei Sei', recorded in 1994, where a newly arrived Korean-Australian boy performed a Korean game with an Anglo-Australian child. This game, with predominantly mimetic movements for most of its course, culminates in yet another version of Scissors, Paper, Rock. At Springfield the unfamiliar section of the game was played in the Korean language while the familiar section ('scissors, paper, rock') was rendered in English, the recognition of this familiar formula contributing to its acceptance by players of different ethnicities. The Korean boy was the dominant performer, empowered through superior knowledge of the game and the medium of the game itself.

During the field-recording period, I witnessed other multi-ethnic groups of children negotiating and performing bilingual and multilingual versions of singing games in a similar manner. For example, in 1993 I recorded a multi-ethnic friendship group spontaneously translating a bilingual Greek/English game, 'Ana Thio Thio' (translated as 'One Two Three'), into their first languages (Cantonese, Tongan and Romanian). In this case, the multiple reiteration of numbers in the text ('Give me a one, one, one, Give me a two, two, two' and so on) was easily translatable into the required languages.

Factors influencing interethnic transmission

In order to understand the processes which affect transmission of the games, it is necessary to understand the context in which game performance occurs. At Springfield Primary School, as in the USA (Merrill-Mirsky 1988), clapping games are most frequently played to alleviate boredom, either during recess times or while waiting for other school activities to commence. The games are played during waiting times partly because they require no equipment and little space. They are most frequently played between peers in a group situation. Games are always played either by pairs of children or in ring formation by small groups which rarely exceed six children. They are usually played by children from friendship groups, though other classmates may join in, particularly when waiting in lines.

The group form of performance operates as a mechanism for social inclusion or exclusion. Jones and Hawes, in their discussion of African-American ring games, describe the ring formation as a 'charmed circle' which 'includes and excludes at the same time . . . surrounds and enfolds while it walls off and repels' (1987: 87). The ring structure is also seen to embody democracy in play: 'The strength of the ring is in its construction. Since it has neither beginning nor end, there can be no ranking of its parts – no strong or weak, big or little . . . no captains, no opposing ranks' (1987: 87).

Whether group performance functions as a mechanism for inclusion or exclusion in terms of the creative variation of games is the subject of some debate. In the USA, Riddell (1990) and Harwood (1992, 1993a, 1993b) see the maintenance of highly prescriptive forms of play as a prime concern of the players: 'the children clearly expected the correct, prescribed behavior. Any slight deviation was audibly and visibly disputed . . . The group . . . serves to criticise those who aren't faithful to the correct ways of playing' (Riddell 1990: 354).

By contrast, Blacking describes the interactive playing of Venda children from the northern Transvaal in South Africa as 'an exercise of individuality in community' (1985: 46), whereby 'the collective effort produced both new cultural forms and a richer experience for the participants' (1985: 46–7). In Venda children's games variation is not only tolerated but socially valued and children may gain prestige by introducing new elements into a known song text (Blacking 1995: 32).

At Springfield, the cooperation between the children which is necessary for successful completion of games seems to lead to an emphasis on inclusion rather than exclusion. The need to be inclusive of all group members is reflected in variants which are consciously made to accommodate the differing performance practices of single members of a group. Individuals or pairs of participants within a group of children may also simultaneously perform differing variants of text, music or movements without comment or dissension, while being fully aware of the differences.

Player 1	Player 2
When Susie was a mother,	When Susie was a mother,
A mother, a mother,	A mother, a mother,
When Susie was a mother,	When Susie was a mother,
She used to go like this:	She used to go like this:
Smack, smack, a-smack smack smack	Mix, mix, a-mix mix mix
A-smack smack smack smack smack smack smack.	A-mix mix mix mix mix mix mix.
When Susie was a grandmother,	When Susie was a grandmother,
A grandmother, a grandmother,	A grandmother, a grandmother,
When Susie was a grandmother,	When Susie was a grandmother,
She used to go like this:	She used to go like this:
Knit, knit, a-knit knit [*silence*]	[*Silence, cracking finger movements*] crack
A-knit knit knit knit knit [*silence*].	[*Silence, cracking finger movements*] crack.

Figure 4.4 Comparison of simultaneously performed verses of 'When Susie Was a Baby'.

This can be seen in the above example (see Figure 4.4) taken from a performance of 'When Susie Was a Baby' by two 8-year-old girls in 1994. In this case, the two players performed two different text and movement 'versions' simultaneously, interlocking the two texts in the 'grandmother' verse.

This cooperative group dynamic appears to assist interethnic transmission of the games in this school. Contributing to this interethnic exchange of material is not only a tolerance of difference between performers, but also the multi-ethnic membership of the friendship groups which form the nucleus of performing groups. Of the 34 performing groups recorded from 1990 to 1996 at Springfield, 26 groups were multi-ethnic in composition.

While mere proximity between children of different ethnicities in the classroom may have some influence on the formation of performing groups in the playground, the conscious practice of many of the infants[5] teachers in creating groups of mixed ethnicity for learning experiences in the classroom is likely to be of greater significance. Because children of different ethnicities are grouped together for lengthy periods of time during formal classroom activities, friendship bonds can be firmly established. A similar influence of classroom practice on formation of multi-ethnic friendships has also been found by Minks (1999) in the USA.

Another factor in the evident acceptance of ethnic difference by the children is the high degree of ethnic diversity in the school. Collins, commenting on the relatively low incidence of racial tensions in Australia, states that 'the evidence suggests that the greater the ethnic diversity, the smaller the chance of racial conflict' (1991: 222). Although there is now a fairly large group of Chinese-Australian children at Springfield, the wide range of ethnic groups represented in the school population tends to mitigate against a construction of non-Anglo-Australians as 'other'. There are so many 'others' with a variety of racial, cultural and linguistic characteristics in the school, that difference is a norm.

Collins also attributes the relative lack of racial conflict in Australia to the bipartisan endorsement of multiculturalism by political parties and by the 'opinion-makers' in the media and academia (1988: 222). At Springfield, the teaching staff, to some extent, take on the function of authoritative opinion makers who, particularly in the infants department, endorse ethnic identity. In addition, the role of the English as a second language (ESL) teachers in modelling an acceptance of individual worth of children from varied ethnic groups, both to other staff and to children, is enhanced by the practice of ESL team-teaching within mainstream classrooms. Both classroom and ESL teachers consciously endeavour to create a classroom climate in which cultural difference is acknowledged and accepted, using strategies such as those discussed by one teacher: 'I . . . go through what their ethnic background is, what languages they speak and then record it on a large sheet so that everyone is able to see it and often refer back to it. So I guess we do constantly want to remind them of their ethnicity . . . so they don't lose it' (Interview with ESL teacher, Springfield Primary School, 15 June 1995).

Knowledge of, and participation in, the games assists both Anglo-Australian children and children from language backgrounds other than English alike to gain social acceptance. Blacking describes this function of game knowledge in relation to Venda children's songs: 'Knowledge of the children's songs is a social asset, and in some cases a social necessity for any child who wishes to be an accepted member of his own social group' (1995: 31).

Despite the tolerance of diversity at Springfield, transmission is still most clearly evident in the learning of many games from the dominant Anglo culture by children from other ethnic groups. The majority of games recorded in the playground have texts either in English or incorporating nonsense words. The repetitive use of formulae within the game texts, and the movement element of the games, which can be learned through imitation only, allows bilingual children with a developing competence in English to participate in group singing games with minimal difficulty. It is possible that the nonsense element of many of the texts may also enable participation in the games by bilingual children regardless of their level of understanding of the words.

The characteristic use of nonsense words in game texts, which reduces the necessity for players to understand the meaning of the words, also facilitates the inclusion of non-English words in the game repertoire. In fact, children seem to legitimize nonsense words by nominating the language to which they are presumed to belong. For example, one of the most popular games in this playground, 'Sar Macka Dora', with a text made up almost entirely of nonsense words, is seen by different players as having various linguistic derivations, one group describing it

Figure 4.5   A multi-ethnic group of 6-year-olds playing 'Sar Macka Dora', Springfield, 1996.

as 'Aboriginal' and another as 'Italian'. The lack of meaning in the words does not lessen their enthusiasm for the game (see Figure 4.5).

'Sar Macka Dora' (also known in this school as 'Son Macaron') is another elimination game, where a clap is passed around the circle on the beat, the child whose hand is hit on the last beat of the song being 'out'. Because the text has no inherent semantic meaning, it is easily and frequently changed, so that many textual variants coexist in the play-ground. Three examples are listed in Figure 4.6. The nonsense element of this game may well have contributed to its intercultural transmission on a larger scale. Segler (cited in Doekes 1992) lists 19 variants from a range of European countries.

In the case of 'Sar Macka Dora', the popularity of the game at Springfield has also been enhanced by classroom transmission. The game (variants of which were collected by two classroom teachers at other schools in Sydney) was disseminated in a teaching kit which I wrote for the New South Wales Department of Education in 1988 and was taught by several of the classroom teachers and two music specialist teachers to all children entering the school in kindergarten. It was used by these teachers in subsequent years for lesson breaks and therefore formed a reiterated template for playground performance, thus becoming well-known by the majority of the children in the school.

Interethnic transmission may also occur because of the children's

Sar macka dora	Son macaron	Emma dio
Eyo maria maria	Son ferio ferio ferio	Chicka charma
Eyo eyo ch ch ch	Leya leya tap tap tap	Emma di emma di
Eyo eyo ch ch ch	Leya leya tap tap tap	Chicka charma chicka charma
One two three	One two three	One two three

(Counting out in the last line is usually to 3 but may go up to 20 in some variants)

Figure 4.6   Three Springfield textual variants of 'Sar Macka Dora'.

inherent interest in novel forms of the games, as outlined by a 12-year-old girl in 1994: 'I think you're attracted to anything you don't know. Like, somebody's doing a clapping game or something and it's one that you don't know how to do it and you hear it and you listen to the words and show it to your friends' (Interview, 'Clara', Springfield Primary School, 12 December 1994).

Certainly the Springfield children are aware of immigrant children as a source of new game material in the playground. One group of 10-year-old girls who had all performed a Korean game taught by a Korean-Australian member of their group ('Hong-Soo') in the previous year, discussed this in 1994:

Annette: . . . as new people come in from different countries and if they have a handclapping game or something, they'll teach us.

Hong-Soo: And as Springfield is quite a—

Alicia: Multicultural school—

Hong-Soo: Multicultural school, yeah . . .

KM: Can you give me an example of what you're talking about maybe? . . . Are there any other games from other countries that . . . ?

Several: Hong-Soo knows one.

Annette: There's a Korean one that I was taught by Hong-Soo but I can't remember it.

(Interview, 10-year-old girls,
Springfield Primary School, 12 December 1994)

The nature and popularity of the games is also perceived to affect the degree of interethnic transmission. The Chinese-Australian girls, when they first showed me the game Black and White TV, stated that it would become a popular game with children in the Springfield playground, regardless of ethnicity, because it was so popular in Shanghai. In a subsequent interview in 1996, members of this Chinese-Australian friendship group, now 12 years old, confirmed that Black and White TV was still played at Springfield and that it was still being learned by other younger children.

However, the degree of interethnic transmission does seem to depend on other factors, such as the relative confidence and popularity of the children concerned, and the circumstances in which the game is learned. The newly emigrated Korean-Australian boy, John's teaching of the game 'Sei Sei Sei' (discussed earlier) was seen by his teacher as being related to his extroverted nature and general popularity. It was also related to the initial circumstances in which it had been imparted. John had first taught the game while he and his friend had been confined to a seat in the playground as a punishment for rough play. With mobility limited, they were unable to play more boisterous games and so spent the time playing the clapping game which was a common pursuit of both boys and girls in Korea.

In the case both of John and the multi-ethnic group who translated the game 'Ana Thio Thio' ('One Two Three'), discussed earlier in the chapter, another contributing factor to the performance of games in non-English languages may be what Isenberg and Jalongo (1993), drawing on the creativity theories of Rogers (1970), refer to as the 'psychological safety' provided by the friendship group. Isenberg and Jalongo define psychological safety thus: 'Psychological safety is . . . dependent upon the existence of a low-risk environment. Children feel psychologically safe when significant others accept them as having unconditional worth, avoid external evaluation, and identify and empathize with them' (1993: 14). For many Springfield children from language backgrounds other than English, the friendship group seems to provide these conditions.

Finally, I return to the importance of the media both to the interethnic transmission and the maintenance of tradition of these games. In their 'dialectic with the media' children have learned to reappropriate their own material from adult-produced written and audio-visual sources. For example, one group of 9-year-old girls showed me in 1993 how they recreated a game from a written text entitled 'Teacher Teacher' documented in popular playlore publications for children (Russell 1990; Factor and Marshall 1992) by improvising a rhythmic rendition and adding clapping patterns and mimetic movements to the text, as shown in Figure 4.7.

In another example of children's reappropriation of their own material from the media, the most popular singing game in this playground from 1990 to 1994 was 'Down Down Baby', an African-American game reportedly learned by most children through the American children's television programme *Sesame Street*, which is broadcast regularly on the national Australian television network (ABC). The continual rescreening of this game on the programme ensures that its popularity is maintained over a lengthy period of time.

Through this and other American television programmes and films, transmission of games and game performance practice between continents is continued. That these influences exist in locations other than

Figure 4.7   Clapping game recreated by children from published text.

Australia is shown by my final example, the text of a Dutch version of 'Down Down Baby', recorded in 1991 (Doekes 1992), and a French version remembered by a parent of some Australian children who had learned the game in the playground of their school in a small French village in 1992. They are compared below with the text of the *Sesame Street* version as performed at Springfield (see Figure 4.8). Embedded in the second to last line of the French version, the word 'Amerika' is a clear indication of its perceived American origins. Versions of 'Down Down Baby' have also been reported in Ghana, though in this instance it is more likely that they have been transmitted indirectly through the media and more directly by Ghanaian children who have learned the song in other countries and taught it to their peers after returning to Ghana (in the same manner as the Shanghai version of Black and White TV discussed earlier) (A. Addo, personal communications, 1997, 2000).

It would seem, then, that the media, classroom practices and the interaction of immigrant groups combine, not only in Australian playgrounds, but in many playgrounds around the world, to transmit game elements from one culture to another. Within this apparent unity there is constant diversity, attributable both to the variety of musical sources and to the constant creative endeavours of the children themselves.

Sesame Street	Netherlands	France
Down down baby	Daun daun lady	Dam dam bebe
Down down the roller coaster	Down daun olé olé	Dam dam a dolika
Sweet sweet baby	Si si bé bé	Trieste trieste bebe
I never let you go.	Si si olé olé.	Trieste trieste a Mexico.
Chimmy chimmy coco pop	Jimmi jimmi jakovo	Shooby shooby cocoban
Chimmy chimmy pow	Jimmi jimmi jéé	Shooby shooby comba
Chimmy chimmy coco pop	Jimmi jimmi jakovo	Shooby shooby cocoban
Chimmy chimmy pow.	Jimmi jimmi jéé.	Shooby shooby comba.
Granma, Granma sick in bed	Akovo akovo akovo	Marseille de letty
She called the doctor and the doctor said	Voorjou.	Qui fait de letty
		Amerika
Let's get the rhythm of the head, ding dong.		Ma? de . . .

Figure 4.8 Comparison of multi-ethnic versions of 'Down Down Baby'.

Conclusion

Performance of playground singing games at Springfield Primary School occurs within the context of friendship groups which provide the psychological safety within which children can accommodate both aesthetic and sociocultural differences. Practice of the games within social groups in this playground is therefore inclusive and tolerant of variation. In fact, constant variation and striving for novelty is a characteristic feature of children's performance of the games.

Participation in the games contributes to group solidarity and appears to assist with the attainment of individual acceptance. At Springfield this is especially important for children who have language backgrounds other than English, or who have migrated into the playground either from other schools or other countries.

The school practice of deliberately integrating children of different ethnicities in classroom activities appears to facilitate the transmission of games across ethnic boundaries, by creating classroom friendship groupings which continue to function in the playground. Endorsement of interethnic exchange is also provided indirectly by teacher reinforcement of ethnic identity and by direct classroom teaching of games which are viewed as having a non-English origin.

Adults often have a tendency to underestimate the abilities of children. While teaching strategies which supported intercultural exchange had been actively implemented in the classroom, few teachers in this school were aware of their ongoing repercussions in the playground where children controlled the teaching and learning. For children in this playground diversity was a feature of their social and auditory environment which was not only actively accommodated but was used to creative advantage. This ability to accommodate and create change enables children to ensure that their play traditions will continue to flourish, despite the dire predictions of adults to the contrary.

Notes

1 In this chapter, I use the term 'playground singing game' to denote a game which occurs in a playground context and involves rhythmic text (either chanted or sung) and movement. Movements include clapping, stamping, jumping and mimetic (mimed) movements. Playground singing games may be played by pairs or small groups of children. In the latter case, the games are usually in ring formation. Using ethnomusicological and sociolinguistic conventions, I refer to the playing of a singing game as a performance and to the players as performers. A performance is defined as a 'framed' event, particularly one involving music, dance or dramatic action. It is delineated from ordinary unregulated activity by a 'frame' (Bateson 1972; Bauman 1984) – a set of culturally determined signals. For example, the beginning of a performance of a clapping game is frequently indicated by a frame of placing the hands in close proximity to those of another player in order to initiate the first clapping movement. The patterned movements and text serve to maintain the performance 'frame' throughout the game.
2 'Springfield Primary School' is a pseudonym, used for ethical reasons.
3 In Table 4.1, language or cultural background is listed according to the designation given in the school's ESL teaching records for 1991 and 1995. These designations are derived from student enrolment forms as completed by parents or guardians of children entering the school and from interviews with older children. This practice accounts for the evident anomalies and possible overlaps in the listing, for example 'Chilean'/Spanish, Arabic/Lebanese, 'Singaporean'/ Malay and 'Yugoslavian'. Despite these anomalies, figures have been calculated in relation to these designations, on the basis that this is the way in which children or parents have themselves identified the cultural or linguistic groups to which they belong.
4 In Russell's (1984) fieldnotes for her study which was published in 1986, she records Black and White, alternatively entitled Or Sam, Sin Sam or Si Sam, as having been played extensively in 1984 by children at a multicultural primary school in Melbourne, Australia. Although the game was played by children of different ethnicities, it had evidently been introduced into the school playground by Vietnamese, Lao and Chinese children, many of whom reported having learned the game in their country of origin. It resembles the game Scissors, Paper, Rock to the extent that children shake their fists three times and then make either a fist or flat-handed shape with their hands. Individual children are eliminated from the game depending on the hand shape they have chosen. It can thus be used as a form of counting out.
5 In Australia, children aged 5 to 8 years in the first three years of school are designated as belonging to the infants department of the primary school.

Appendix

Table 4.1 Language or cultural backgrounds of children at Springfield Primary School

Language or cultural background grouped according to region		No. of language speakers, March 1991	% of school population, 1991	No. of language speakers, May 1995	% of school population, 1995
East Asia	Cantonese	32		45	
	Chunga	0		1	
	Hakka	0		1	
	Huanese	0		1	
	Japanese	1		2	
	Korean	10		16	
	Mandarin	2		42	
	Shanghainese	0		8	
		Total: 45	8.3	Total: 116	17.4
South-East Asia	Burmese	1		1	
	Cambodian	0		1	
	Filipino	6		5	
	Indonesian	5		2	
	Malay	2		0	
	Singaporean	1		0	
	Tagalog	9		0	
	Thai	1		0	
	Vietnamese	13		13	
		Total: 38	7	Total: 22	3.3

Table 4.1 (cont'd)

Language or cultural background grouped according to region		No. of language speakers, March 1991	% of school population, 1991	No. of language speakers, May 1995	% of school population, 1995
Indian Subcontinent	Assamese	1		1	
	Bengali	1		2	
	Gujerati	0		1	
	Hindi	15		11	
	Nepalese	0		1	
	Punjabi	2		1	
	Sinhala	1		0	
	Tamil	7		0	
	Telugu	0		1	
		Total: 27	5	Total: 18	2.7
Middle East	Arabic	10		10	
	Egyptian	2		0	
	Hebrew	2		0	
	Lebanese	3		0	
	Persian	2		0	
	Turkish	12		5	
		Total: 31	5.7	Total: 15	2.3
Eastern Europe	Albanian	2		2	
	Croatian	9		3	
	Hungarian	2		4	
	Polish	5		4	
	Romanian	2		1	
	Russian	1		6	
	Serbian	0		1	

Region		School 1	Total 1	% 1	School 2	Total 2	% 2
	Ukrainian	0			1		
	Yugoslavian	0			1		
			Total: 21	3.9		Total: 23	3.5
Southern Europe	Greek	13			6		
	Italian	12			1		
	Maltese	1			0		
	Portuguese	6			4		
	Spanish	9			9		
			Total: 41	7.6		Total: 20	3
Western Europe	French	6			3		
	German	5			2		
			Total: 11	2.2		Total: 5	0.75
Pacific	Fijian	6			1		
	Maori	1			0		
	Samoan	0			2		
	Tongan	5			4		
			Total: 12	2.2		Total: 7	1.1
West Africa	Temne	1			0		
			Total: 1	0.18		Total: 0	0
South America	Chilean	0			1		
			Total: 0	0		Total: 1	0.15
Total children with language backgrounds other than English			227	42.08		227	34.2
Total school population			541			666	
Number of language groups			41			41	

5

'We like singing the Spice Girl songs ... and we like Tig and Stuck in the Mud': girls' traditional games on two playgrounds

Elizabeth Grugeon

In the UK, current anxieties about standards in education have led to an increasingly prescriptive curriculum and a heavier workload for young children. The 'time out' which morning and lunch breaks provide is in danger of being eroded. A recent longitudinal study of children's own views on their needs has made this need abundantly clear (Blatchford 1998). This time of 'festival' (Sutton-Smith 1990), when children have a degree of autonomy and are allowed to choose activities that lie outside adult jurisdiction, is becoming increasingly rare in their lives and is often undervalued or simply ignored by adults. Yet, as I hope to show, a great deal is going on that should be of interest and concern not only to folklorists but to educationalists, linguists, sociologists, psychologists, musicologists and anthropologists. In this chapter I will document the ephemeral existence of a number of traditional games on two primary school playgrounds in Bedford on a couple of days in summer 1997. On other days I might have found more or fewer games and certainly, different versions of similar texts. Where possible I have tried to trace the provenance of these games by reference to Iona and Peter Opies' scholarly collections (1969, 1985, 1997).

In 1994 I encouraged groups of student teachers studying to be language and literature specialists to collect data in morning break times at local schools. The examples of rhymes, jokes, clapping and skipping games which they collected encouraged me to return to these schools for a brief update in the summer of 1997. I was curious to see whether 5- to 9-year-old girls were playing the same games as they were in 1979, when I had first visited my daughter's school playground, or those I had recorded on subsequent visits in 1986. The following account provides evidence of continuity and change in the oral culture of young girls on these two playgrounds.

The lower schools in Bedford are for 5- to 9-year-olds. The two that I visited are both urban multicultural schools. One draws on a fairly wide catchment as it is one of the two Roman Catholic lower schools in the town. The children come from a range of backgrounds, including Irish, Italian and multi-ethnic families of low and middle income. The other draws on the immediate surroundings, an area of private and former local authority housing bordering a large industrial estate, again with children from low- and middle-income families. Although the children on both playgrounds could also be seen to be playing a variety of running, chasing and ball games while I was there, I have focused on singing games as these seem to be unique to girls' play.

'Girl power' on the playground

As a teacher, a mother and a teacher educator, I have spent part of my time in the last 30 years collecting samples of children's playground rhymes and games which I refer to in my teaching of language and literature. My main interest has been in the gendered nature of the content of the singing games played by girls in the first four years at school, in the way these games parody adult norms and behaviour, often dealing with taboo subjects through mocking and subversive texts (Turner *et al.* 1982; Opie and Opie 1985; Grugeon 1988). I have observed the way that these games involve close collaboration and physical interaction through skipping, clapping and dancing routines.

In the summer of 1997 the Spice Girls' song 'Wannabe' was at the top of the pop music charts in the UK and it seemed that every young girl from 5 to 15 wanted to be a Spice Girl. On playgrounds across the country, groups of girls were copying the singing and dancing routines, imitating their new icons and role models, 'Posh', 'Ginger', 'Scary', 'Sporty' and 'Baby' Spice:

> I'll tell you what I want
> What I really, really want!
> So tell me what you want,
> What you really, really want?
> I wanna, I wanna, I wanna,
> I wanna, oh, what I really, really want
> Is zig-a-zig-aah!
>   (Version sung by 9-year-old girls, Bedford, July 1997)

Teachers and parents had mixed views; the Spice Girls' singing and dancing routines were explicitly sexual and provocative, and aggressively loud. The Spice Girls' song 'Wannabe', with its insistent rhythm and repetition, dialogic format and nonsense phrases has similarities with girls' playground rhymes. It seemed likely that it would, like many other pop songs before it, become absorbed and gradually adapted by the playground culture. I saw this beginning to happen in Bedford in 1997 as I watched a group of 9-year-old girls snap from a performance of 'Wannabe' to singing 'We Are the Teenage Girls'; both songs were accompanied by elaborate actions. The gendered and sexual content was unashamedly explicit and provocative; as Kathryn Marsh has described in Chapter 4, this process of adapting media texts to the playground involves 'a curious balance between parody and emulation of adults' (see p. 83). It also suggests the ease with which the popular culture and mass media can be absorbed into children's play; minutes later these girls had moved on, using one of the many traditional counting-out rhymes in preparation for their next game – switching from the subversive back to the conventional, as June Factor has suggested in Chapter 1.

From the time that I recorded my 5-year-old daughter's version of 'When Susie Was a Baby' (a daring game in 1979 with its references to bras and knickers), I had been interested in the texts of the games played by 5- to 9-year-old girls. They seemed both to anticipate their adult roles and explore archetypal themes: birth, courtship, sex, marriage and death. These serious and often taboo subjects were dealt with via a mocking bravado. When my daughter played the clapping game

> My boyfriend's name is Tony,
> He comes from Macaroni . . .

I doubt whether she was aware of the significance of the lines

> I jumped in the lake and swallowed a snake
> And came up with a bellyache.
>
> (Jessica, aged 5, Bedford, 1979)

However, this suggestion of pregnancy recurs in many of the games that I recorded in later years, such as

> Meet my boyfriend Fairycake
> He gave me a cake and a bellyache
> Mama, mama, I feel sick,
> Call for the doctor, quick, quick, quick.
>
> (8-year-old girls, Bedford, 1995)

Humour and bravado typify these games.

Resistance and domesticity

When I first started to consider the reason for the continued existence and significance of these singing games for pre-pubescent girls, I suggested that the texts which seemed to be played exclusively by girls could be interpreted as subversive acts of resistance while still predicting a future of marriage, domesticity and childrearing (Grugeon 1988). James has also suggested that they provide a 'cultural framing for gender during childhood' and 'an opportunity to experiment with many different stereotypes of femaleness' (James 1993: 194). In the 1990s a new 'stereotype of femaleness' seems to have appeared; at the end of the century, the concept of 'girl power' was manifested in the mass media by girl bands like the Spice Girls, and in the workplace and education by a new concern for equal opportunities. Both of these may be having an impact on the way children now behave on school playgrounds. Despite the defiant tone and content of many of the songs they sang, the girls I had recorded in the 1980s tended to be marginalized on the edges of the playground as boys monopolized the centre space to play football. The two schools I visited in 1997 seemed to be aware of this and were developing positive ways of making playground space more accessible for all.

In 1993 the publication of Iona Opie's *The People in the Playground* had reminded me that a great deal of evidence of childlore could be collected in a short space of time: 'A remarkable number of games can be fitted into the fifteen minutes of playtime if they are minor transient games . . . The children play these games rapidly, one after another, instant decisions being instantly translated into action' (Opie 1993: 4). A problem for the onlooker who is attempting to record and analyse 'minor transient games', however, is that the games played by girls aged from 5 to 12 on school playgrounds are typically a combination of meaningful and nonsensical verbal patterns with elaborate and highly patterned musical and movement routines. The written transcript can only be a pale reflection of a vibrant, three-dimensional performance.

Lower school 1 (4 July 1997): the Spice Girls are banned

My first visit to this school was to see whether it would be worth returning with a camcorder. Explaining to the playground supervisor that I was interested in recording any traditional games that the girls might be playing and was particularly interested in singing games, she responded by telling me, 'The Spice Girls are banned on this playground'. Perhaps the teachers did not approve of the sexually precocious dance routines. The significance of this remark did not occur to me until after I had visited the next school. The playground at the first school has a large asphalt area and a spacious playing field. As the bell rang, girls came out slowly, often in pairs, holding hands, sometimes in groups. Almost at once, I noticed a small group 'dipping' (counting out):

Each peach pear plum,
Who's your best chum?

Two girls had skipping ropes. Another group sat down in a circle on the grass. They appeared to be deciding what to do. Soon they stood up and started to play a singing game. This was 'In and Out the Dusty Bluebells' which involved complex movement in and out of a circle as one girl tapped on the shoulders of another and claimed her as a partner. They were absorbed, concentrating on the sequence of movements, going in and out of arches made by the players' joined hands.

I asked them how they had chosen this game and whether they could tell me about other games that they played. I asked what they were doing earlier when they had been sitting down. They said that they were choosing which game to play:

EG: Right, what were you choosing?
Girls [*calling out*]: 'Red Rover', British Bulldog, Stuck in the Mud, It, 'In and Out the Dusty Bluebells', Mums and Dads and Baby [*embarrassed laughter at this*].
Girl: And then we had a vote and we chose 'In and Out the Dusty Bluebells'.
EG: How did you choose that, did you dip?
Girl: We picked whoever put her hand up first.
EG: Right, which is your favourite game?
Girls: 'Red Rover' [*repeated with enthusiasm by many of the group*].
EG: Can you explain 'Red Rover'?

They tried to explain but decided to show me how the game actually worked. Two teams faced each other several yards apart, holding hands. When a number was called, one person ran across and tried to break through the hands of the opposite team. If they broke through they then joined that team.

EG: Do you do anything with skipping ropes?
Girl: Yeah. Cross skipping – and we tie them together and put them round our ankles and we go—
Girls [*chanting*]: 'England, Ireland, Scotland, Wales, inside, outside, inside, on'.
Girl: And we also do two ones together [i.e. two ropes are tied together] and we go like that and that and we say, 'Iddy addy over, are you in the clover kissing __ ?', say a boy, then you choose a boy, then you say, 'Is it true he loves you? Yes, no, yes . . . he loves you. How many babies did you see? How many babies did you have? How many rings did he give you?'
EG: Yes. Anything else?
Girl: I like coffee, I like tea, I like Jack in with me. I don't like coffee, I don't like tea, I don't like Jack in with me.

At this point the bell for the end of playtime went and the children lined up in classes to go back into school.

It is my habit to check the provenance of each new text that I encounter. When I looked up 'I Like Coffee, I Like Tea', I found that it is a very old rhyme that has evidently been used for skipping since the nineteenth century. The Opies cite an example of a fragment recorded in the USA in 1886 (Opie and Opie 1985: 358). What was also interesting about this visit was the fact that, although the girls had democratically chosen to play the very demure 'In and Out the Dusty Bluebells', another singing game with a long pedigree (Opie and Opie 1985: 366), they evidently preferred the much more boisterous 'Red Rover'. The way they played it was the same as that described by the Opies in *Children's Games in Street and Playground* where it appears in the category of 'exerting' games and is described as a 'particular favourite with girls in Scotland' (Opie and Opie 1969: 239).

I returned on the next day with two helpers and a camcorder and recorded a range of games being played by 7- to 9-year-old girls during the 15-minute morning break. These included a number of clapping and skipping games.

A clapping game with two players

A rhythmic chant regulated the claps:

Mrs D, Mrs I, Mrs F-F-I-
Mrs C, Mrs U, Mrs L-T-Y.

The Opies claim this as a skipping rhyme and trace it back to 1910 (1997: 175).

A clapping game for two with chanted words, actions and clapping

Pepsi Cola
Pepsi Cola
Boys have got the muscles
Teachers got the brains
Girls have got the sexy legs
And here we go again.
[*Change rhythm*]
Hypnotize,
Paralyse,
Turn around and faint.
[*One girl turns and falls backwards into the arms of her partner – this involves impeccable timing and trust*]

Looking for the origins of this game, it would seem to be an extract from what was once a version of a popular song. The Opies recorded a song 'My Name's Diana Dors' in Hampshire in 1975, which includes the refrain 'Boys have got the muscles . . .'. But the Opies also have an earlier version, recorded in 1972, which is much closer to the Bedford one:

The boys have got the muscles [*everyone flexes their biceps*]
The teacher's got the pay [*stretch out hands*]
The girls have got the sexy legs [*lift skirt showing off leg*].

(Opie and Opie 1985: 416)

This suggests that these lines were already being used, as they were in 1997, as a separate game.

A clapping and singing game played by two girls

I had a little dustbin girl
Her name was
Eye [*hand to eye*]
Shoe [*hand to shoe*]
Anna.
And all the boys
On the football pitch
say
Eye Shoe Anna
[*Change to faster rhythm*]
How is
your mother?
All right.
Died in the fish shop
last night.
What did she die of?
Raw fish.
How did she die?
Like this.
[*One partner turns and falls back into arms of the other as for 'Pepsi Cola'*]

A version of this also appears in the Opies' book *The Singing Game*, (1985: 480) as 'I Know a Little Dutch Girl Called Hie Susie Anna'. It had been recorded in Hampshire in 1983. In the Bedford version of 1997, the Dutch girl has become a 'dustbin girl'.

A singing and dancing game involving a group of more than four players

In and out the dusty bluebells
In and out the dusty bluebells
Tippy tippy tap tap
On your shoulders

Tippy tippy tap tap
On your shoulders
Tippy tippy tap tap
On your shoulders
You will be my partner.

'One of the most popular song games in the present day' (Opie and
Opie 1985: 366), it was first recorded in an embryonic form in 1916,
again in 1925, and has been going strong ever since. The Opies also add
that it is deceptively demure; the 'tippy tappy' can involve thumping
and, as the line of girls gets longer, skirts are often pulled down, adding
much to the excitement and general chaos as the game draws to an end.

A skipping game using a rope

The rope is stretched between the ankles of two girls who are standing
about five feet apart. One or two players were involved. The accompanying chant reflects the jumping movements back and forth across
the rope:

England, Ireland, Scotland, Wales,
Inside, Outside, Inside, OUT.

A song sung by a group of eight girls

The girls clapped in pairs for the first six lines and then skipped round
with arms linked to 'I yi yippy yippy yi':

I found a box of matches
Behind the kitchen door, door, door,
And when I opened them
They were dancing on the floor, floor, floor,
Singing I yi yippy
I yi yippy yippy yap.

This was sung to the tune of 'She'll Be Coming round the Mountain
When She Comes' and would seem to illustrate the way 'scraps of rhythmic utterance' are included in these games 'as if they were magic incanta-
tions' (Opie and Opie 1985: 428).

A skipping game using a long rope

Several girls jumped together, chanting the alphabet. When someone
tripped on the letter G, they chose a boy's name (George Newton) and
continued:

Iddy addy over
I saw you in clover

Kissing George Newton
Is it true you love him?
Yes, no, yes, no, yes . . . [*until a player trips*]
How many babies will you have?
1–2–3–4–5 . . . [*until someone trips and they dissolve in paroxysms of laughter at the number of babies*].

This type of divination game is particularly popular with the older girls as it gives scope for public statements about boyfriends and much ribald teasing and taunting of the boys by the girls. The Opies describe many games of this kind and trace versions back to the nineteenth century: 'The fantasies children indulge in today are, apparently, no more detailed than were those of their grandparents and even great-grandparents in the nineteenth century' (Opie and Opie 1997: 248).

A clapping game played by two players

My boyfriend gave me an apple
My boyfriend gave me a pear
My boyfriend gave me a kiss on the lips
And kicked me down the stairs
I gave him back the apple
I gave him back the pear
I gave him back the kiss on the lips
And kicked him down the stairs.

Despite the fact that a reference to this extract appears in *The Singing Game* under the title 'Twelve Less Popular Singing Games' (Opie and Opie 1985: 478), it seems to have continued to be popular in Bedford. I have collected a version similar to this one almost every time I have visited a playground since the 1980s. However, it also appears as one verse in a longer clapping game, 'I Am a Pretty Little Dutch Girl' (Opie and Opie 1985: 450–2), where the Opies remark that the text in this case is 'an assemblage of all the component parts of the story which stem from different places' (p. 452). It also appears as a skipping rhyme in *Children's Games with Things* (Opie and Opie 1997: 288) where it is described as 'part of street play (mostly while skipping) in both Britain and America since the nineteenth century'. It seems it was originally part of a skipping rhyme which has been adapted for clapping.

Our video ended with a close-up of three girls playing Cat's Cradle. One, who was clearly the expert, was teaching the others as the children lined up to go back into school.

This visit provided evidence of the continued existence of a number of traditional games. Interestingly, in this school, where the Spice Girls were banned, there was no evidence of any other recent media influence. This was not the case at the next school.

Lower school 2 (11 July 1997): 'they have asked for a Spice Girl corner'

The school building on the main road out of town is late Victorian, complete with an ornate clock tower; behind it is a 1960s hall and utilitarian brick classrooms; beyond these are an attractive group of single-storey classrooms, a nursery unit and a landscaped playground; tiled paths and flower beds lead to a wide field. The school has about 150 pupils from the immediate locality. Some thought has been given to the layout and play equipment on the various playground areas. The headteacher told me that when the Year 2 children (6- and 7-year-olds) had been consulted about their designated space, they had asked, among other things, for a basketball net and a Spice Girl corner. She added that she thought the Spice Girls were 'rather sweet'.

As we had only one chance to visit the school we did not know what to expect and began recording immediately. We videotaped a number of traditional games in 15 minutes on the Year 4 (8- to 9-year-olds) playground. These girls seemed to prefer playing in groups of six to eight players; their large circle games were accompanied by singing, clapping and complex, synchronized movements such as the splits. All the games conformed to well-defined rules and required a high level of concentration. By the end of this 15-minute playtime we had recorded an impressive number of different games with accompanying texts.

'Saint Mary Anne'

Sitting in a large circle the girls clap round the circle – one girl dancing in the middle is replaced at the end of each round by the one whose hand is clapped on 'trois':

> Saint Mary Anne, Mary Anne, Mary Anne
> Saint Gloria, Gloria, Gloria
> Laya laya pi pi pi
> Laya laya pi pi pi
> Un deux trois.

This was a version of a game that my students had recorded when they visited both these playgrounds in 1994. At first I was unable to track it down but have recently been informed by Kathryn Marsh that she had recorded 35 performances of a very similar game, 'Son Macaron', on a Sidney playground. She writes, 'the text is highly variable but the movement elements and associated rhythmic features of music and text are what identifies it' (Marsh, personal communication, 1998). She also refers to another version recorded in the USA.

It was possible that there were at least two versions going on while we were videoing, as another large group of girls were standing in a circle clapping and chanting while gradually doing the splits until they sat on the ground. They were too far away for the rhyme to be audible but it ended 'un deux trois'.

'Cat's Got the Measles'

This was played by a large group sitting in a circle; clothes (cardigans, shoes, socks) were dropped in the middle of the circle and retrieved by different players at the end of each round of the song:

> Cat's got the measles
> Dog's got the fleas
> The baby's got the chicken pox
> And so have we.

This again would seem to be a fragment of a longer text, possibly 'See, See My Playmate' (Opie and Opie 1985: 474–5) which has the lines 'Because I've got the flu, Chicken pox and measles too', although with such a bouncing rhythm it could be a ball game.

'We Are the Cow Girls'

Two lines of girls with linked arms skipped back and forth, chanting:

> We are the cow girls
> Ready to fight them
> Come and get it
> We want [*name of chosen victim*].

The victim was then dragged over to the opposing side and the chant resumed:

> We are the Indians
> Ready to fight them . . .

While this seemed at first to share some of the features of the energetic 'Red Rover' played at School 1, it became apparent that it was almost certainly a version of the singing game 'Romans and English', described by the Opies as 'a dramatic dialogue between two lines of girls who advance and retreat as they sing alternate verses' (Opie and Opie 1985: 281). It was a rather truncated version which did not have the extended text nor the ritualized fight ending described by the Opies; the children at School 2 ended with a tug of war and chanted rather than sang the challenge. Nonetheless, it has antecedents in the nineteenth century and has been interpreted as a struggle between the Roman Catholic and Protestant churches (Opie and Opie 1985: 281). In Bedford in 1997, as we watched the children at School 2, we could see and hear that this was a particularly popular game; a number of versions using different names for the opposing teams were going on at the same time:

We are the tiger cubs
Ready to fight them
We want Sonia
Ready to fight them.

'Knickerbocker Glory'

This was a smaller circle clapping game played by a group of six to eight players clapping with complex movements round the circle:

Knickerbocker glory
My mum's poorly
It's so boring
It's so boring.

It seems likely that this is another example of a snippet from something that has been part of a much longer song, as indeed the next example seems to be.

'Mrs Right Had a Fright'

This was played by a large group who were clapping an elaborate pattern of claps round the circle:

Mrs Right had a fright
In the middle of the night
Saw a ghost
Eating toast
Halfway up
The lamp post.

Consulting the Opies, this seems likely to have been a ball-bouncing rhyme at some point, as it has much in common with

Mrs Brown went to town
With her knickers hanging down.

(Opie and Opie 1997: 143)

The Opies suggest that such fragments often have resonances of older traditional verses and that children very often produce hybrid rhymes that are very difficult to identify (1997: 142).

'Cancan'

This was a vigorous version of the cancan which the children have no doubt absorbed from television and popular culture. It involved dancing in a chorus line with synchronized high kicks accompanied by the cancan tune, 'La la, la la la la la la', ending with a defiant display of knickers. This would come under the heading of 'impersonations and dance routines' in *The Singing Game*, as would the girls' performance of 'Wannabe': 'Pop songs are sung on the playground either with the actions believed to have been performed by the pop groups singing them on television, or more often, with actions fitted to them by the children' (Opie and Opie 1985: 414). Thus these songs and movements become absorbed into their culture.

'We Are the Teenage Girls'

A group of five Year 4 girls positioned themselves in front of the camera and sang, 'We Are the Teenage Girls', each line illustrated by exaggerated mimed actions:

> We are the teenage girls [*dance about with exaggerated wiggle*]
> We wear our hair in curls [*curling actions on either side of head*]
> We wear our dungarees
> Up to our sexy knees [*hands by knees*]
> I met a boy last night
> He paid me 50p [*loud slap of hand*]
> To go behind a tree
> To have it off with me [*action not clear but much mirth*]
> My mother was surprised
> To see my belly rise [*gesture to indicate large stomach*]
> My daddy jumped for joy
> It was a baby boy [*mimic babe in arms*]
> My mum had fifty tits [*much hilarity*]

A much more innocent version of this song appears in *The Singing Game* under the heading 'Less Popular and more Ephemeral Clapping Songs' (Opie and Opie 1985: 78). It had been recorded in Glasgow in 1975 but later appeared on a gramophone record which may explain why it has not been as ephemeral as expected:

> We are the barbie girls,
> We wear our hair in curls,
> We wear our dungarees
> To hide our dirty knees.
> We wear our father's shirt,
> We wear our brother's tie,
> And when we want a guy
> We simply wink the eye.

(Webb 1983)

The Opies could not have foreseen the potential for adaptation and change that seems to have taken place. The girls were consumed by giggling at the parts they evidently considered rudest. The idea of 'fifty tits' seems to be a logical mishearing in the context of this song which is entirely in keeping with its Rabelaisian humour; the phrase 'fifty fits' would be quite unfamiliar to this generation. This rhyme is typical of the subversive nature of many of the playground rhymes which both mock authority and rejoice in taboo topics. When I interviewed them later the girls were eager to tell me, 'We never tell teachers. We never do'.

'Wannabe'

There was a spontaneous rendering of the Spice Girls' song 'Wannabe' – a large group of girls performed to an imaginary audience. The words and movements of the song were impressively imitated and sung with gusto. Like the cancan, this was much more of a performance than a game. Their games tended to be played holding hands in inward-looking and private circles with no need for any outside audience.

Not all the games were played by large groups. A number of clapping games were also being played by two players. We recorded two, as follows.

'High Low'

This clapping game had complex hand movements:

High low chickali
Chickali high low
Chickali chickali chickali
High.

'I Went to the Chinese Restaurant'

Two girls played this as a combined clapping and miming routine.

I went to the Chinese restaurant
To buy a loaf of bread, bread, bread,
I wrapped it in a five pound note
And this is what they said, said, said,
'My name is Elvis Presley
Girls are sexy
Sitting on the doorstep
Drinking Pepsi
Having a baby
Sitting in the navy
Boys go kiss, kiss [*hands to mouths and blow*]
Girls go woo' [*lift skirt to show knickers*].

The Opies have almost exactly the same version ('back seat' instead of 'doorstep') which was recorded in Virginia Water, Surrey, in 1983 (Opie and Opie 1985: 467). My 5-year-old daughter's version of this in 1979 excluded Elvis and Pepsi but included a long drawn-out nonsense refrain:

> Elli, elli, chickali, chickali
> Chinese chopsticks
> Wily, willy whiskers
> Pow, pow, pow.

This later became

> Rom pom pooli
> Willa, willa whiskers
> Injun chief say
> How, how, how.

'Under the Apple Tree'

This was a clapping game played by two players:

> Under the apple tree
> My boyfriend said to me,
> 'Kiss me, hug me, tell me that you love me
> One, two, three.'

This could be another example of a fragment from a much longer clapping game, possibly 'Under the Bram Bush' (Opie and Opie 1985: 453–5). On this playground there seemed to be a number of games that used only fragmentary references to longer texts in order to accompany shorter and simpler games.

At the end of break, we caught up with a group of girls in time to have a brief interview:

EG: Tell me something now – what I want to know is how did you know these?
Girl 1: Oh we've been doing them since—
Girl 2: We made them up at school—
Girls [speaking together]: We made them up . . . we've been doing—
Girl 2: We've been making them up since we've been in the 4+.
Girl 3: Yeah we just made them up . . .
Girl 1: Yeah.
Girl 2: That rude one, um, I got off my sister, though – told every-body else.
Girl 1: I got it from my friend, Jade.
Girl 3: And we all put it together.
Girl 1: We never tell teachers.
Girl 3: We never do.
EG: It's not the sort of rhyme you tell to teachers, I agree, no, but it's still fun for playing.
Girl 1: Yeah.
EG: Right, anything else?

> *Girl 1*: Sometimes we dance around because we like singing the Spice
> Girl songs—
> *Girls*: Yeah.
> *Girl 1*: And we like Tig and Stuck in the Mud.

The Spice Girls it seems are no more significant than any other game they play. Yet, on this playground where the Spice Girls were welcome, there was a confident and noisy exuberance about their games which seemed to reflect that of the girl band in, for example, the 'Cow Girls' game. Kicking legs in a chorus-line style, the girls with linked arms surged towards each other in two opposing lines, chanting the challenge 'Coming to get you', pulling the nominated victim from one team to the other in a show of controlled aggression or what almost seemed like female solidarity. Boys on the periphery looked on. Occasionally they attempted to join in and were pushed aside. Watching the video it is interesting to speculate how much this media-generated sense of 'girl power' is affecting their play. Certainly, what is evident from watching these two video recordings is the cooperative and collaborative nature of the games they are playing and their inclusiveness; girls, unlike the boys, can be seen to break into games that are in midstream, simply picking up the words, rhythm and often split-second timing as they join in the clapping or dancing circle.

What is there to learn from this?

What was particularly impressive about the visits to these schools was not simply the confirmation of the continued existence of a variety of traditional games and a vibrant oral culture, but further confirmation of the importance of break time in the school day. I have not attempted here to discuss theories as to why these games seem to be so important for the young girls who continue to play them; there is considerable analysis of their significance in the processes of maturation and socialization (Sluckin 1981; Grugeon 1993; James 1993; Blatchford 1998) and of their contribution to the participants' linguistic and literary development (Grugeon 1988, 1999; Widdowson, Chapter 7); nor should the significance of the music of the singing games to the players' aesthetic development be underestimated (Harwood 1992; Hall 1993).

For these 5- to 9-year-olds, the traditional texts of playground folklore seem to be both empowering and reassuring; the culture of childhood allows them to explore dangerous adult themes while remaining children. As the 9-year-olds told me, 'We like singing the Spice Girl songs . . . and we like Tig and Stuck in the Mud'. In those carnivalesque moments at break time, largely out of earshot, young people have a unique opportunity to explore the boundaries of their experience within a safe and conservative environment. These games challenge common-sense classification and suggest that things are not always what they seem. Nonsense appropriates the forms and institutions of everyday life and rearranges them; play with taboo topics becomes possible precisely because nonsense introduces a state of anomaly and ambivalence – the games create a context which can never be contextualized and never takes place in the real world. Thus the events that take place in the 'Cowgirls' game and the crude dramatization of the 'Teenage Girls' song, take their place alongside 'whopper-telling stories' and the use of extravaganza in speech and literature – the Rabelaisian humour to which Bakhtin refers (1968). The playground texts can be seen as part of an ongoing process of interpretation of different domains of discourse which have constantly shifting boundaries. On the playground these traditional games create a particular and unique context in which the 'metaphorical behaviour of nonsense, play and paradox is removed from everyday life, cut off from its reality-generating conversations and contexts, and limited to the "never-never land" context of playground, ritual and fiction' (Stewart 1979: 61).

Since 1997, with the advent of a new urgency in the requirement for all primary schools in England and Wales to adopt a daily 'literacy hour' and a national literacy strategy, I have become concerned to help students who are training to be primary school teachers to recognize and understand the resource already available in children's learning on the playground, which is every bit as rich and complex as the early stages of the formal introduction to reading and writing in the classroom. Children's oral playground lore and language can provide insights into the way personal literacies exist alongside, and complement, school literacies. In the past, attention has been paid to these games as part of a process of socialization (James 1993) or as an alternative culture (Blatchford 1994). Less attention has been paid to the linguistic features of oral playground rhymes and the possible contribution to literacy development that Widdowson illustrates in this book (see Chapter 7). It is possible that the threat to playtime may hinder or stifle a motivating, personal and cultural pursuit that is a vibrant and important part of young people's (and particularly girls') linguistic and musical development.

Acknowledgement

I would like to thank the children of Saint John Rigby Lower School and Goldington Green Lower School, Bedford.

6

The saga of Susie: the dynamics of an international handclapping game

Andy Arleo

According to Iona and Peter Opie (1985: 440), the popularity of handclapping games has waxed and waned in Europe since 'Pat-a-cake, Pat-a-cake, Baker's Man', first recorded in 1698. After a peak at the end of the nineteenth century and up until the First World War, handclapping receded until roughly the 1950s, at least in several English-speaking countries. In Britain during this period, 'the art of hand-clapping did not exactly die out; but it came a poor third to ball-bouncing and skipping amongst the games of agility. It was not till the wave of sparkling and spirited chants came over from America that it could be said to enjoy a revival' (Opie and Opie 1985: 443). Since the 1960s handclapping games have become popular among schoolgirls in many European countries and around the world. Part of their success surely lies in the sheer fun of performance, in the synchronized rhythmic acting out of patterns of language, sound and movement, where the player is at once storyteller, actor, singer and dancer.

Variants of the handclapping game known in English as 'When Susie Was a Baby' (Opie and Opie 1985: 458) have been collected in Australia, Britain, Cyprus, Denmark, France, Ireland, Israel, South Africa, Spain, the USA and perhaps elsewhere, in at least five languages: English, Danish, French, Greek and Spanish (see Table 6.1). This chapter examines some of the patterns of language, music and body movement associated with this game, and attempts to capture the apparent complexity of an activity performed so naturally and holistically by schoolgirls. My aim is not only to document the international diffusion of the 'Susie saga', but also to address some general issues that arise in the study of childlore. How does one account for the success of a particular rhyme, song or game within children's oral tradition? Given the variation that is inherent in oral tradition, which elements of an item of childlore remain stable and which change? To what degree do linguistic and cultural factors contribute to the process of variation? How do the patterns of sound and movement contribute to memorization and oral transmission?

The first section summarizes the data regarding selected versions of 'Susie' in different languages and presents the results of previous studies of this game. Possible historical sources of the game are then discussed in the next section. The following section is devoted to a fairly detailed study of the poetic, musical and kinetic organization of two French versions of 'Quand Delphine [Fanny] était un bébé'. This analysis is then extended to versions in other languages and cultures in the next section, with an emphasis on the narrative structure. Finally, the conclusion attempts to account for the success of this game within children's oral tradition.

The data and previous studies of 'Susie'

Before presenting the data, it is necessary to consider the terminology that has been adopted here. First, I use the term 'handclapping game', rather than 'handclapping rhyme', which refers in a more limited way to language, or 'handclapping song', which refers more to music. Although 'Susie' may not be a game in the strict sense, as there is not usually an outcome with winners and losers, it certainly is a form of play and a game in the looser sense. As suggested above, 'Susie' is a story, a song, a mime and undoubtedly other things as well. 'Game' translates best the multiple facets of this activity.

Second, we must look at the criteria that have been used to define 'Susiehood'. 'Susie' is used here as a cover term for the protagonists in different languages, and for the game itself, since this is a name that occurs frequently in the literature (for example, Opie and Opie 1985). In folklore in general, and in children's folklore in particular, there is rarely a clear boundary between items belonging to Family A and items belonging to Family B. Instead of strict membership of a well-defined set, we have fuzziness and overlapping, with some items on the edge of categories. This 'messiness' is of course exacerbated in a cross-linguistic and cross-cultural study that tries to deal with performance features, such as music and body movement, as well as text. To deal with this problem, I will consider that elements of childlore form 'radial categories' (Lakoff 1987: 91–114). From this perspective, certain items are seen as central or core members of a family of texts or games, while other items are viewed as more peripheral. The following textual and performance features are used as a rough guide in determining centrality. When all the features are respected, the item can be considered as a core member of the 'Susie family'. On the other hand, when only a few features are present, the item is on the edge of the radial category, a distant relative of the core 'Susie'.

Textual features:
- the narrative concerns a named central female character as she goes through stages of life, from infancy to death and beyond;
- the text displays poetic structure, such as division into verses and lines, and uses repetition.

Performance features:
- the text is used for handclapping among children, usually elementary schoolgirls;
- the text is sung or chanted to a regular beat;
- the verses alternate with mimed sequences, which contribute to the narrative content.

Table 6.1 presents selected variants of 'Susie' in ten countries and in six languages. As can be seen, all the data were collected from the late 1960s to the 1990s, with the notable exception of two Danish versions (Heft 1943; Nielsen 1994). The Danish version from the 1930s is a girls' singing game performed in a circle. Although it does not involve a named female, since each verse begins with 'When I shall be *x* years', it does involve life stages from 8 ('into school I go') to 500 years old ('I walk around as a ghost'). I will therefore consider this version as a peripheral example of the 'Susie family', as it deviates in several respects from the criteria mentioned above. We may observe that two classes of text emerge: those that designate a third person, named female (a dissyllabic first name except in the Cypriot version) and those that designate the first person singular 'I'.

Several researchers have commented on the narrative of this handclapping game. Brinton (1985: 159, quoting Roberts 1980: 97) writes about a French version: 'This clapping song, which catalogues life from babyhood through marriage to death, has been described as "a comic drama of the many ages of man"'. She notes the 'childish logic' of two alternative endings to the rhyme: 'Quand j'étais un microbe' and 'Quand j'étais grand-microbe' ('When I was a microbe/a big microbe'), with a pupil explaining that the players pretend to be a microbe on a chair. Thus 'a traditional story – a "life history" – is given a surrealist twist, with a typically ghoulish touch' (Brinton 1985: 161).

Jorgensen (1980: 63) notes that jump-rope and handclapping rhymes

> often carry with them partially hidden attitudes, values, and feelings which are particularly important to female children of this age group of approximately five to twelve years. At this time in their lives, young girls are beginning to consider the possibilities inherent in adult life and the new roles which they will soon be encountering, especially ones such as girlfriend, wife, and mother.

The popular handclapping rhyme, collected in Jorgensen's study under the name 'When Lucy Was a Baby', is 'amazingly specific in detail and

Table 6.1   Selected variants of 'When Susie Was a Baby'

Geographical area	Language	Name	Document type	Source	Year collected
Australia	English	Susy	T	Factor 1988	1980s
Australia (Melbourne)	English	Suzy	TVG	McKinty 1998	1984
Britain (Bedford)	English	Susie	TMG	Opie and Opie 1985	1975
Britain (Berkshire Downs)	English	Susie	T	Opie and Opie 1985	mid 1970s
Britain (W. Yorkshire)	English	Susy	TMGA	Hubbard 1982	1979–80
Britain (Andover)	English	Suzy	TMG	Roud 1984	1983–4
Cyprus	Greek	Aliki Vouyouklaki	TV	Panayi-Tulliez c. 1992	c. 1992
Denmark (Naestved)	Danish	'I'	TGM	Nielsen 1994	1930s
Denmark	Danish	'I'	Unknown	Heft 1943	Unknown
France (Provence)	French	Fanny	TGA	Brinton 1985	1979–82
France (St-Nazaire)	French	Delphine/ Fanny	TMGA	Arleo 1985	1985
France (5 locations)	French	Fanny	TMGV	Bustarret 1998	1991–2
Ireland (Tralee)	English	Susie	A	Webb 1983	1975
Ireland (Donegal)	English	Susie	T	Harlow 1994	1992
Israel (Jerusalem)	English	'I'	T	Eifermann 1971	Unknown
South Africa (Johannesburg)	English/ Afrikaans	Unknown	T	Opie and Opie 1985	1969
Spain (Madrid)	Spanish	Unknown	TMAV	Fribourg 1991	1991
USA (N. California)	English	Lucy	T	Jorgensen 1980	1977
USA	English	Unknown	V	Hawes 1969	Unknown

Key:
A = audio recording
G = description of gestures
M = musical transcription
T = text
V = video recording

quite comprehensive in terms of the many life situations which are discussed' (p. 63). Jorgensen also observes that although this rhyme models possible roles that girls may experience in their lifetimes, and even speculates about the hereafter, it does not mention other possibilities, such as a career.

Factor (1988: 175) notes that the Susie game, which is 'performed by Australian girls in playgrounds all over the country', shows 'freedom from customary propriety'. This is especially evident in the verse in which Susie, as a 'provocatively sexy' teenager, says:

Ooh, aah, lost my bra,
Left my knickers in my boyfriend's car.[1]

Factor underlines the subversive nature of this game: 'It is all mockery, a child's version of *commedia dell'arte*, with the raucous energy of the young reconstructing an unsentimental facsimile of adults' division of time' (1988: 176). It is no doubt this disturbing subversiveness that led a primary school headmaster in Victoria (Australia) to ban 'a collection of children's rhymes from the school because it contained the Susy saga' (1988: 176).

Lecourt (1998: 40), commenting on a version of the French 'Quand Fanny était un bébé' in which Fanny is first a little seed ('une petite graine'), notes that the narrative as well as the musical form is based on a cyclic rather than a linear conceptualization of time, which recalls Indian philosophy.

Other authors have stressed the value of this handclapping game for children. Harter (1998: 37) claims that it contributes to sensorimotor skills (such as rhythm, precision, speed, coordination, lateralization); memory and intelligence (language and general learning skills in particular); sociability, affectivity and creativity. Bustarret and Hurel (1998) see 'Quand Fanny était un bébé' as a model for memorization and show how the game uses different types of memory: procedural, episodic, sensorial, lexical, visual, semantic and musical.

Historical aspects

Who are Susie's ancestors in oral tradition? Iona and Peter Opie state that this handclapping game, taken up enthusiastically in the late 1960s, emerged from an earlier singing game 'When I Was a Lady' (1985: 458). In this game players imitate the actions of types of person or profession: lady, gentleman, baker, teacher and so on. Many of the versions cited extend back to the nineteenth century. We note a version published by Cecil Sharp in 1909 entitled 'When I Was a Schoolgirl'. Although these versions do not usually involve life stages, there are some similarities with 'When Susie Was a Baby'. Besides the mimicry, we also find the same syntactic inversion of subject and object found in many recent versions of 'Susie': 'When I was a lady, a lady was I'. The tune for 'When I Was a Lady', although it is in 3/4 metre, has a similar melodic contour to 'Susie'. Elizabeth Wein provides extensive notes for 'When I Was a Lady', extracted from an unpublished dictionary of singing games compiled by Roger Abrahams (personal communication, 1994). Among the alternative titles she cites are 'When I Was a Young Girl (Shoemaker) (Sailor)', 'When First We Went to School' and so on. She also sees similarities between 'Susie' and the singing game 'Jenny Jones', also cited by the Opies.

There is reason to believe that some of the versions of 'Susie' cited in Table 6.1 derive from the English-language tradition. For instance, the earliest reports of the French 'Quand Fanny était un bébé' I have found are from the late 1970s (Brinton 1985: 158). Moreover, the grammatical construction suggests that this version may be a translation of an English version. In standard French one would say 'Quand Fanny était bébé', omitting the indefinite article 'un'.

An analysis of 'Quand Delphine [Fanny] était un bébé'

We turn now to the analysis of a performance of 'Quand Delphine était un bébé' which I tape-recorded on 23 January 1985 at the Maison de Quartier de Kerlédé, a recreation centre in Saint-Nazaire, France. This version was performed by two girls, aged 9 and 10 years. I have provided several variants from another version, 'Quand Fanny était un bébé', tape-recorded in a classroom at the École Primaire Jules Simon in Saint-Nazaire on 9 February 1985, and also performed by two girls aged 9 and 10 years.

Quand Delphine était un bébé

Figure 6.1 Music notation for 'Quand Delphine était un bébé'.

French	*English translation*
1 Quand Delphine était un bébé, Un bébé, un bébé, Quand Delphine était un bébé, Elle faisait comme ça: [*Spoken*] 'Areu.'	When Delphine was a baby, A baby, a baby, When Delphine was a baby, She used to do this:

[*Variant: sucks thumb*]

| 2 Quand Delphine était une p'tite
    fille . . .
[*Spoken*] 'Un, deux, trois.' | When Delphine was a little
    girl . . .
'One, two, three.' |

[*Variant, spoken: 'Bigoudi bigouda' and imitates making curls. A 'bigoudi' is a hair-curler*]

| 3 Quand Delphine était une jeune
    fille . . .
[*Spoken*] 'Allo, chéri.' | When Delphine was a young
    girl . . .
'Hello, dear.' |

[*Mimes holding receiver*]

| 4 Quand Delphine était une
    maman . . .
[*Spoken*] 'Chh, bébé dort.' | When Delphine was a
    mummy . . .
'Shh, baby's sleeping.' |

[*Index in front of mouth and then mimes rocking baby to sleep*]

| 5 Quand Delphine était une
    grand-mère . . .
[*Spoken*] 'Ouille, mes reins.' | When Delphine was a
    grandmother . . .
'Ouch, my back.' |

[*Right hand on lower back, bends over in pain*]

| 6 Quand Delphine était un
    squelette . . .
[*Spoken*] 'Ououou.' | When Delphine was a
    skeleton . . .
'Oooooo.' |

[*Variant: spreads lips and chatters teeth*]

| 7 Quand Delphine était une
    poussière . . .
[*Spoken*] 'Balaie-moi.' | When Delphine was a dust
    speck . . .
'Sweep me.' |

[*Mimes sweeping*]

| 8 Quand Delphine était invisible . . . | When Delphine was
    invisible . . . |

[*Performers stop suddenly on the last syllable*]

| [*Variant: waves and says: 'Salut,
les gars.'*] | 'Hi, guys.' |

The poetic organization of 'Quand Fanny était un bébé'

In these two versions we have eight 'narrative blocks' corresponding to eight life stages, from 'babyhood' to 'dust' and ultimately 'invisibility'. Each narrative block includes a sung verse, accompanied by a repetitive three-stroke handclapping pattern (see below), which is followed by a mimed sequence in which the performers act out the life stage. We note a shift from a third-person perspective in the verse to a first-person perspective in the mimed sequence. The use of the imperfect tense (était) in the verse also underlines the narrative function. In this handclapping game the players are alternately narrators and actors. On the whole, the verses, with their repeating rhythmic, metrical, melodic and kinetic patterns are characterized by regularity and structural constraints, while the mimed sequences are freer, more individualistic and more expressive. There is of course a reason for this: successful performance of handclapping is a collaborative activity which requires synchronization between players and therefore tends to be rule-governed.

The verse is analysed here as a quatrain, as shown below:

1 Quand Delphine était un bébé,
2 Un bébé, un bébé,
3 Quand Delphine était un bébé,
4 Elle faisait comme ça.

I will refer to Lines 1 and 2 as the first couplet and Lines 3 and 4 as the second couplet. A line may be subdivided into two hemistichs (half-lines), as in Line 2, where 'un bébé' is a hemistich. Unlike many forms of written and oral poetry, including children's rhymes, these poetic divisions are not based on rhyme schemes, but on a general principle of repetition. In this case, the end-of-line rhymes in Lines 1, 2 and 3 are simply the result of the repetition of a noun phrase ('un bébé') and a when-clause ('Quand Delphine était un bébé'). Eliminating the repetitions, the grammatical structure of each verse can be reduced to the following construction:

Quand + DISSYLLABIC FEMININE FIRST NAME + était + LIFE STAGE + 'Elle faisait comme ça'.

The verse is actually a single complex sentence, consisting of a subordinate when-clause ('Quand . . . LIFE STAGE) and a main clause ('Elle faisait comme ça'), that is expanded through repetition. The last line uses the expression 'comme ça' as a transitory element that points ahead to the action in the mimed sequence. This poetic structure might be called a 'frame and slot' model, consisting of a relatively stable frame with two slots into which variables can be plugged. From one version to another, the first name of the protagonist may change and within one version the life stage changes from one verse to the next. This simple repetitive structure eases the burden of memorization and facilitates oral transmission, while allowing room for innovation.[2]

The melody and rhythm

The tune for each verse is a simple hexatonic melody, which might be described as a major scale without the fourth degree. The first two bars, which outline a major chord, are the same as the beginning of the well-known French Christmas carol, 'Il est né le divin enfant' ('The Divine Child Is Born'). Although the players may not be aware of the connection, it is interesting to note that both the carol and the handclapping song refer to an infant. Bars 3 and 4 extend the melody of Bar 2 by rising to the second degree of the scale (A) in Bar 3 and then to the third degree of the scale (B) in Bar 4. Bars 5 and 6 then repeat Bars 1 and 2. Finally, Bars 7 and 8 bring us from the dominant back to the concluding tonic.

There are several parallels between the melody and the grammatical structure. First of all, the repetition of 'Quand Delphine était un bébé' corresponds to the repetition of the melody. Furthermore, the repetition of 'un bébé' corresponds to a rising three-note melodic and rhythmic figure: D G G, D A A, D B B. The end of the first musical phrase (on the third 'un bébé') is suspensive (that is, we sense there is more to come), while the end of the second musical phrase (on 'ça') is conclusive. Grammatically, the subordinate when-clause ('Quand Delphine était un bébé') is also suspensive, whereas the main clause ('Elle faisait comme ça') is conclusive. It is likely that this parallelism between melody and grammatical structure also facilitates the task of memorization.

The rhythmic pattern is very simple with only two values, noted here as crotchets and minims. Using the relatively fast crotchet beat (approximately 196 beats a minute), which corresponds to the claps, as the basic time unit, we note that the whole verse has 32 beats (counting the rests at the end), each couplet has 16 beats, each line has 8 beats and the hemistich 'un bébé' has 4 beats. This binary organization, based on powers of 2, is quite frequent in children's rhymes and no doubt contributes to effective oral transmission (Arleo 1997). Finally, we see that the longer rhythmic values (that is, the minims) all occur at the end of textual divisions, making it easy to sense the poetic organization of the song.

The handclapping patterns

Below is a description of two handclapping patterns collected for 'Quand Delphine [Fanny] était un bébé':

A	B	C	A	B	C	A	B
Quand	Del-	phine	é-tait	un	bé-	bé,	
C	A	B	C	A	B	C	A
Un	bé-	bé,		un	bé-	bé,	
B	C	A	B	C	A	B	C
Quand	Del-	phine	é-tait	un	bé-	bé,	
A	B	C	A	B			
elle	fai-	sait	comme	ça.			

The two players are standing and facing each other.

Delphine
   A Palm of right hand turned upwards, palm of left hand turned downwards. Clap partner's hands.
   B Hold hands vertically in front of chest with palms facing partner. Clap partner's hands.
   C Hold hands vertically in front of chest and clap own hands together.

Fanny
   A Clap both hands against own thighs.
   B Hold hands vertically in front of chest and clap own hands together (same as '*Delphine*' C).
   C Hold hands vertically in front of chest with palms facing partner. Clap partner's hands (same as '*Delphine*' B).

We notice that in both versions the three-clap patterns are 'out of phase' with the eight-beat lines, that is, Line 1 begins with Clap A, Line 2 begins with Clap C and Line 3 begins with Clap B. In reference to this game, Bruckert points out that the superimposition of a binary rhythmic structure and a ternary handclapping pattern creates a 'décalage d'accent très complexe' [a very complex shift of accent]' (1998: 30). Kathryn Marsh also notes that this polymetric pattern is very widespread in Australia (personal communication, 1998). We may conclude that this handclapping game allows children to learn in an informal way how to maintain a pattern of body movements that is to some degree independent from the poetic and musical organization.

The narrative organization

As mentioned above, the narration is handled both verbally and, through the mime, non-verbally. The verse introduces a life stage that is subsequently illustrated in the mimed sequence, which presents stereotyped events, behaviours and speech associated with a particular age or status. Thus, 'thumb-sucking' represents babyhood as does the enigmatic two-syllable 'areu' that all French babies are supposed to utter just before beginning to speak the language of Voltaire. Delphine/Fanny is not a career woman, juggling professional and family responsibilities, as one might see in contemporary film or fiction. In these two versions she performs traditional roles, such as curling her hair, chatting on the phone with her boyfriend, rocking baby to sleep and becoming a grandmother.[3] One might see this as a survival from the past, as often happens in folklore, or rather as a lighthearted parody of the traditional role, a mockery or *commedia dell'arte* in the terms of June Factor. This latter interpretation seems more plausible, especially since handclapping texts as a whole tend to be satirical, but of course this depends on the age and the attitude of each child.

Figure 6.2 The words in the mimed sequence are chanted to a regular beat.

'Susie' around the world: a comparative approach

We now turn to a comparative analysis of 'Susie' in several languages. First, I will compare 'Quand Delphine Était un Bébé' to English-language versions of 'When Susie Was a Baby' provided by Hubbard (1982) and McKinty (1998), focusing on the poetic organization, music and handclapping patterns. I will then look at the narrative content by analysing the life stages in versions from six countries.

'Delphine' and 'Susie'

In the English-language versions of 'Susie' the verses and mimed sequences usually alternate as well. For example, Hubbard (1982: 253) states that 'throughout the verse, the children perform the clapping pattern, then during the last line they perform actions to fit the words'. However, in contrast to the French versions, the words in the mimed sequence are chanted to a regular beat (see Figure 6.2). While chanting this immortal line, the English equivalent of the French 'areu', the players pretend to suck their thumbs, as in the French version.

The poetic and grammatical structure of the verse of the Australian version (see Appendix) is nearly identical to the French versions shown above:

1 When Susie was a baby,
2 A baby, a baby,
3 When Susie was a baby,
4 She used to go like this.

There are also some musical similarities between the French versions and the English-language versions. The melodies are in a major key, begin with an ascending major fourth and end with the same four notes leading from the dominant back to the tonic. If an English version was the source for the French versions, which seems likely, we might reasonably speculate that the French tune was influenced both by the source tune and by the beginning of the well-known indigenous carol.

It is interesting to note that the texts of the French 'Delphine' and the Australian 'Susie' can be almost perfectly aligned, as shown below for the first line (the Xs above the text show where the minim pulse occurs):

```
X              X              X        X
Quand  Del-   phine  était   un   bé-  bé,

        X              X        X
When   Su-   sie      was    a    ba-  by,
```

The main rhythmic difference is that the English version begins with an upbeat, with the downbeat falling on the first syllable of 'Susie', whereas the French version begins with a downbeat. This no doubt stems directly from the well-known differences between the English and French stress systems. In English, it is natural to stress the even-numbered syllables ('Su-', 'was', 'ba-', etc.) and it would be extremely unnatural to stress the odd-numbered syllables ('when', '-sie', 'a', '-by', etc.) Thus, the minim pulse (approximately 95 beats a minute) is aligned with 'Su-', 'was', 'ba-' and so on. In French, the situation is reversed: the minim pulse (approximately 98 beats a minute) is aligned with the syllables 'Quand', '-phine', 'un', '-bé' and so on. This shows that, even when texts are translated almost word for word from one language to another, subtle melodic and rhythmic adjustments must be made due to the differences between the respective phonological systems.[4]

The Australian version also has a three-clap pattern that is identical to the French 'Delphine' version. On the other hand, the handclapping pattern described by Hubbard (1982: 253–4) is a four-clap ABCB pattern. Unlike the French and Australian patterns, this pattern is in phase with the musical and textual divisions – that is, each bar and each line begins with the same clap. Some of the claps are of course the same as in the French version, such as 'clap your own hands' (*'Delphine'* C clap) or 'clap partner's hands' (*'Delphine'* B clap).

The Susie saga in five languages

I will now look at the different life stages in selected French, English, Danish, Greek and Spanish versions, summarized in Table 6.2. In order to facilitate comparison, I have set up life stages that fit as closely as possible the data across languages. As can be seen, some versions do not have a particular life stage, whereas other versions have several verses about one life stage. The Danish version, for example, omits infancy, but, on the other hand, has several verses devoted to motherhood. Only the two English versions have a pregnancy stage; in the American version pregnancy follows marriage while in the British version it precedes it. The Spanish version, which begins directly in the courtship stage, deviates notably from the other versions since it deals with marital conflict and separation. In fact, there is an embedded sub-narrative, left out for reasons of space, that explains the reason for the separation: the central character's boyfriend no longer loves her and stole her necklace. Only the Australian version has a career stage, where Susie becomes a teacher, perhaps not a coincidence as this is a highly feminized profession.

Table 6.2 Life stages in five languages

Life stage	France: St-Nazaire (Arleo 1985)	Britain: Berkshire Downs (Opie and Opie 1985)	USA N. California (Jorgensen 1980)	Australia Melbourne (McKinty 1998)	Denmark (Nielsen 1994)	Cyprus (Panayi-Tulliez c. 1992)	Spain (Fribourg 1991)
I Infancy/early childhood	1 bébé	1 baby 2 toddler	1 baby	1 baby		1 baby	
II Childhood	2 p'tite fille	3 schoolgirl	2 schooler	2 schoolgirl	1 8 years into school	2 primary school	
III Adolescence	3 jeune fille	4 teenager	3 teenager	3 teenager	2 14 years out of school	3 secondary school	
IV Courtship					3 18 years I get a sweetheart	4 engaged	1 we met 2 now we're friends
V Pregnancy		5 a-pregnant	4 pregnant				
VI Marriage		6 a-married	5 married		4 20 years we stand before the parson	5 married	3 we got married
VII Motherhood	4 maman		6 mother	4 mother	5–7 22 (24, 26) the first (second) (third) child I get	6 gave birth	4 we had a child
VIII Career				5 teacher			

Table 6.2 (cont'd)

Life stage	France: St-Nazaire (Arleo 1985)	Britain: Berkshire Downs (Opie and Opie 1985)	USA N. California (Jørgensen 1980)	Australia Melbourne (McKinty 1998)	Denmark (Nielsen 1994)	Cyprus (Panayi-Tulliez c. 1992)	Spain (Fribourg 1991)
IX Separation							5 I no longer love you 6 because you don't love me 7–11 because you stole a necklace from me . . .
X Old age	5 grand-mère	7 a granny		6 grandmother		7 got old	12 now we're old
XI Death	6 squelette	8 a-dying	7 a goner, she went to heaven	7 skeleton	8 60 years walk with crutches 9 70 years go down into the grave	8 died	13 now we're skeletons
XII After death	7 poussière 8 invisible	9 an angel 10 a devil 11 a nothing	8 turned honest 9 went to hell 10 was a ghost 11 was a statue		10 100 years rise from grave 11 500 years, ghost		14 now we're nothing

Note: Arabic numerals refer to the order of verses. The Cypriot, Danish and Spanish versions are given in English translation.

A most interesting stage is (after) death, for here we have much variation, and perhaps an inkling of the child's conception of death. In three
versions death eventually leads to nothingness, after intermediary stages
(from 'skeleton' to 'dust' to 'invisible' in the French version; from 'angel'
to 'devil' to 'nothing' in the British version). In the American and Danish
versions the central character becomes a ghost. Religious themes like
heaven, hell and resurrection are evoked in the English and Danish
versions.[5]

Carey (1985: 65) points out that 'the landmarks of the human life cycle
are as inevitable as they are bewildering: infancy, childhood, adolescence,
adulthood, old age' and that, for example, 'the maintenance of personal
identity through the life cycle is beyond the young child's understanding'.
Furthermore, 'by age 5 or 6, children know that as they grow they keep
the same name, but they have a very fragile idea of any other senses in
which they stay the same person. They do not yet have a concept of an
individual person's life cycle (let alone of a plant's) around which to
organize their sense of personal identity' (p. 68). According to Carey, the
problems in understanding growth are due not only to a lack of biological
knowledge, but also to difficulty in conceptualizing time. In the light of
these findings, the 'Susie saga' is particularly interesting as it provides
a window into how time and growth are conceptualized by the elementary schoolgirls who perform this game. While some stages correspond to
natural and universal events, such as pregnancy and childbirth, others
are linked to cultural and institutional divisions of time, which have
become increasingly standardized around the world. School strongly
influences the child's notion of time for both short periods, such as
the daily timetable, and longer periods, such as the organization of the
school year. It is therefore not surprising that many versions of the 'Susie
saga' refer specifically to a 'schoolgirl' stage. From the child's viewpoint,
Susie moves from the known to the unknown. From the familiar initial
stages that the players have experienced personally, Susie advances into
uncharted territory, such as motherhood, which has been observed
but not experienced, and finally reaches the unknowable stage of death.
This progression through the life stages may therefore be considered as
a representation of existing notions, as a reinforcement and reminder
of the culture's temporal divisions, and as a way of understanding the
growth process. How each player interprets this material will of course
depend, among other factors, on her age and cultural background. With
its endearing mixture of realism and fantasy, the game simultaneously
rehearses and mocks the conventional categories of time and growth.

Conclusion

As was noted in the introduction, handclapping games are great fun
because of their combination of movement, language and music. But why

has this particular game become so attractive to schoolgirls in different parts of the world? Although the uninformed adult observer may be impressed by the complexity of this game, it is actually the simple repetitive structures, which emphasize the parallelism between text and music, that make 'Susie' easy to learn, remember and pass on to others. This structural advantage is enhanced by a fanciful, facetious and ultimately tragic-comic narrative that deals lightheartedly with fundamental and universal issues like growing up, falling in (and out of) love, sexuality, motherhood, ageing and death. Such themes no doubt strike a resonant chord in schoolgirls at a crucial transitional period of their life, as they leave elementary school and childhood.

The 'Susie saga' also offers a case study in the study of variation within children's oral tradition. It has often been observed that childlore spreads like the flu across social, political, linguistic and geographical barriers. Although we have noted some divergences as the saga moves from one play community to another, these appear to be outweighed by the many similarities that show the strong appeal of this narrative for young girls around the globe.

Researchers may wish to explore further this delightful handclapping game by collecting and examining variants from other cultures and languages. An additional line of investigation might involve gathering data on the players' own interpretations of the 'Susie saga'. More generally, this study suggests that the field of childlore should benefit from research that adopts an international perspective, in which performance analysis, focusing on the interactions among text, music and movement, is combined with cross-cultural and cross-linguistic comparison.

Appendix: Australian version of 'When Suzy Was a Baby'

Videotaped by Heather Russell at the Debney Meadows Primary School, Melbourne, 1984. Words and gestures transcribed by Judy McKinty. Music transcribed by Andy Arleo. There are slight melodic and rhythmic variations, for example, in Verses 3, 6 and 7, to accommodate the trisyllabic life stages such as 'teenager'. The tonic rises nearly a whole tone in Verse 3 (to B flat), then falls a semitone in Verse 5 and again a semitone in Verse 6 (back to A flat) (see Figure 6.3).

  1 When Suzy was a baby, a baby, a baby,
    When Suzy was a baby, she used to go like this:
    'Waah, waah, waah waah waah.'
    [*With crying action: rubbing eyes*]

  2 When Suzy was a schoolgirl, a schoolgirl, a schoolgirl,
    When Suzy was a schoolgirl, she used to go like this:
    'Write, write, write write write.'
    [*With writing action on hand*]

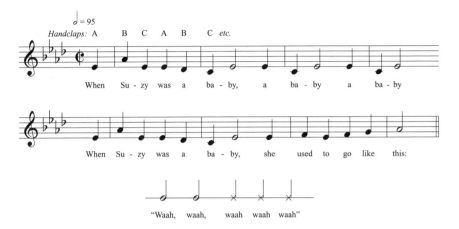

Figure 6.3 Australian version of 'Susie'.

3 When Suzy was a teenager, a teenager, a teenager,
When Suzy was a teenager, she used to go like this:
'Ooh, aah, I lost my bra in my boyfriend's car,
I don't know where my knickers are.
Ooh, aah, there they are—
Hanging in my boyfriend's car.'
[*Action: on 'Ooh' cross arms over chest, on 'Aah' cross arms over crotch*]

4 When Suzy was a mother, a mother, a mother,
When Suzy was a mother, she used to go like this:
'Smack, smack, smack smack smack.'
[*With smacking action*]

5 When Suzy was a teacher, a teacher, a teacher,
When Suzy was a teacher, she used to go like this:
[*Action only, no words. Index finger extended, shaking it up and down as if telling
someone off. Finger is shaken in rhythm, e.g. shake, shake, shake shake shake*]

6 When Suzy was a grandmother, a grandmother, a grandmother,
When Suzy was a grandmother, she used to go like this:
'Knit, knit, knit knit knit.'
[*With knitting action using index fingers*]

7 When Suzy was a skeleton, a skeleton, a skeleton,
When Suzy was a skeleton, she used to go like this:
[*Action only, no words: let body go limp and start to fall*]

Handclapping pattern

The two players are standing and facing each other.

A Palm of right hand turned upwards, palm of left hand turned downwards.
Clap partner's hands.

B Hold hands vertically in front of chest with palms facing partner. Clap partner's hands.

C Hold hands vertically in front of chest and clap own hands together.

Notes

1 This particular verse appears to be widespread in the English-speaking tradition (see Appendix and Hubbard 1982). Mavis Curtis (personal communication, 1999), commenting on a version she collected in 1993 in Shipley, West Yorkshire, which also contains the 'teenage verse', speculates convincingly that 'it will be very stable because it is very daring'.

2 Rubin (1995) provides detailed evidence that shows how the combined constraints of language and music contribute to the memorization of texts within oral tradition.

3 Chauvin (1999: 112) provides an example in which Fanny says, 'Au revoir, les enfants, j'vais au boulot [Goodbye, children, I'm going to work].

4 Arleo (1998: 88–90) examines this point in greater detail.

5 On the child's conception of death, see Carey (1985: 60–5).

Part 3

Widening perspectives: the possibilities of play

It is encouraging to note that the social, psychological and educational benefits of free play activities in middle childhood have recently begun to command a similar level of attention as research into the play of preschool children (see, for example, Kirshenblatt-Gimblett 1976; Sluckin 1981; Grugeon 1993, 2000; James 1993; Smith 1994; Pellegrini 1995; Blatchford 1998). The chapters in the final section of this book contribute to this important area of debate from three complementary angles.

The acquisition of linguistic skills among children in their informal play, already touched on by Marsh, Grugeon and Arleo (Chapters 4, 5 and 6), is given detailed consideration by J.D.A. Widdowson in Chapter 7. He underscores the importance of an alternative 'three Rs' in the verbal play of children – rhythm, repetition and rhetoric – as essential factors enabling the effective mastering of language skills. Through copious examples, Widdowson demonstrates the linguistic sophistication of much childlore at all linguistic levels, from phonology to semantics, and in the use of figures of speech and rhetoric. He argues that much of this largely unconscious learning, acquired in play, forms an important resource on which teachers could draw more extensively in the formal language lessons of the classroom.

As highlighted by Widdowson and in the Introduction to this book, our cultural traditions, many learned in childhood, are pivotal in form-ing and expressing our sense of cultural identity. Traditions are thus potentially divisive as well as integrative in that they may define who is an insider and who is an outsider (for example, Jansen 1965). The work of the Traditional Creativity through the Schools project, run by Simon Lichman in Israel, is a vivid demonstration of the positive potential of folklore in promoting intercultural understanding in a divided society. In Chapter 8 Lichman describes the project's use of children's play traditions in joint activities between Arab and Jewish schoolchildren and their family members. The exchange of games and the fun of playing together provide a non-threatening environment in which members of these groups can establish contact, experience peaceful coexistence and explore common interests.

The fun of informal play activities is also a central theme of Chapter 9 by Carole Carpenter. In it, we come full circle to the concern discussed at the outset of this book – namely, that traditional games are in decline. Carpenter finds some evidence for this in the play of boys in Toronto. She suggests, however, that this is partly due to adult interference in children's self-directed play, particularly the teaching of organized sport as a substitute for free play. She argues that the channelling of children into league hockey in Canada has produced a concomitant decline in the folk game of 'Shinny'. The emphasis on winning, physical aggression and expensive equipment in organized hockey has taken the fun out of the game. This loss of the play element for its own sake has helped to sap the ingenuity, vitality and self-esteem of young boys. Nevertheless, Carpenter points to signs that children are once more being allowed the space to organize their own games, including Shinny, in order to counter this decline.

7

Rhythm, repetition and rhetoric: learning language in the school playground

J.D.A. Widdowson

Published work in the field of children's folklore has focused primarily on form, variation and historical provenance, and the central role of childlore in the acquisition of social and linguistic skills has received comparatively less attention. Even a cursory exploration of available material reveals a wealth of information on the contribution of this lore to the development of language, especially in the context of traditional play. From early childhood through to adolescence children encounter and absorb a remarkable range of linguistic skills through a process of informal learning of which they are largely unconscious. Beginning with the apparently simple but actually complex interaction with parents and other carers – a vertical process of transmission – through to the rich variety of traditional material passed on from child to child within peer groups during schooldays – a horizontal process – the native language is acquired, developed, refined and above all revelled in. Virtually every aspect of language is involved in these informal playful exchanges: the rhythm and intonation of speech; the fundamentals of phonology, lexis, grammar and syntax; the appropriateness of language use in its social setting; culturally specific usage such as traditional sayings and proverbial forms; linguistic dexterity and virtuosic performance; storytelling skills; traditional humour such as pun, irony, sarcasm, innuendo and the testing of linguistic taboo; and familiarity with the essentials of literary analysis – rhythm, rhyme, alliteration, assonance, simile, metaphor, personification and other figures of speech. This chapter investigates the nature and function of traditional informal modes of language learning in the child's world in order to demonstrate their indispensability to the linguistic and social development of the individual.

Folklore is part of each one of us, and we in turn are part of the infinite variety of traditions which characterize the culture in which we live. Much of this traditional knowledge is acquired during the formative years of childhood, and a significant proportion of it persists throughout our lives. Among other things (as Lichman demonstrates in Chapter 8), it contributes to our sense of identity, of belonging to our culture, whether at the micro level of family and local community or at the macro level within the complexity of the wider social and national spheres. One of the obvious primary functions of tradition is to help each one of us to locate ourselves in both time and space. Most of us have vivid memories of those playground activities where we first experienced in play so many of the situations, roles and strategies which we encounter in our adult life. These memories are often so indelibly imprinted in our young minds that they stay with us for a lifetime and are clearly recalled even in old age. Despite their pervasiveness it is all too easy to underestimate or ignore the seminal influence of these early experiences, for they are so much a part of us that we simply take them for granted and, like so much of our folklore, regard them as unremarkable.

In recent years, however, there has been a reawakening of interest in childlore in Britain and indeed farther afield, not only in academic research (Roberts 1980; Opie and Opie 1985, 1997; Moore 1986; Bronner 1988; Grugeon 1988, 1996, 2000; Dargan and Zeitlin 1990; Butt and Small 1993; Everitt 1993; Glass 1993; Opie 1993; Robson 1993; Widdowson 1993; Sutton-Smith *et al.* 1995), but also in the teaching profession, and more widely among the general public in Britain. There is much to be gained by exploring the contribution which traditional play can make to educational development across the curriculum at the primary level. Such play has a useful and practical role in the acquisition of at least basic knowledge and skills in English, mathematics, history, geography, religious education, music, art and physical education, not to mention memory skills, communicative facility, hand–eye coordination and physical dexterity. Comparatively few studies (for example, Sanches and Kirshenblatt-Gimblett 1976; Roberts 1980) have directly addressed the role which childlore plays in the development of language and literacy in the primary school years. Indeed, the teaching of English language and literature at both primary and secondary level usually maintains a lofty and even frosty distance between formal and even informal work in the classroom on the one hand, and whatever goes on in the playground and/or in peer group interaction outside school hours on the other. This unnatural divorce means that for the most part teachers fail to capitalize on the wealth of material informally learned by children within the traditional culture of the playground. In my own experience of observing playground activities over the past 20 years, when I ask about children's traditional play at the primary school level, teachers typically say that the old games have either died out or are rapidly disappearing, and that nowadays the children in the playground 'just run around being silly' or some similar dismissive expression.[1] These observations are corroborated and elaborated by Factor (see Chapter 1). Some teachers, on the other hand, along with dinner ladies, care assistants and voluntary helpers, take an active interest in everything going on around them and at times participate in it, contribute to it and even initiate it, perhaps, in so doing, handing on the traditions of an older generation. Nevertheless, at the end of the playtime or lunch break this material is usually left behind in the playground and rarely crosses the threshold of the school building – a threshold which truly separates the informal and the formal worlds.

Virtually all the traditional activities in children's play involve language in all its rich variety; and knowledge, skills, and understanding of speaking and of language variation figure prominently in Key Stages 1 and 2 of the National Curriculum. Yet, in Britain our teaching concentrates on extending and developing skills in reading and writing, focusing primarily on literacy and proficiency in the written word, and leading ultimately to a knowledge and appreciation of literature. By contrast, the playground culture is almost exclusively oral. Notwithstanding the recent and continuing efforts through the National Curriculum to encourage effective and confident self-expression in speech, assessment at all levels foregrounds the testing of knowledge and skills concerning the written language, thus maintaining the primacy of print as the measure of academic achievement. For some unaccountable reason oracy is relegated to minimal status in this process, in spite of the fact that speech is the normal and habitual mode of everyday human interaction.[2]

Acquisition of language and lore

When children enter primary school, they have normally already acquired the essentials of spoken English, which is the foundation for all subsequent linguistic development. It is worth reminding ourselves that this knowledge is learned by informal traditional means within the family. Mothers and other carers initiate, encourage, extend, develop and refine linguistic knowledge and skills. Linguistic competence and performance are imparted largely through an extensive range of traditional verbal interchanges between adults and children, often in a playful mode enjoyed by both. The informal teaching is characterized by constant repetition and reinforcement – an effective traditional form of pattern practice. Adults also guide children in the acquisition and use of spoken greetings, leave-takings and other forms of language within a social context (Widdowson 1976; Lewis 1978).

Catherine Snow (1976) points out that, for most children, the process of acquiring language in infancy and early childhood is very fast, relatively painless and seemingly automatic, so it often goes unnoticed how much time and effort the children themselves and their older caretakers invest in the process. She adds that:

events and experiences ... which may contribute to the acquisition of linguistic and communicative skills ... include:

1 'Conversation-like' interactions in early infancy.
2 Having one's first communicative efforts responded to.
3 Receiving linguistic input of a simplified and repetitive nature.
4 Having adults respond to one's signals that their communicative efforts are ineffective.

(Snow 1976: 63)

Such linguistic interaction in early childhood normally provides a solid grounding in traditionally learned language, not to mention at least some experience of preschool rhymes, games and stories, whether transmitted orally from memory or read aloud, often in a distinctive way which exaggerates intonation patterns and utilizes the visual images in children's books, aiding the association of words with their referents, first on the printed page and later in real life. In recent years these skills and this knowledge have been built on and extended in nursery and reception classes, often in ways which mirror the home environment. A significant difference now, however, is that this learning process has progressed from a one-to-one experience to one shared and participated in by a group of children with diverse backgrounds and experience of traditional forms, including, of course, a multicultural dimension. Although these early preschool rhymes, games and stories are shared by the peer group and may remain in memory throughout the life of each individual, they rarely find a place in the playground, except perhaps in parodic form. The traditional playground activities seem to develop independently, though no doubt drawing on their precursors in the preschool years. 'The people in the playground', as Iona Opie has so aptly termed them (1993), are for the most part in sole charge of their activities in a world of play which, though open for all to see, is essentially close-knit and secretive. To investigate it in any depth one first needs all the skills of fieldworkers such as the Opies in establishing a sufficient rapport with the children that one is accorded the privilege of being invited into this hidden culture and allowed to share at least some of its secrets. So strong are its protocols and policing, however, that the owners of the information, the young people themselves, use self-censorship and other powerful means to control access and, if they think it necessary, to conceal information and/or withdraw cooperation.

Research at the National Centre for English Cultural Tradition (NATCECT) at the University of Sheffield,[3] reveals that while 5-year-olds in reception classes at primary school, and sometimes also 6-year-olds in Year 1, are fully aware of the preschool lore from their home environment, they may know little if anything of the wealth of traditions of those a few years older which are going on all round them in the playground. They acquire a knowledge of this material, and the skills to perform it, by a gradual process of observation and by transmission from slightly older children. This process is usually established by the age of 7, if not before (Grugeon 1988: 161–5), each peer group developing its own unique and eclectic mixture of traditional activities from the available repertoires. The range of this school-age lore transmitted from child to child is extensive, and virtually all the activities involve language, often exclusively. Halpert (1971) provides a useful summary list:

Jeers, taunts, reproofs.
Defiance and retorts.
Calls, cheers, chants and yells.
Mockery of school, teachers, school subjects, etc.
Humorous narratives; modern topical verses and songs.
Parodies, mock speeches, backwards and nonsense verses, etc.
Other verbal play: abbreviations, epithets, euphemisms, insults, tongue-twisters, trick spelling, trick languages, put-offs, catches, wisecrack answers, etc.
Games and game rhymes: counting-out and choosing; ball-bouncing; rope-skipping; marching chants; singing games; non-singing games (without equipment); games with equipment.

Such an inventory immediately calls attention to the potential for language learning in such activities. As in the informal learning in early childhood, linguistic knowledge and skills are largely acquired in the context of play and as part of the socialization process within the group. The learning ranges across the whole field of language, contributing to knowledge and performance skills at all five analytical levels: phonology, lexis, grammar, syntax and semantics, and beyond these to at least a basic familiarity with spelling and even punctuation, as well as certain essential features of literature, storytelling, role-play and humour.

Before briefly exploring each of these in turn, however, it is important to draw attention to three pivotal elements in traditional linguistic play which have a key role in the language learning process. They are the alternative three Rs: rhythm, repetition and rhetoric. Collectively these are the central pillars of a pervasive traditional system of education which takes place in a parallel universe. Both in preschool and playground interaction, rhythm underpins not only rhymes and songs but also much other verbal play, often emphasized or complemented (as in clapping games, for instance) by rhythmic physical action. Rhythm is, of course, fundamental to the whole process of language learning and to the development of musical skills. While one might lament the recent apparent decline of singing games in the playground, as evidenced by my own research in Sheffield, the chants which have often replaced them re-emphasize the rhythmic basis of these activities. The importance of repetition in the acquisition of language in the preschool years is mirrored in playground rhymes and games. Young children delight in repetition for its own sake, playing the same game over and over again, and so imprinting it firmly in the memory along with its language. As for rhetoric, it seems that teachers pay little attention to the range of figures of speech and other devices which become familiar to children during play. More significantly, when such features are explored in the classroom, usually at the secondary level, no account seems to be taken of this prior informal knowledge. What could and should be a bridge between informal and formal language skills remains unrecognized or ignored, to the detriment of the learning process as a whole. The failure to acknowledge and build on this acquired knowledge is both short-sighted and perverse, as indeed is the persistence of artificial barriers in teaching which so often separate oracy and literacy and discount their interrelationships.

Phonology, lexis, grammar, syntax and semantics

Turning now to the acquisition of specific linguistic skills, it is clear that the traditional play of schoolchildren within the peer group makes a significant contribution to the learning process across the full range of language, in terms of both knowledge and performance. This is immediately evident from the available published and archival data.

Phonology

At the phonological level, for example, traditional play re-emphasizes characteristic features of pronunciation and intonation of current spoken English and encourages facility of articulation; for example, through counting-out rhymes, tongue-twisters and tangle talk in which rhythm and repetition are reinforced by alliteration, assonance and unusual or strongly contrasted patterns and pairings of individual consonants and vowels. Deviation from normal pronunciation may be stigmatized by name-calling and nicknaming. As Sanches and Kirshenblatt-Gimblett (1976: 92) put it in their groundbreaking study, 'the child's interest in phonology . . . helps to account for the high degree of morphophonological patterning generally found in children's speech play productions', and they add: 'It is not accidental that young children should employ gibberish which is rhythmic and highly patterned phonologically . . . Gibberish is purely phonologically motivated and it appeals to younger children because phonology, as compared to semantics and syntax, is far more highly developed in the younger child's language'. The importance of nonsense words in playground games 'reduces the necessity for players to understand the meaning of the words' and 'also facilitates the inclusion of non-English words in the game repertoire' (see Marsh, Chapter 4, p. 88; cf. Arleo 1999).

Examples of phonological skill and dexterity in traditional play include the derisive intonation pattern in the tune of 'Cowardy, Cowardy Custard' and similar taunts, as well as such examples as:

Did you eever, iver, over,
In your leef, life, loaf,
See the deevel, divel, dovel,
Kiss his weef, wife, woaf?

No I neever, niver, nover,
In my leef, life, loaf,
Saw the deevel, divel, dovel,
Kiss his weef, wife, woaf.
                    (Sanches and Kirshenblatt-Gimblett 1976: 93–4)

I scream
You scream
We all scream
For ice cream.
                    (Sanches and Kirshenblatt-Gimblett 1976: 95)

How much wood would a woodchuck chuck if a woodchuck could
chuck wood.
                    (Sanches and Kirshenblatt-Gimblett 1976: 97)

Eeny, meeny, mackaracka,
Air, aye, dominacker
Chicker Pocker, lollipopper,
Om pom push.
– and numerous variants
                    (N. Williams, Oxford, 1977, SLF/Archives of
                        Cultural Tradition, ACT 99-014/CS12719)[4]

Jink, jink, pom, pink
Inky, pinky, perky, pun.

                                        (Kelsey 1983)[5]

The Opies also mention the alteration of names for humorous effect:
'Clara Dace becomes "Clear-a-space", and Fred Maddox becomes "Fresh
Haddocks"' (1959: 158).

Lexis

It is, of course, at the lexical level that we have overwhelming evidence
of children learning a wealth of words and expressions, not only during
traditional play and games but also in the everyday interaction among
the peer group and in the wider context of the playground culture as a
whole. Much of this vocabulary belongs to the children's world and is
central to its characterization. As the Opies amply demonstrate (1959:
154–74), this extensive inventory of words is learned as part of the code
of oral legislation – for example, in gaining possession of items, claiming
precedence, obtaining respite by using truce terms and so on, as well as
in the invention and use of nicknames and epithets, and in jeering,
taunting, defiance and retorts. The process of acquisition is aided by a

collective indulgence in an extraordinary range and complexity of traditional linguistic play, typified by a delight in puns and other wordplay (Sanches and Kirshenblatt-Gimblett 1976; Roberts 1980: 117–19). In all these activities children are amazingly creative, exploring every facet of language use, including abbreviation, euphemism and terms through which they learn to exercise power and assertiveness by the deployment of insults, witty responses and the like. Each generation also acquires its own characteristic vogue words, including greetings, leave-takings and terms expressing a liking for or dislike of something. This generational language normally accompanies a particular age group of speakers throughout their lives. The Opies discuss the nature, form, extent and use of these lexical inventories, especially in *The Lore and Language of Schoolchildren* (1959), and present substantial and detailed lists of words and expressions, grouped into a series of typical categories. They also provide numerous examples of favourite endings and other morphological characteristics which clearly demonstrate that young people of this age become familiar with the structure of words during their play, and acquire the fundamentals of word formation. A particularly favoured morpheme is the diminutive ending -y/-ies, humorously tested in the trick question 'Where did Napoleon keep his armies?' – 'Inside his sleevies' (Widdowson Fieldwork Collection).

The Opies' research discovered a range of regional dialect words for a given notion, and they present the evidence for words claiming precedence, truce terms, words for playing truant, and the use of the dialect term *mardy* for a spoilt child or cry-baby in the form of a revealing map of their distribution (1959: 177). The development of vocabulary through traditional play is part of the social bonding process, both within the peer group and beyond. The deployment of individual inventories, often in the context of competition in which humour,[6] frequently in the form of puns, plays a major role, also builds a degree of self-assurance at both personal and group level. The sheer enjoyment of playing with words is central to this process of acquisition and performance, familiarizing the users with terms they may not as yet fully understand, but at the same time preparing users for their appropriate use in later life, as illustrated in a 10-year-old's facetious manipulation of the lexis in 'I presume that your presumptions are precisely incorrect. Your sarcastic insinuations are too obnoxious to be tolerated' and 'If you insinuate that I tolerate such biological insolence from an inferior person like you, you are under a misapprehended delusion' (Sanches and Kirshenblatt-Gimblett 1976: 101).

When young children are asked to describe a game, they often demonstrate an extraordinary range of fully assimilated vocabulary specific to it, together with a remarkable economy of expression, as in this example of a ball-bouncing game from London:

After 'plainsie' you go overs, then upsies, downsies, dancies, clapsies, digsies, twisties, blinksies, other blinksie, winksie, other winksie, legsie, other legsie, hopsie, other hopsie, jumpsie, alairsie, one handsie, curtsey, bowsie, dropsie, floorsie, bendsie, shoesie, thumbsie, gatesie, farsie, nearsie, smallsie, tallsie, milkman, policeman. When it goes 'farsie' you jump away, for 'nearsie', you jump towards the wall, for 'smallsie' you go down when it says so, for 'tallsie' you got to get up a little bit more, for 'milkman' you got to quickly go down and touch the floor, for 'policeman', you just bow like a policeman does.

(Girl, Dalston, London, in Kelsey 1983)

The class shifting of words is also characteristic of children's speech, for instance the transference of nouns to an adjectival function in vogue words expressing a liking, such as *'cool'*, *'mint'*, *'top'*, or *'wicked'*. Class shifting, along with reversed compounding and other unexpected, inventive, amusing and accessible linguistic features, both lexical and grammatical, are evident in 'As I walked down to the wayrail station, I met a bark and it dogged at me. I pulled a hedge out of a stake and necked its knock out' (Opie and Opie 1959: 24).

Indeed, young people are bold, innovative and highly creative in their use of words, revelling in them for their own sake, and greatly developing their linguistic knowledge and skills in the process. The fundamentals of spelling are present in traditional play, as for example in counting-out rhymes ending with 'O-U-T spells out' and variants, partisan rhymes requiring the spelling of a place or person (Opie and Opie 1959: 351), and such tricks as:

If a feller met a feller in a feller's field
Would a feller tell a feller what a feller means?
How many 'f's' in that?

(K.W. Turner, West Butterwick, Scunthorpe, 1969,
SLF/ACT 98-589/CS10824)

Round and round the rugged rocks
The ragged rascal ran.
How many 'r's' are there in that?
Now tell me if you can.

(Opie and Opie 1959: 68)

and the ubiquitous 'Constantinople is a very hard word. Spell it' (J.D.A. Widdowson, Filey and Bridlington, East Yorkshire, 1967, SLF/ACT 97-020/CS12292).

Grammar

It is often at the grammatical level that young children experience difficulty in the language learning process, not least because grammatical forms in regional speech may differ markedly from those of standard English, which are, of course, central to language teaching in schools. Interestingly, the vast majority of published examples of traditional rhymes appear to conform to the rules of standard grammar. Anyone who tape-records children's language, and especially their narratives, in the playground, however, usually finds that the children use the grammatical forms of their local dialect. This is certainly the case in my own experience of recording childlore. Paradoxically, viewed from a generational perspective, I have found that the youngest and the oldest members of society in England utilize regional dialect to a much greater extent than the intervening age groups. For example, children in the Sheffield area often use dialectal variants in the past tense of verbs: 'I was stood', 'They were sat', 'It sempt' (it seemed), etc. There are vestiges of older grammatical forms, such as the plural noun inflections in such rhymes as:

I saw two ghostes,
Sitting on postes,
Eating toastes.

(Widdowson Fieldwork Collection)

It comes as something of a surprise, however, to find that young children are apparently aware of the rules of concord in such trick questions as 'Which is correct: "The yolk of an egg *is* white" or "The yolk of an egg *are* white"?' (J.D.A. Widdowson, Chesterfield, Derbyshire, 1967, SLF/ACT 97-020/CS12183), which seem to mimic the kinds of question which were once fashionable in school examinations. However facetiously, even grammatical categories are mentioned:

Masculine, Feminine, Neuter,
I went for a ride on my scooter . . .

(Opie and Opie 1959: 19)

Syntax

The acquisition of syntax is a complex and little understood phenomenon. It centres on the ability to string words together in a meaningful way, beginning with the linking of words in pairs and progressing to longer utterances with the addition of verbs. Traditional preschool and playground play and games allow children to extend and develop their syntactical skills. While teachers at the primary level encourage children to augment their vocabulary by using a wider range of descriptive words, many children have already acquired this skill in an informal way. Stimulated by the competitive edge in the context of exchanging jocular insults, for example, a child as young as 7 who can concatenate an utterance such as 'A silly, soppy, sentimental, disconnected, over-heated, prehistoric drainpipe' (J. Osborne, Sibthorpe Hill, Nottinghamshire, 1970, SLF/ACT 00-003/CS13496) has already mastered at least the rudiments of syntax. What is more, the playful tone, double meanings and appropriateness of the utterance demonstrate a grasp of language use far beyond the mechanics of sentence construction. Listing words in a set order, as, for instance, in rhymes for counting fruit stones, etc., such as 'Tinker, tailor, soldier, sailor, rich man, poor man, beggarman, thief', both aid the acquisition of vocabulary and the concatenation of heterogeneous terms in a syntactical string.

Rhyme, rhythm, metrical patterning and musical tunes in singing games also contribute to the acquisition of syntax, often based on the typical interaction patterns of different types of utterance: statements, questions, exclamations and so on. Sanches and Kirshenblatt-Gimblett (1976: 97–8) provide a detailed analysis of the rhyme:

> Are you the guy
> That told the guy
> That I'm the guy
> That gave the guy
> The black eye?
>
> No, I'm not the guy
> That told the guy
> That you're the guy
> That gave the guy
> The black eye

and show that it involves a process of embedding, based on four sentences, which demonstrates competence in handling syntactic complexity. Rhymes of this kind also require careful spoken delivery, with appropriate intonation and parsing which reflect the syntactic structure in a way not dissimilar to punctuation in the written language.

Semantics

Moving on now to semantics, young people take particular delight in punning and wordplay, as we have already seen, and this obviously has a key role in learning the meanings of words and expressions. Once again, this process is aided by the humour, competitiveness and sheer exuberance of interaction in the peer group and also across the age groups. Most children have been caught out by failing to identify the semantic trap in such rhymes as:

> Adam and Eve and Pinch-me
> Went down to the river to bathe
> Adam and Eve got drowned
> Who d'you think was saved?

> (Kelsey 1983)

– a trick often perpetrated by children on those younger than themselves. Most of us will also remember that in childhood a number of words and expressions were as yet somewhat peripheral to our knowledge. Their meaning was eventually revealed, though in the meantime we pretended that we knew what they meant.

Figures of speech and rhetoric

The acquisition of meaning leads on to familiarization with figures of speech and rhetoric, and the symbolic use of language. Children encounter many of these usages in the course of their traditional play and interaction, so much of which is after all in rhymed metrical form. In theory at least these encounters might pave the way for the recognition and interpretation of such rhetorical devices when they are met with later during the study of literature in the classroom. As the detailed discussion of the full range of rhetorical figures in Sanches and Kirshenblatt-Gimblett (1976) amply demonstrates, much can be learned from developing an awareness of these devices and of their precursors in traditional play, and from a more extensive exploration of their inter-relationships. The following preliminary listing is intended as a starting point for further investigation.

Alliteration

This is a ubiquitous feature of traditional rhymes and linguistic interaction, children revelling in its repeated patterns, as for example in such tongue-twisters as 'Peter Piper picked a peck of pickled pepper . . .' (Kelsey 1984), the rhymes 'Charlie, Charlie, chuck, chuck, chuck . . .' (Opie and Opie 1959: 159), 'Dunce, dunce, double D . . .' (Kelsey 1979), 'See-saw, see-saw, sitting on a see-saw . . .' (Kelsey 1983), 'Tell tale, tit . . .' (Kelsey 1984), and the Punjabi clapping rhyme 'Zig zag zoo . . .',[7] as well as innumerable examples of two alliterating words either following each other or in close proximity.

Anaphora

This is the successive repetition of an initial word or phrase. It is common, reflecting young people's enjoyment of repeated forms and patterns:

When I was one . . .
When I was two . . .

(Kelsey 1984)

Plainsie to America
Plainsie to Japan . . .

(Kelsey 1983)

One more day at school
One more day of sorrow . . .

(Kelsey 1983)

and in part of the Punjabi clapping rhyme 'Zig zag zoo':

| Khabie oppear | Sometimes up |
| Khabie nichay | Sometimes down |

Khabie sithay   Sometimes facing you
Khabie photay.   Sometimes away from you.[8]

Antithesis

This is a common feature of playground language, notably in often unexpected and bizarre appositions of words and ideas which, among other things, play a central role in much of children's humour. The creativity and sense of fun which characterize these contrasts show that children are fully capable of manipulating quite complex notions through language, fascinated as they are by the attraction of opposites:

I went to the pictures tomorrow
I got a front seat at the back . . .

(Kelsey 1983)

One bright morning in the middle of the night . . .

(Kelsey 1984)

Finders, keepers
Losers, weepers.

(Kelsey 1984)

Assonance

As might be expected, this is very much in evidence in playground rhymes in a variety of metrical forms, for example, in 'Each, peach, pear, plum . . .' (Kelsey 1983), 'If I lie I promise to die . . .' (Opie and Opie 1959: 124), 'Inky pinky, pen and inky . . .' (Opie and Opie 1959: 48), 'Peter's pop kept a lollipop shop . . .' (Opie and Opie 1959: 160), and the Punjabi counting-out rhyme:

Eessie Peessie nack pareessi
Garae wun garae peessie.[9]

Bathos

As with antithesis, children's love of contrasts in their play inevitably leads to the juxtaposition of the sublime and the ridiculous, not least in parody, which is one of their favourite indulgences. Anticlimax of course is essential to such narratives as the shaggy dog story, but is particularly effective in parody:

Good King Wenceslas looked out,
On the eve of Stephen,
Someone donked him on the snout,
And made it look uneven.

(Kelsey 1983)

Gradatio

The repetitive structure and patterning of traditional rhymes means that step-by-step progression of clauses, often with overlapping of words, phrases and meanings is likely to occur, especially in the longer rhymes. Such progression may also lead to a climax, often an unexpected one, as in certain rhymes intended to scare the listeners:

> In a dark, dark street,
> There was a dark, dark house,
> In the dark, dark house,
> There was a dark, dark room . . .

(Kelsey 1983)

Hyperbole

The fiercely competitive nature of much children's play is an open invitation to boasting and exaggeration, whether jocular, ironic or more serious. Young people constantly vie with each other across the full range of their interaction and activities, often on their own behalf but also on behalf of the peer group as a whole, especially in football chants and other expressions of partisanship:

> Ipswich Town are rubbish,
> Liverpool are the best,
> No one can beat them,
> Nor can the rest.

(Kelsey 1983)

Metaphor

Long before young people are formally introduced to metaphor they are already aware that words can have meanings and referents other than the literal ones. Once again it is children's enduring fascination with wordplay which enables the addition of this important further dimension to their language skills, even though the vast majority of rhymes and other traditional forms are literal rather than metaphorical. A great deal of wordplay involves quite complicated juggling with literal and metaphorical meanings, as in the following examples: 'Up the little wooden hill to blanket town' (going to bed) (Widdowson Fieldwork Collection), 'armoured cow' (corned beef) (Opie and Opie 1959: 163) and 'murder on the Alps' (rice pudding with jam on) (Widdowson Fieldwork Collection).

Onomatopoeia

From the outset, traditional modes of language play and interaction include a greater proportion of echoic forms than in normal adult speech.

Perhaps beginning with such baby-talk preschool usages as *'baa lamb'*, *'chuck-chuck'* (hen), *'quack-quack'* (duck) and *'tick tock'* (clock), children progress to employing a wide range of usages echoing the sounds of both the real and the imaginary world (Widdowson 1976: 45–6). They imitate, for example, the sound of aeroplanes, cars, cats, dogs, explosions, fighting, guns, horses, insects, musical instruments, rockets, sirens, spaceships, trains and vomiting, often as part of the fun and creativity of acting and pretending games. In other games and rhymes, onomatopoeia is also often in evidence:

> bells: Ting-ling-ling . . .
>
> (Kelsey 1983)
>
> hiccups: Too many radishes – Hick! Pardon me.
>
> (Opie and Opie 1959: 18)
>
> knocking at a door: Rat tat tat, who is that?
>
> (Opie and Opie 1959: 11)
>
> laughter, often ironic: Ho! Ho! Ho! He! He! He!
>
> (Kelsey 1983)

along with such words as *'bang'*, *'bash'*, *'bop'*, *'bump'*, *'fizz'*, *'guck'*, *'plonk'*, *'pooh'*, *'slurp'*, *'splat'*, *'splosh'*, *'squish'*, *'whizz'*, *'yuck'* and a host of onomatopoeic expressions from television, video games, comics and other sources in the all-pervasive mass media.

Oxymoron

Witty absurdities, often involving an apparent contradiction, are a common occurrence in traditional rhymes and verbal play. As with antithesis, they are characteristic of children's humour:

> The sausage is a cunning bird
> With feathers long and wavy;
> It swims about the frying pan
> And makes its nest in gravy.
>
> (Opie and Opie 1959: 22)
>
> 'Twas in the month of Liverpool
> In the city of July,
> The snow was raining heavily,
> The streets were very dry.
> The flowers were sweetly singing,
> The birds were in full bloom,
> As I went down the cellar
> To sweep an upstairs room.
>
> (Opie and Opie 1959: 24)

Simile

Traditional rhymes and repartee include a range of comparisons, often humorous and/or bizarre, which introduce children to simile:

Oh, Judy, you're a funny 'un
With a face like a pickled onion,
A nose like a squashed tomato,
And teeth like green peas.

(Opie and Opie 1959: 171)

face like a chimpanzee

(Opie and Opie 1959: 171)

like a sausage in the air

(Opie and Opie 1959: 184)

Summary

This chapter can do no more than draw attention to some of the ways in which traditional play can contribute significantly to the acquisition of language skills. In addition to the elements outlined here, this early experience introduces young people to rhyme, metre and most if not all of the essentials of poetry, as well as to the skills of storytelling. We need to remind ourselves that some children as young as 5 are capable of sustaining a spoken narrative for 15 minutes or more (Widdowson 1979). This process of informal learning is also a vital stimulus to creativity, not least in acting and pretending games, which allow free rein to the imagination and instil the rudiments of drama long before the formal study of literature in school. Traditional play and interaction ensure that young people acquire the knowledge and skills to use language in all its rich variety. For the most part, this is achieved by a process of unconscious learning within a context of playful interaction. The children's infectious enthusiasm for language, their fascination with sounds and words, and the sheer sense of fun which characterizes the learning process, all combine to ensure its effectiveness.

All through childhood, and extending into adolescence, young people discover for themselves most of the key elements of language and literature which they will meet again in the more formal context of the classroom. This information, however, usually remains latent, its potential largely unrealized. It may be rudimentary in some respects, but in spite of all the pressures for change in childlore today, it provides a sound basis for potential educational development. For those of us working in the field of children's language and folklore, this material presents no 'triviality barrier' (Sutton-Smith 1970). For us, everything children say and do is meaningful and revealing.

It is important that teachers be aware of, and give due recognition to, the informal linguistic knowledge and skills which children acquire through traditional play and interaction. Armed with such awareness we shall be able to capitalize on at least some of the acquired knowledge and skills, and to recognize their contribution within the formal educational process. As Roberts puts it, 'it seems self-evident that the more thoroughly a teacher knows her pupils – and children generally – the more sensitive she will be to their needs' (1980: xv). Even if this results only in a greater degree of self-confidence among the learners, it will be a distinct advantage. If, on the other hand, even a fraction of the enthusiasm, verve, creativity and enjoyment which characterize traditional play can be harnessed in the classroom, the exercise will be more than worthwhile. Each one of us acquired the essential elements of language by traditional means in the home environment and in the playground: 'It is in childhood that a language is learned and a culture planted' (Montgomerie and Montgomerie 1985: 3). By the time children go to primary school they have already assimilated the indispensable foundation on which more formal education can build. Whether we acknowledge it or not, this process of traditional learning is indeed the gateway to language skills.

Notes

1 The fact that such responses are so common provides clear evidence that many teachers are unaware of the wealth of childlore in the playground.
2 For a penetrating and informative discussion of the transition from oracy to literacy, see Grugeon (1988).
3 Founded in 1964, NATCECT is the only higher education institution in England devoted to the study of English cultural tradition and folklore. Its ongoing Survey of Language and Folklore gathers data on the full range of these subjects throughout the country. NATCECT's extensive Archives of Cultural Tradition include substantial holdings on children's language and folklore.
4 The Survey of Language and Folklore (SLF) is a national survey of linguistic and traditional material throughout England. Information contributed through the survey constitutes one of the major collections in the Archives of Cultural Tradition.
5 The Kelsey Collection consists of children's rhymes and games collected between 1962 and 1984 in inner London by N.G.N. Kelsey, bequeathed to the Archives of Cultural Tradition (ACT 97-013) in 1991.
6 For a full and highly revealing discussion of humour in childhood, see Wolfenstein (1954).
7 I am grateful to Mavis Curtis (personal communication, 2000) for this item, collected in Keighley in the 1990s.
8 Collected by Mavis Curtis in the 1990s (personal communication, 2000).
9 Collected by Mavis Curtis in Keighley in the 1990s (personal communication, 2000).

8

From Hopscotch to *Siji*: generations at play in a cross-cultural setting[1]

Simon Lichman

Traditional Creativity through the Schools is a folklore project which takes place in Israel and addresses a number of issues that face many societies today: cultural and religious pluralism; transmission of home culture between generations; and coexistence between neighbouring but different communities.[2] As pointed out in the previous chapter, 'one of the obvious primary functions of tradition is to help each one of us to locate ourselves in both time and space', contributing to 'our sense of identity, of belonging to a culture'. This becomes increasingly problematic within multicultural societies, with so many people turning away from their home cultures in search of 'modern' identities. The Traditional Creativity through the Schools project is based on building long-term relationships between neighbouring Jewish and Arab communities, with children learning about each others' cultures as they experience their own and stimulating a refreshed relationship between the generations.[3]

Cultural distinctions in Israeli society are determined by ethnicity and religious practice in both the Jewish and Arab sectors. The wide range of ethnic groups among the Jewish population reflects the many countries throughout the world in which Jews have lived.[4] Among the Arab population there are three major religious groups: Muslim, Christian and Druze. There are also nomadic and settled Bedouin communities. In both Jewish and Arab sectors, there are differences between rural, village, town and city ways of life. Some Israeli towns and cities have a mixed Arab and Jewish population, while most of the smaller settlements are either Arab or Jewish.[5]

No matter where they live, Jewish and Arab societies both have to deal with the complexities of 'modernization'. Younger generations, often with higher levels of formal education, are faced with the dilemma of seeing themselves as having 'progressed', perhaps coming from traditional societies but looking to the West for their cultural aspirations and behavioural models. Children have tended to become increasingly alienated from their parents and grandparents, dismissing their home cultures as irrelevant to their modern lives, while the older generations lose their traditional audience for the transmission of their culture. The process of creating a unified national culture and integrating immigrants from diverse backgrounds has also created pressure to join a mainstream.

In 1991, I set up the Centre for Creativity in Education and Cultural Heritage, a non-profit-making organization, based in Jerusalem, which designs and implements education projects which encourage a climate of cultural pluralism and intergenerational understanding. As a folklorist, I felt that children needed a different way of seeing their home culture and those family members who represent and transmit that culture. Since the rich and varied cultural resources of this new society were seldom reflected or acknowledged in the education system, it seemed that the school setting might be a suitable vehicle through which to learn about folklore and give tradition-bearers a credibility that society was, by and large, undermining.

While there is a national school curriculum in Israel, all schools can determine their own balance between compulsory subjects and special projects. The Centre for Creativity in Education and Cultural Heritage established such a project, called the Traditional Creativity through the Schools project, which brings together pairs of Jewish and Arab school communities.[6] It is characterized as a folklore project not only because of the subject matter but also because of its approach to coexistence work, running between communities through the involvement of the extended family, rather than being limited to a singled-out group within each community (who in this case would be the schoolchildren). The use of folklore offers a profound basis for neighbouring Jewish and Arab populations to develop positive relationships with each other that can be sustained.

The programmes of this project are ongoing from one school year to the next and include the same children (10- to 13-year-olds) meeting each other over a two- to three-year period. New pairs of classes are added every school year. The target populations are the Arab and Jewish school communities, beginning with the children in each participating class, their families, school staff and gradually including other people in the community. With the project as part of each participating school's curriculum, the pupils are automatically in the programme. Since their 'homework' is about aspects of their own folklore or home culture, the children need to include their parents, grandparents, aunts, uncles and siblings in their research.[7]

While we have developed a basic programme structure, we adapt it to suit each class community. In the first year of the programme, fifth-grade children (10- to 11-year-olds) learn about their families' traditional outdoor games, play areas, dolls and stuffed toys, as well as studying examples of games and toys from around the world. In the second year of the programme, the sixth-grade children (11- to 12-year-olds) learn about the history of foodways and do research on their own families' traditions of breadmaking, food preservation, farming and herding, building up a picture of how access to food has changed.

The project team consists of the director, Arab and Jewish programme facilitators, and an evaluator. In weekly lessons, a member of the project team works with pupils and class teachers in the Arab and Jewish schools separately. In these lessons the children study particular traditions; they learn how to gather material at home from parents and grandparents and how to present this information to their classmates; and the classes are prepared for meeting each other. The paired Jewish and Arab classes come together for joint activities that last for a complete school morning. These are held in alternate schools every six to eight weeks, taking into account the Jewish, Muslim and Christian religious calendars and their different school holiday periods and exam schedules.

Each joint activity has its own folkloric focus – for example, traditional outdoor games, traditional dolls or traditions in pickling. These joint activities are designed around parents and grandparents who, in their expert capacities as tradition-bearers, work together with mixed groups of Jewish and Arab children. Between 2 and 15 parents and grandparents from both the Jewish and the Arab classes come to each joint activity. There is usually a core group of family members in each class who, having come once, try to come as often as they can. Since the joint activities take place during school hours, working parents and grandparents who want to participate need to take time off work.

Throughout the programme, the children assemble 'active archives' of the information they collect from their families, including descriptions and rules of games, recipes, photographs, family trees and oral histories, which ideally become part of their communities' resources, housed in the schools' libraries. The children design ethnographic exhibitions to display in their schools. During the year the children also become acquainted with the cultural and religious calendar of the other community (for example, the festivals of Ramadan, Passover, and Christmas), through the first-hand accounts of their counterparts. When possible, they visit local mosques, churches, synagogues, craft workshops, museums and parks together.

We see the class teachers as the key to their class community and welcome their input into programme content and implementation. Through their experience in this project, they are encouraged to look at the out-of-school world of the child and to place value on the informal learning process that exists in traditional contexts. Meanwhile, the children are encouraged to look at their home cultures as a means of understanding the world around them, with parents and grandparents as sources of interesting and useful information as to how this world came about.

We work with different kinds of societies (rural and city), which gives us experience of the diversity of cultures and living situations in Israel. There are various reasons for pairing particular Jewish and Arab schools. For example, the communities may be neighbours, in which case participants in the programme may begin to recognize each other when passing in the streets or markets, becoming more at ease in these chance contacts. This is the case in Ramle and Jaffa, two towns in central Israel where we work, which have mixed Arab and Jewish populations. In other cases, the schools or communities may have common interests that make them particularly compatible. For example, two schools in Jerusalem have a joint science project and want to develop this relationship by learning about each other's way of life. An urban Jewish school in the centre of Jerusalem is paired with a rural school that services two Arab villages close to the city, both schools having in common a strong sense of themselves as community schools. A school in a large Arab town near Jerusalem is paired with a nearby Jewish school that services the neighbouring *kibbutzim* and *moshavim*.[8] These two populations have much work-related contact but want to develop cultural and educational ties that would bring the communities closer.

In this chapter I will concentrate on traditional play, the subject of the first year of our programme, to show how the project works and how we use folklore to realize and reinforce connections across generations and between cultures. We use play as the constant common denominator in our activities. All cultures and generations have their own repertoire of games and each individual can be an expert in his or her own traditions. When considering play, everyone is a child and everyone knows best. When playing, everyone wants to have fun.

We usually begin our classwork by showing the children a selection of toys ranging from the traditional to the mass-produced. We encourage them to think about the relationship between kinds of toy and kinds of play; the relationship between the world in which their parents and grandparents grew up where toys were often home-made, and a 'ready-made' world where many of the toys are popular due to television shows or Disney films. Even where a family's economic situation might prevent a child from owning some of the in-fashion toys, most children in Israel are aware of toy emporiums in which they can see the 'real thing', colourfully packaged and 'reasonably priced'. The message here is not 'this is bad, this is good', but that Barbies, Care Bears and Ninja Turtles, for example, arrive at home with names, genders and a story-world, whereas making a doll or toy is part of the play process, the personality of rag dolls, for example, being determined by their maker's personality and relationship to the materials used. The visual impact of rag dolls, teddy bears, Ninja Turtles, sock puppets and Aladdins sitting together on the table gives the children a tangible example of the continuum between 'now' and 'then'.

Having triggered the children's imagination with the display of toys and dolls, we move to a discussion of outdoor games as the most immediate way in which they can experience being part of different traditions, both 'current' and 'old'. In class, the children compare two paintings. Brueghel's famous sixteenth-century Flemish painting shows outdoor games being played around a town square. In John Allin's painting, children are playing in the enclosed courtyard of a 1930s block of flats in the East End of London.[9] The children examine the games they find in these two paintings, which are divided by 400 years, and note the contexts in which these games were played. They then compare them to their own games and play areas. The next step is for them to gather information from home. The dialogue goes like this: 'Ask your parents what games they played when they were children. Where did they play them? Describe them and explain the rules'. Invariably some of the children call out, 'They didn't play games!'; we ask, 'How about your grandparents?'; 'Certainly not' reply the children. They are urged to ask their families these questions anyway.

The following week the children return to class with lists of games their parents and grandparents miraculously seem to have played, often accompanied by pictures they have drawn together of these games *in situ*. The children demonstrate these games to each other, still in their separate classes. We examine specific traditions – for example, in skipping, Hopscotch or Marbles, in order for the children to see the similarities and differences between these traditions over generations and from the various cultural backgrounds within their own class. They are often surprised to realize that their class, as a group, has its own multicultural repertoire of games.[10] Where possible, we hold these lessons in the playground. If not, we transform the classroom into a play space.

One of the clearest examples of the way the programme works in the classroom can be seen when we focus on Hopscotch. The class is asked, 'Do you know how to play Hopscotch?'; 'Yes, of course'; 'Okay, how many kinds of Hopscotch do you know?'; 'We all play it the same way'; 'Would somebody like to come and draw it on the blackboard?' Just as the chalk moves through a flourish or two, hands shoot up and voices pipe out, 'That's not right'. By the time each dissenter has had a turn, we have a blackboard full of different Hopscotch versions.

In Figure 8.1 we see the Hopscotch repertoire of a Jewish fifth-grade class. The first example, in the middle of the blackboard, is a 'straight up and down' Hopscotch court, going 'boy, girl, number, letter, colour, end' (each group of players fills in the specific information). In another version, on the right-hand side of the blackboard, we find Abraham, Isaac and Jacob in heaven at the top of the court. Some scholars describe Hopscotch as a progression from earth to heaven.[11] In a French version played by a French Moroccan mother, 'Paradise' (not reproduced here) is written in the top of the court, and 'Hell' is written into the tip of this section. If you throw the stone too far you end up in Hell, and then you are out of the game. In the Arab tradition, the Hopscotch courts tend to be identified by names that refer to their shape. Figure 8.2 is a collection

Figure 8.1 Classwork: children showing each other versions of Hopscotch. Ben Zvi School, Ramle, 1993.

Figure 8.2 Classwork: children's drawing of Hopscotch courts. Ein Rafa/Ein Naquba Elementary School, 1997.

of Hopscotch courts drawn by children in an Arab fifth-grade class. We see, for example, the 'flower' (top left-hand side of the picture); beneath it the 'minaret'; the 'child' is next to this; and next to the 'child' (on the same line) is a version of the 'snake'.[12]

In another example of this classroom research, we might surprise teachers by putting some small stones into their hands, saying, 'Did you ever play Five Stones?'. To murmurs of 'Look, teacher's playing', the children see the game actually played with stones as opposed to the neat little metal cubes, or jacks, that come complete with leather case or string bag. Many children go on to discover that someone in their own family also played with five stones or sheeps' knuckles (which they might have noticed in the Brueghel painting).

In addition to bringing different versions of games they themselves play, children often bring games to class which they have newly learned from their families. For example, in one of the Arab classes, a child tried to teach *Hach*, a game in which a chip of wood is hit and the hitter must run around a 'goal' or 'wicket' made up of two 'towers', bridged by a stick. The headmaster had come into the classroom to see what we were doing. Once he realized that the children were bringing information about games, he pushed the desks back, exclaiming, 'You can't play games in a space full of tables'. He then stood to the side of the room in an observer role but, after a few fumbling minutes of *Hach*, he burst into the game as a participant and 'informant' from the parent generation, taking the 'bat' and saying, 'Now, this is how you play it'.

Based on the information the children have brought from home, we design each joint activity around specific parents and grandparents who can come to teach their games. Although it might be some years since they have played their games, they enjoy being interviewed and are excited to be invited to play. Before each joint activity we work hard on preparation with each class separately. As well as understanding the roles of 'host' and 'guest' in different cultures, the children need to consider how to be tolerant of unfamiliar behaviour and how to communicate without a common language, since very few of the children speak both Arabic and Hebrew with any fluency. Then, even though they will find that they have many games in common, the rules are often quite different. It can be frustrating to teach each other versions of familiar games but the children's curiosity and love of playing usually turns these exchanges into fun. They also have to learn how to clarify the rules of popular games, such as football.

A typical joint activity on traditional outdoor games begins with a 'formal' welcoming ceremony and refreshments which have been prepared by the host class. After refreshments, the games begin. The two classes, of 50–70 children and 5–15 adults, usually take over the school playground for the morning. They are divided into mixed groups of 8–12 Jewish and Arab children in each, with at least one adult per group. The adults stay at their playstations and the children gradually move

Figure 8.3   Joint activity: Flipping the Cat. Grandfather and granddaughter show mixed groups of children Tippecat. Ein Rafa/Ein Naquba Elementary School.

around the playground, from one playstation to another. Games found in most joint activities include Hopscotch, skipping, Elastics (known elsewhere as Chinese Jump Rope), Marbles, Five Stones, Seven Stones, *Gogo'im*, handclapping games and football. Once in their 'group', children tend to connect, getting on with the business of play even when the group has been 'artificially' created by a member of the project team or school staff. The moment we get into play, the atmosphere is relaxed, with three to four generations of childhood actively and simultaneously represented on the playground.

In Figure 8.3, a Jewish grandfather demonstrates a street game he learned in London in the 1920s, played with a bat and a carefully bevelled chip of wood, which he calls Tippecat. He explains to the children how making the equipment had always been an essential part of the game. He describes playing three versions of the game in which the hitter a) runs up and down a straight 'pitch'; b) runs round a circular area (as in rounders); or c) touches a box the players have drawn at the beginning of the game (on the edge of an agreed-upon player's left- and right-hand span). The 'cat' is tipped into the air by striking one end with the 'bat' and struck again (in mid-air) as far away as possible. When the cat is fielded by the other team, the batting team stops with the amount of

Figure 8.4   Joint activity: Building the Tower. Mother shows mixed groups of children Seven Stones. Ein Rafa/Ein Naquba Elementary School, 1996.

'runs' or points it has managed to score. The team with the most runs wins. The same morning, an Israeli-born Jewish mother, two generations younger, brought her version of Tippecat, called *Doodes*, *Alambulic* or *Hakafot* (which means 'going round'), which also has similarities to the *Hach* game found in Arab communities. She brought the tools to make the bats and chips of wood with the children, who were fascinated by these two play experts exchanging trade secrets.

In Figure 8.4, an Arab mother is teaching Seven Stones to a group of Jewish and Arab children. It is another game most of the children do not know. It is usually found in the Arab communities, although some Jewish grandparents of Iraqi origin also know the game. The children collect large flat stones and are shown which ones are suitable for balancing on one another. One team then builds a tower of seven stones. The other team throws a ball, and must knock the tower down. The first team quickly tries to rebuild the tower while the other team needs to hit all of the opposing field players with the ball before the tower is rebuilt. Any player who is hit is 'out'.

Figure 8.5   Joint activity: *Gogo'im*. Ein Rafa/Ein Naquba Elementary School, 1998.

A Jewish great-uncle, visiting from London, brought a similar game called Cannon, which he had played in the mid-1920s. Two pieces of wood are placed in a cross over one end of a tin can. One team calls out, 'One, two, three, Cannon', and tries to knock the sticks down with a ball. If successful, the player tries to hit as many of the opposing team with the ball while they race to reassemble the 'cannon'. This great-uncle would usually have played Cannon with two or three children in each team so as to have a good chance of getting the other team out, or of reassembling the 'cannon'. On this joint activity morning, he played the game with groups of about 15 children clustered around him in chaotic harmony.

In Figure 8.5, a Jewish mother surrounded by children teaches an Israeli Marbles-type game called *Gogo'im* or *Adjo'im*, which is played with apricot pips. She has successive groups of ten children quietly playing in pairs over a wide area of playground. Parents tell us how they would collect the pips throughout the summer, gaining kudos depending on the size of their collection. Many of the children play this game although it is becoming less popular.

Siji, in Figure 8.6, looks like a complex mixture of Draughts and Noughts and Crosses. An Arab mother explained that players need to find two distinctive sets of counters. On this day they used light and dark stones. The 'board' is usually marked out as an indentation in sand, but can also be drawn with chalk on a concrete surface. The Jewish children have never seen this game while some of the Arab children know a basic

Figure 8.6   Joint activity: mother teaches *Siji*. Ein Rafa/Ein Naquba Elementary School, 1998.

version. The group of children in this picture worked very hard together to learn this game. Their common interest in it formed the basis of a friendship over the next two years.

By looking at their own traditions and seeing which aspects of their games depend on their innovative use of the play area, children come to understand the narratives in which grandparents and parents describe their childhoods – how they would assess the terrain and the range of available scrap materials needed in order to play. The children see how, for their parents and grandparents, the very possibility of playing would depend on the '*bricoleur*'[13] skills of the players to 'make do' with and 'fit into' the natural settings of their play (cf. Chapter 2). The Three or Five Sticks game, which is still widely played, begins with the players searching for appropriate sticks which are set at an agreed-upon starting distance from each other. The sticks are gradually moved further apart so that the players must keep lengthening their stride or jump. The sticks for this game, the stones for Seven Stones or the apricot pips for *Gogo'im* cannot be bought, and each generation of players still needs to choose the best wall, ground indentation or smooth surface for these games. Even in games like football and basketball, they can appreciate the difference between a pitch or a court defined by goalposts or baskets as opposed to any space available for a run-around, and they see how they themselves take for granted having a ball rather than needing to devise one from rags.

The second joint activity of the traditional play component of the programme is usually making traditional dolls, since in both the Arab and Jewish class communities there are parents and grandparents (and sometimes the children themselves) who made, or still make, dolls and stuffed toys. Parents and grandparents describe the types of scrap material they would use, such as wooden sticks for the frame of stick dolls; cloth and wool as hair and as filler for the doll's body; worn-out socks or gloves for hand puppets; buttons or bits of coal for the eyes; mud or clay for the heads; not to mention the natural colouring agents in fruits, flowers and charcoal. They often send something they have made especially for their child to show in class. During the joint activities the children are taught how to make particular dolls according to the different doll experts who have come in that day. The children learn from each other as well as from parents and grandparents, the boys being as involved in making dolls as the girls. When the dolls are made, we have a period of bilingual 'doll talk' (Arabic and Hebrew) in which the dolls 'meet' each other, or the children put on short plays. At the end of the day, participants take home the dolls they have made.

The atmosphere of the meetings between the Jewish and Arab schools is determined by both the development of their relationship over time and the balance between structure and fluidity in each joint activity.[14] Creating the right atmosphere is of crucial importance to the success of each individual morning, and to the paired classes' series of meetings over the two years of the programme. Through careful observation and the continual sharing of perceptions during each joint activity, the project team and school staff monitor the sense of ease between participants, and try to determine the balance between the educational content, the experience of the transmission of folklore and the element of fun. The formal structure of the programme ensures that there will be interaction among the participants, even where there is anxiety and shyness, since they communicate in the course of learning or teaching. In the structured framework of working in mixed groups no one has to feel responsible for initiating personal contact until they are comfortable enough to do so.

The joint activities also have to be fluid enough for the children to feel that they have autonomy over what they are doing, despite our overall plan. For example, during the games, some children may not want to move to the next playstation, preferring to continue playing one particular game, perhaps in a smaller group or in a different formation. Again, we assess when to encourage the flow,[15] or when to insist on the plan being followed. We also need to be aware that any new mix of children should include pupils from both schools, although there are times when some children clearly need to revert to groups of their own classmates.

The overall atmosphere is also affected by how the generations feel about being together. Are the children anxious, self-conscious, proud or at ease about having their parents or grandparents in the schoolyard? How do they view each other's parents? Are they treated with respect?

Are the parents and grandparents nervous or relaxed about being in the schools? When one of the mothers came to school for her son's class's first joint activity, on traditional outdoor play, she told me, 'I'm rather upset. My son said I could come but I mustn't skip and I love to skip'. We had to decide whose childhood was most important, whose sense of the day had priority. She felt she should not skip and I agreed, neither of us wanting her son to spend the morning feeling embarrassed or uneasy. Almost as soon as the games started, her son sidled past me and said, out of the corner of his mouth, 'She can skip'. In the end, as well as demonstrating what is known in the USA as Double Dutch (two ropes) with a group of 'adults' (parents and teachers) from both schools, his mother taught many aspects of her skipping repertoire, such as the 'crossover jump', to mixed groups of children who spent the rest of the morning 'practising'. Meanwhile, her son spent the morning with his group of Jewish and Arab children, playing games with other parents and grandparents. His mother became a regular participant in project activities, contributing her considerable skills in such traditions as doll-making and, in the second year of the programme, pickling olives and vegetables.

In subsequent joint activities and during their own regular school break times, we often see children spontaneously break into versions of handclapping games, Elastics, skipping and Marbles that they have learned from the other community or from each other. These games and versions of games become part of a separate repertoire of play they share when they meet. They may also enter the general repertoire of their own schools. For example, an Arab skipping song, learned by Jewish children in their first meeting, has become part of the playground repertoire of the Jewish school, where the children have kept the song current and passed it on to other children. Similarly, Tippecat is now often played by a group of boys in one of the Arab schools.

The experience of coexistence is reflected in the joint activities themselves. Most of the children enjoy the content, be it playing, making a traditional item or singing traditional songs to each other. All the children relate to one another on some positive level, from simply enjoying working side by side, smiling at one another or passing materials and tools, to playing the same games as part of the same team, knowing names and gradually learning more about each child as an individual and as part of a community. The children wait to see each other with enormous anticipation, often bringing small gifts. During their separate classwork each week, they are aware that the 'other' class is doing the same work as preparation towards their next joint activity, and in this way they keep each other in mind.

As the programme runs between each pair of Arab and Jewish classes over a period of two to three years, it is exciting to see how not only the children but the adults too begin to look forward to seeing each other again. When parents and grandparents play together and with each other's children, the boundaries between them seem to decrease or even disappear.

They then translate the intimacy they share within the world of play to the 'social situation', during the breaks, when they can converse over refreshments. They often end up discussing their perceptions of visiting each other's 'space', their experiences playing with each other's children, and the pleasure they derive from seeing their children play together.

Although making personal friendships is not a criterion by which the project judges its success, there are groups of children who form strong, direct bonds with one another in every pair of Jewish and Arab classes. These relationships reflect the atmosphere of the project in which developing friendships is possible. When participants discuss the political 'situation', it is from the perspective of having people to talk to who have already shown interest in their lives and views. Children and families in our programmes express concern for each other as well as outrage at acts of violence in which members of either Arab or Jewish communities suffer. They feel that they can reach across religious, ethnic and political boundaries once they have the opportunity of being together and seeing beyond the stereotypes they often have, both of each other and of themselves.[16]

Reflecting on their home cultures, the children see that their societies are in fact in a constant state of 'coming into being'. In understanding their parents' and grandparents' part in this process, they become aware of their own roles in the cycle, especially through the world of play. For all participants in the project, the playground becomes a symbol of a world in which different cultures and generations can be together in a dynamic atmosphere of creativity, mutual interest and natural coexistence.

Notes

1 I would like to thank the British Council and the British Academy for travel and subsistence grants that enabled me to attend the conference at which the paper on which this chapter is based was first presented.
2 Rivanna Miller, the co-founder of this project, has taken most of the photographs that appear in this chapter. She works on evaluation and programme design in the project and is a partner in creating slide presentations and published papers.
3 See Lichman (1997) for a discussion of the application of folklore in education.
4 There are Jewish communities on all the five continents. The ethnic variety is reflected in Israel's population by such diverse groups as Moroccan, Yemenite, Ethiopian, Kurdish, Iraqi, Eastern and Western European, and American (see Gilbert 1981).
5 See Landau (1969: Chs 1 and 2) and Rosen (1970: 12–16).
6 When the State of Israel was created in 1948, the Arab communities chose to maintain a separate school system in which Arabic was the language of learning. In both Arab and Jewish schools, the class may comprise children with family backgrounds from several countries, various ethnic groups and various religions. In both sectors, schools range from those with little religious instruction to those which are orthodox. Contact between Arab and Jewish

communities, even those living side by side, is often limited to the workplace, with little opportunity of gaining direct, positive knowledge of one another. Information coming through the media often reinforces negative stereotyped images.

7 I would like to thank participating children, their families, schoolteachers and principals for the enthusiasm, opennness and warmth that radiates through this project. To date we have worked with ten school communities, approximately 500–700 children and their families per year. Some of these communities have worked together now for seven years. The amount of time the project runs between each pair of schools is usually determined by funding constraints. The project has been supported by institutions and foundations such as the Israeli Ministry of Education; the education departments of local authorities; the Jerusalem Foundation; the Abraham Fund; the Doron Foundation for Education and Welfare; the Belsize Square Synagogue, London; the Josephine Bay Paul and C. Michael Paul Foundation; the Rodgers Family Foundation; the British Embassy; the Embassy of the United States of America (Regional, Professional and Technical Cooperation Program).

8 Communal settlements originally founded around agriculture.

9 See Roberts (1982) and Allin and Wesker (1974).

10 In this chapter I have described games as they have been brought into our programmes by particular participants of all ages and cultural backgrounds. For an informative and fascinating study of games and variants similar to those we have found, see Opie and Opie (1997).

11 See Grunfeld (1975: 164–7). The Abraham, Isaac and Jacob Hopscotch was collected in Ben Zvi Elementary School, Ramle, Israel, in 1993.

12 Collected in Ein Rafa/Ein Naquba Elementary School, Ein Rafa, Israel 1993–8.

13 Claude Lévi-Strauss (1966) uses this term to describe the ingenious and spontaneous creativity of ritual performers.

14 In the analysis of ritual, Victor Turner (1977) refers to this dynamic as 'structure and anti-structure'. See Caspi (1986) for a discussion of the relationship between structure and fluidity in play.

15 Although used specifically in the analysis of ritual, Victor Turner (1974) describes the significance of 'flow', offering it as an anthropological concept that helps explain how the ritual world is created.

16 For a description of one of these exchanges, see Lichman and Sullivan (2000: 66–75).

9

'Our dreams in action': spirituality and children's play today

Carole H. Carpenter

Among the many current agenda of childhood concern, matters of spirituality seem of little account. Yet it could well be argued that a growing malaise of the youthful soul lies at the heart of much that is troubling about childhood in societies which value balanced books before emotional, even physical, let alone spiritual well-being.

Here I address issues of spirituality in childhood by offering another perspective on a subject of much popular and scholarly comment – that is, the contemporary status of traditional children's games. Ongoing research suggests that their worldwide demise is much exaggerated. Yet, in recent decades the time many North American children have for free play has diminished sharply owing to the adult agenda for childhood as documented by Elkind (1988) among others. Omnipresent media and powerful market forces have commodified and transformed childhood. These forces are driving the mammoth entertainment, sports and toy industries which compete with children's traditional culture for space in their lives. Further, dedicated early childhood education specialists, as well as concerned scholars from many disciplines and many well-meaning parents, clamour for children to use their available time supposedly to best advantage by acquiring measurable skills. Concurrently, Hopscotch has entered the elementary curricula in some Canadian school districts – evidence of adults' perception of its value, yet also proof that this game at least is no longer part of many children's own oral tradition.[1]

Here I will decry adult interference with this traditional lore, specifically in terms of some boys' games, while reporting on very recent circumstances in Canada publicizing diminution of play for fun as a serious cultural loss. However, I will also show that some immediate circumstances do bode well for the continuation of children's oral culture and free play, paradoxically *because* of the very forces which appear to threaten the traditions most.

The Canadian circumstances to be discussed pertain to hockey, the game inextricably linked to 'Canadianness'. In the public mind, and hence in popular discourse, there is a deeply rooted connection between the play of Canadian children, the soul of the nation and Canada's continued well-being. The voluminous literature on play likewise underscores its spiritual dimension, an aspect Johan Huizinga emphasized in specifying human beings as *Homo Ludens*: 'Man the Player' ([1938] 1950). Both before Huizinga and since his seminal work there have been legions of arguments proclaiming the need for play among humans around the world and, on occasion, the detrimental effects of its absence, as argued by Cox in *The Feast of Fools* (1969). A central aspect of this need for play involves celebration of the life-force – joy in and through living that enables psychic well-being. According to Robert Neale, 'the individual who sees himself consistently as one who is at play in the world is expressing his state of inner harmony' (1969: 24).

The rhetoric and research of various disciplines converge on the significant point that we achieve our full humanity through play – activity that simultaneously engages body, mind and spirit. This point, while certainly not new, deserves to be emphasized in keeping with Schiller, who wrote in his *Aesthetical Letters and Essays*: 'For to speak out once for all, man only plays when in the full meaning of the word he is a man, and he is only completely a man when he plays' (quoted in Caillois 1961: 162–3).

If we agree with Horace Beck, one of the great elders of American folklore studies, that 'play is our dreams in action' (personal communication, 1998), then it follows that play is in effect an active experience of wonder, a 'secondary world' in J.R.R. Tolkien's terms, capable of providing the escape, reconciliation and consolation offered by experiencing well-crafted alternative realities ([1947] 1975: 43–62). There are those who argue that fantasy is potentially harmful to young readers in that it may interfere with their ability to distinguish what is real. Might not some activity designated as play similarly carry the possibility of a comparable negative outcome for young participants?

Play may provide Dionysian freedom to move beyond the bounds and restrictions of everyday living; it stimulates vision and experience of alternatives; it offers glimpses of Wordsworth's 'celestial light', views of a greater reality. So play can come to illuminate and foster joy in our existence. But play must also be seen to have the potential to attack our humanity and diminish our being. There may actually be play that is bad, or at least negative aspects to play when it is clearly contained, manipulated and exploited by adults so as to achieve their agenda for children without due regard for either the cultural traditions of children or the best interests of the young. If one accepts the argument of Bateson and Martin (1999), among many others, that children's free play promotes exploration, manipulation and mastery of the social, natural and emotional worlds in which children live and leads to their acquisition of important life skills, then, logically, restricting play opportunities detracts from significant learning. Such negative results are well-known to many a contemporary scholar, educator and others regularly involved with children. One of my informants, a 50-year-old teacher and hockey coach, reported that his high-school students had developed insufficient active skills to organize themselves into teams and play a game of hockey without adult intervention.

Another logical, but ill-recognized consequence of restricting children's play is the diminution of their 'joy in being', the very words used as a definition for play late in the nineteenth century.[2] Any loss of such joy is (or at least should be) alarming, especially given the recent dramatic increases of late in youth suicide. Canada has seen the rate of suicide among its youth almost triple since the 1960s, resulting in the third highest rate worldwide[3] in this country, rated by the United Nations as the best place in the world to live.[4] The phenomenon is of course not limited to Canada. As reported by Slaby and Garfinkel, '60% of all high school students [in the USA] have thought about their own death or about killing themselves' (1994: 3).

Investigation of the state of games among pre-teenage boys in Canada since the Second World War will serve to illustrate a marked decline in free play of games involving interpersonal activity, a situation which arguably has produced detrimental spiritual effects on youth. The focus here is on the three most prevalent circumstances in which contemporary pre-teen males play actual games: school playgrounds, the home/ street, and organized teams.[5] These milieux share in social trends characteristic of Canada's population as a whole, namely: over three-quarters of Canadians today live in urban centres; the population is increasingly diverse such that the largest single group in the country is now persons of mixed heritage; and recent immigration has resulted in a very high proportion of schoolchildren in metropolitan centres being newcomers to the country.[6] Before the Second World War, just over half of Canada's population was urban, the largest single group was of British extraction, and newcomers were a decided minority in most city schools. Consequently, from the end of the war to the 1960s, most children had abundant open space and freedom to play without the concerns for their safety so common in today's urban areas. Also, the prevailing children's traditions in English Canada (the prime focus of this discussion) were those of the English-speaking community worldwide, and a strong 'Anglo' norm was operative in childhood culture.[7]

My fieldwork for this study was conducted in the Greater Toronto area between 1997–9 and involved a comparison of the games played by contemporary pre-teen boys in the three specified milieux with those played by their age peers in the two decades following the Second World War. Changes in the extent, nature and outcome of game playing were studied to determine the differences, if any, in the reported or inferred spiritual dimension of the activities. The data presented here were obtained from observation of several hundred contemporary boys at play; informal, unrecorded and relatively brief discussions with approximately 35 boys, sometimes in groups (including one hockey team); similar discussions about their childhood game playing with some 20 young adult and adult males; more extended conversations with eight young men and tape-recorded conversations with six adults. These informants are generally representative of the social and ethnic diversity, as well as the skill range, of the majority of hockey-playing males in English-speaking Canada.[8]

The study targets males for two reasons: first, the circumstances in the three game-playing venues have changed far more for boys than for girls; second, the suicide rate among young male Canadians vastly exceeds that among females (by about 4:1 in the last census). This identifies boys as a particularly high-risk group for whom living sometimes holds little, and all too often insufficient, joy.[9]

In the post-war decades it was typical for girls to be excluded (by school regulations as well as the rules of childhood culture) from the more rough-and-tumble playground activities, particularly such traditional games as British Bulldog, Piggy-Back Duelling or Buck, Buck, as described by Fowke (1988: 36, 64, 76). Schoolyard play tended to be sexually segregated, with the boys having a greater (often virtually total) reign over the playing fields, which generally were dirt rather than grass, as later became more common. At smaller schools and during sanctioned periods of integrated play at the larger ones, girls tended to participate in somewhat gentler games which are still sometimes played on the constricted, but commonly integrated, playgrounds of today. These activities include ball and circle games such as Monkey in the Middle (Fowke 1988: 24); racing games such as Duck, Duck, Goose (p. 57); chasing games such as Spud (pp. 21–2) and Marco Polo (p. 34); and numerous variations on Tag. Girls of the post-war era seldom tossed pennies for keeps or played Marbles, and hardly ever played knife games like Mumbly-peg (as my older informants most commonly called the game described as Chicken by Fowke 1988: 65), and today physical conditions or restrictions are such that no one can.

In the home and on the streets, most girls played domestic games, Hopscotch, singing and clapping games, and Let's Pretend, all of which are still possible if caregivers permit street or yard play. Finally, fewer girls than boys played any team sports other than for the school or in required physical education classes. Less access to the playing fields at school, limited availability of or restrictions on participation in outside leagues, and general societal expectations of female behaviour mitigated against girls' involvement in sports except those identified as feminine or appropriate, generally such individual activities as gymnastics, skating and swimming. Percentage participation of females in organized sport has definitely increased in the past several decades with the establishment of more girls' leagues and the removal (sometimes through court challenge) of male-only restrictions on some sports. Yet, only a very few girls have ever taken part in 'Canada's game', hockey, to be discussed in depth subsequently.

Like many playgrounds throughout the industrialized world, Canada's elementary schoolyards have transformed almost beyond recognition since the Second World War. But our efforts to control and contain what occurs on these traditional loci of children's culture may have been greater than elsewhere. For Canadians are a nation dedicated to preserving 'peace, order and good government', cultural goals designated in the British North America Act (1867) as the purpose of founding the nation. My research in the mid-1970s into games played by children approximately 5 to 12 years of age on multicultural school playgrounds in Toronto revealed far more evidence than exists today of traditional games among the boys, including all those mentioned above as well as duelling games such as Conkers (Fowke 1988: 67), exerting games such as 'Red Rover, Red Rover' (p. 72), collector (especially hockey) Card Toss and Exchange, and strategy games such as Rock, Scissors, Paper (p. 17).

Today some of these activities can still be found, but primarily on the fringes, marginal rather than the focus of child-directed energy. Some that were traditionally played in the dirt, such as Marbles, are now physically impossible because most playgrounds are paved in their entirety except for a closely monitored, and most often grass, sports field reserved for organized play. Rare indeed is the urban school without large stretches of asphalt marked in part for Hopscotch and possibly Dodge Ball, but largely dedicated to half basketball courts. Likewise, adventure playgrounds are ubiquitous. India rubber balls are banned along with many rougher, 'dangerous' games such as British Bulldog. Play is structured and carefully supervised even during recess, once viewed as an outlet for children's pent up emotions and energy but now, according to my younger informants, the venue for aerobics classes at some Toronto schools attended by 12- to 15-year-olds. Such restrictions and changes are in keeping with the overall efforts of adults to redirect children's free time to supposedly more useful and decidedly more measurable and disciplined training in academic, artistic or physical endeavours. As observed on location and described by my most youthful informants, the whole scene is carefully patrolled by numbers of teachers along with student 'peacemakers'. These youngsters are self-selected or chosen by school administrators and then specially trained in 'dispute resolution'. Marked by a sash and armed with moral rectitude, they ensure that there are no taunts, jeers or name-calling and intervene in conflicts as necessary in the absence of adult authorities. A policy of 'zero tolerance' is quite common; punishment for transgressions is swift and often severe, not infrequently involving immediate suspension.

These playgrounds are not, then, 'alternative realities' offering abundant opportunities for 'sublimation of frustrations and desires', or 'loci enabling play' in which, according to Sutton-Smith, 'each individual differentiates himself from his own entrapment and in so doing becomes, momentarily at least, a free spirit' (1972: xiii). Nor are they conducive to a 'play-mood', which James Sully identified in 1902 as 'an attitude of throwing off restraint' (Millar [1968] 1975: 20). Rather, ever-encroaching adult control has made for an unhappy, negative environment for many boys who sulk and skulk about, unable to find a means to develop and demonstrate prowess and prestige among their peers. Contemporary playgrounds give precedence to a small minority of strong, athletically gifted and physically well-developed youngsters – quite distinct from the playgrounds described with reference to Vancouver by Sutherland (1986: 37, 43–4, 46–9) and comparable to those remembered by my older informants. For them, disparate traditional pastimes offered a greater variety of exploration, manipulation and mastery leading to shifting groups of players with varying skills in different groups. Thus, each boy had more possibility to develop prowess within some group and thereby enhance his presence among his peers and nurture his self-esteem.

What many boys reported having done recently, and I observed others actually engaged in on playgrounds, is worth noting. There is increased betting and gambling of various sorts, so that 12-and-unders are frequent (illegal) players in commercial sports lotteries. One informant reported having made, spent and lost several hundred dollars in this fashion as an 11-year-old. Similarly, there is more evidence of sexual behaviours and dangerous risk taking, including increased smoking, drug and alcohol use, despite the counter-education campaigns to which these children have had lifelong exposure. This free activity – while covert and subversive like much traditional play – must be seen to have some negative outcomes, for it certainly diminishes well-being and, it can be argued, offers only momentary and spiritually unsatisfying thrills distinct from the life-affirming empowerment and joy potentially attainable through genuine play.

Moves to greater control are coincident with the increase in the amount and severity of bullying documented in studies by Craig and Pepler of children's aggression, observed through extensive remote audio-visual documentation of Toronto school playgrounds (1995, 1997, 1998). In the waning of the traditional subversive behaviour that is children's own lore, a much more dangerous form of subversion of *all* authority has emerged, giving rise to increased proto-criminal activities such as dominance, extortion and threatened, if not actual, violence. The majority of boys are perceived as weak by the bullies who demand, threaten and terrorize them, making the schoolyards effectively an assault on their spiritual as well as physical being.

Turning to boys' games at home, informants both younger and older note the increase of video and computer games which now almost totally eclipse the common home games of earlier years. These included a variety of board games; imaginative play with model trains, planes or boats; building activity with a diversity of construction sets or kits; trading and other games with collectible cards; fantasy games associated with legendary and super heroes; or a multiplicity of street games permitted far more then than now. Many an urban home has lately acquired a fixed or free-standing basketball hoop which serves as a diversion (and often, parental relief) from the electronic play that boys find so addictive. Perhaps the fact that the majority of girls continue to resist the marketing efforts to engage them in electronic games means that young females will increasingly be the keepers of tradition.

Only a few technologically minded, computer-gifted boys can find playing electronic games empowering, for this minority can master these activities, on occasion even adapting and programming their own variants. When reflecting on their more youthful play, most of my informants in their late teens/early twenties indicated at least some awareness of being manipulated and controlled by such games, restricted to exploring what and how the computer permits. This play is passive even if energetic, neither active nor free, and certainly not joyous and fulfilling but rather intense and hypnotic. Again, for most it is ultimately demeaning, sapping rather than feeding the spirit and thereby contributing at least to some degree to widespread young disillusionment and depression.

The final venue is sport, in which the majority of Canadian boys participate now as in the past. What has changed markedly over time is the parental and societal pressure to take part in organized team sports in preference to traditional games, including street or playground versions of the sports. It is widely argued that organized sports are character building and prepare children for life in a modern, competitive society. Claims to the contrary seem to fall increasingly on deaf ears, as apparently did Mary and Herbert Knapp's assertion in 1976 that 'folk games which involve verbal competition and individual judgement are a more useful map of the territory ahead than organized sports, which emphasize physical competition and submission to authority' (p. 49). These scholars warned that 'those who believe that the discipline and narrow focus of organized sport will prevent juvenile delinquency, build character, and add to [national] prestige' are mistaken, in that 'often supervised sports produce only obedient specialists' and 'there's more to sports than victories and records that are supposed to make some pseudo-Darwinian point about a player's or a nation's fitness' (p. 267).

It is children who seem to recognize the limitations of organized sport, but are inhibited by them rather than goaded into constructive alternatives. Consequently, as the organization of most sports has increased, play at the grass roots has decreased, leading to what one hockey coach characterized as an outright unwillingness among his teenage team to engage in playing the game 'just for fun on [sic] their own time'.

The following discussion specifically concerns hockey, though as my informants insist, the situation in Canada is very similar for childhood versions of all sports that have become highly organized, professionalized and commercialized.

Professional hockey

- National Hockey League (NHL)
- Senior A
- Junior A

League hockey

- House Leagues: open to anybody
- All-Stars/Selects: selected from House League players
- Minor Leagues: highly selective
- School/college
- Organizations, e.g. York University Faculty
- Old-Timers
- Girls

Shinny

- Ice hockey
- Street/road hockey

Figure 9.1   An outline of hockey in Canada.

There are, in fact, three forms of hockey in Canada, as illustrated in Figure 9.1. First, in terms of public profile internationally, there is professional hockey, the commercialized gladiator sport familiar through media broadcasts to most people in the industrialized world. This version of the game offers employment and fame to a very small number of players who tend to be physically enormous and paid handsomely to participate in violent play during which fist-fights are not only permitted (though penalized) but also applauded by fans.

Second, there is organized or league hockey at various levels, commencing for children at age 5 and continuing through to 19. League hockey is ubiquitous, involving more players than any other form of the sport. Virtually any small Canadian town has an arena and play continues around the clock in many (especially urban) facilities. It can be a costly sport, generally requiring a great deal of equipment – on average $500-worth per year, though some can usually be obtained second-hand. The games are very structured – in many leagues all players (no matter their skill levels) get equal ice time and the whistle blows at regular intervals to ensure shift changes. There are referees; the rules are strictly enforced; adults are in command and 'play' is decidedly organized. Indeed, the sport often seems to be *for* adults, many of whom are deeply involved, often (according to my informants) living out their own fantasies or single-mindedly directing their sons toward the dream – the National Hockey League (NHL). The organization and control of children's play tightens over the years, but the sport is competitive from the very beginning with the aim generally being to win rather than to develop skills or simply have fun.

In addition to mainstream leagues, there are organized teams of a girls' version of hockey called ringuette. Also, through the feminist movement and anti-discriminatory legislation, girls now participate in most regular leagues (even once the NHL) and, as of 1998, in Olympic competition. There are 'Old-Timers' leagues as well for players aged 25 and over and such phenomena as the York University Faculty team, a flexible group of dedicated players drawn from faculty, graduate students and administration, which has existed over the 40 years since the university's inception and which now includes numerous retired people. They play first and foremost 'just for the pure fun of it', said my informant who went on to describe the importance of camaraderie both on and off the ice and the exhilaration and freedom of the ice time.[10]

Third, but far from least in the memories of my informants, there is Shinny, the folk game which is played almost exclusively for fun. It is derived from a winter game common in some traditional North American indigenous cultures which must have reminded British settlers of the Scottish game Shinny or Shinty, resembling grass hockey and played with a ball and curved sticks. Contemporary hockey descends from the Native not the Scottish game even though, according to *A Dictionary of Canadianisms on Historical Principles*, the term 'Shinny' refers in Canada to 'a loosely organized game of hockey played on ice without referees' (Avis *et al.* 1967). This type of play was well-known among the European settlers and their descendants by the early nineteenth century. Shinny can be played on any available stretch of ice, usually outside – a frozen pond, lake or slough, a flooded backyard groomed into a flat surface, or a constructed rink – by any number of players with a bare minimum of equipment (essentially some form of stick for each player and one puck) and a variably negotiated set of rules. The players are almost always boys and range in age, with the older fellows helping, protecting and serving as models for smaller boys. Games can go on for hours and, while there may be 'regulars' among the participants, play is generally democratic and not restricted to any group. It is in Shinny that most of the finest players from North America – many of the great NHL players, for instance – honed their skills, for good skating and stick-handling are necessary when there is a minimum of equipment and relatively unrestricted play. Street hockey is a variant which used to be more frequently played in the off-season, though now is favoured by younger boys throughout the year and sometimes by older youth on roller-blades during the warm seasons.

Overall, a very high percentage of boys in Canada have played one form or another of hockey at some time, though very few indeed ever make the professional leagues. Today, a great many boys stop playing before their teens, which raises the question of why they do so. My informants in this category, including my own 21-year-old son, said almost uniformly, 'Because it was no longer fun'.

Hockey and its role in the lives of Canadian boys have radically altered since the post-Second World War era in the following ways, as specified by my informants. First, the game has become increasingly violent, requiring more protective equipment and favouring size and strength over actual game skills. Consequently, many less aggressive or smaller players quit, usually around the age of 12 or 13 when 'body-checking' is permitted. This form of interference with the opposition involves purposeful body contact, often at considerable speed and with painful results. Some boys simply find playing so violently, hitting other players gratuitously, and winning at all costs meaningless and demeaning rather than fun. Such a game is an assault on them personally as well as on the spirit of play.

Second, winning has become paramount. Thus, the minor leagues are so competitive as to not infrequently be corrupt and to involve the bribing of players onto teams with gifts and favours. Team spirit, camaraderie and commitment, once the hallmarks of amateur sport, are sacrificed through releasing lesser players of long-standing in favour of potentially winning newcomers from out-of-district.

Third, the game is more expensive – in terms of ice time, state-of-the-art equipment, hockey schools and camps – all of which are deemed necessary for a boy to remain competitive, literally at the cutting edge. Hence, the game is increasingly restricted to groups privileged financially and, typically, mainstream ethnicities; it is no longer the broad-based game of the populous at the grass roots that it once was.

Fourth, and ultimately most significant, there is much less Shinny or 'folk hockey'. Many ponds are gone, victims of urban sprawl and infill. It costs too much to maintain abundant outside rinks or to reserve indoor ice for what one informant called 'simply messing around'. Streets are too busy to permit much road hockey where most people now live; in fact, the game is actually banned in some locations to ensure safety and avoid interruption of traffic flow. Besides, youngsters are heavily programmed and seldom left to the 'joyful anarchy' one informant dubbed his free play in the 1950s and early 1960s. It was this same informant who emphasized the significance of the fantasy associated with Shinny, saying that once he laced on his skates, he could believe himself to be his idol, Toronto Maple Leaf star Frank Mahovolich, or any other hockey superstar, even if he in fact was a somewhat stout, uncoordinated and basically not very athletic boy.

Last, but not least, Canada no longer 'rules' in hockey, either in being the source of the best players for the NHL or in competing internationally. This fact is causing considerable concern that is reverberating throughout the sport and the culture right down onto the Shinny rink.

These five factors have been developing for some time, in fact, from the Second World War to the present when hockey is being described as 'a game in crisis' (Houston 1998). A powerful and very public call has come from the highest levels of the sport for the recognition, celebration and encouragement of the play element in what has become all too much of a commercial enterprise. This call emanates from those with sufficient influence, incentive and capital to actually make it happen. For instance, in a retirement speech at the end of the 1999 season, Wayne Gretsky – arguably the greatest hockey player ever – poignantly expressed how much he had loved to play, what fun he had had every day and how he would miss the play. All my informants agreed that bringing play – that is, fun – back into hockey was necessary, but none could see how it could happen unless 'the big guys' (meaning those who control the purse strings and shape the expectations and direction of the sport, such as league governors, managers, coaches and superstars) got involved. They finally have because hockey matters so much to Canadians – financially, to be sure, but spiritually as well, for hockey and its vitality are popularly linked to Canadian identity and the spirit (soul) of the nation.

Perhaps now the professional leagues will put money into the minor leagues to reform and democratize them, to re-educate players and coaches to reduce violence and reward them for doing so. This support might filter down to maintaining local rinks for pick-up street hockey thereby reviving and sustaining Shinny, the nurturer of skills and hockey in its essence as play. Among children, by children and for children it is possible, as indicated by the following account from Roy McGregor, in an explication of the significance of hockey in Canadian life:

> In winter I help flood the schoolyard down from our house. I do it with a man named Dave who shares my love of the game and still plays old-timer hockey. We *talk* hockey while we work . . . we can stand there and bitch happily about how kids don't play shinny any more the way we did when we were kids.
>
> Dave's son Danny and my son Gordie are both six and have started playing on this rink . . . And over the last two winters an older group of neighbourhood boys, the ones we'd given up on, have started coming out to play as well . . . First time out they asked me if I'd referee and I foolishly agreed. Then they spent ten minutes arguing about rules. Where would they have face-offs? How many 'steamboats' would they have to count for a penalty? I threw the puck down and walked home where, from a bedroom window, I was able to see that eventually they worked everything out. No face-offs, no penalties, and they played magnificently for three hours and went back the next afternoon.
>
> So don't tell me there's no hope for this game . . . Organized hockey may be out of control, greed may be too much in control – but when a game can still draw children to a raw outdoor rink in February there is reason to cheer.
>
> (Dryden and MacGregor 1989: 271)

A former NHL goalie who is now general manager of the Toronto Maple Leafs, Ken Dryden, summarizes the joy to be had from hockey when it is play:

It is like a kid's game, in a backyard or on a pond or playing field. There, kids learn to sort things out themselves, to decide their own rules; they learn to be fair. Introduce a referee, a judge, a higher authority, and everything changes . . . But with no referee you become your own referee, and 'getting away with it' ceases to be a game. And a game becomes play . . .

It is play we [old-timers] seek. I schedule other things around Monday nights and every Monday night I'm not here I resent whatever keeps me from it. I love the physicality, the feeling of moving . . . I feel powerful, even graceful, when I skate. I am amazed at how recklessly, excitingly fast I can go, able to feel my own crisp breeze, to bite loud, crunching ridges into the ice as I move.

(Dryden and MacGregor 1989: 260–1)

The highlighting of play and the rebirth of Shinny or any other hockey for fun can perhaps bring about support for other play venues through heightening awareness of the general need for free play. To make a significant difference to children's lives, though, average adults must reshape their agenda for childhood by withdrawing pressures on the young to grow up, thereby allowing them to grow. Adults owe children the opportunity to exercise their cultural rights *as children* and ought to be enabling their freedom and safety to pursue their own games and other traditions in their own manner. For, as the Knapps conclude, we may 'like to see children's folklore play a larger role in their lives, but there is nothing we can do directly to promote it. Its whole value lies in the fact that it is not ours to promote. It is our children's lore. All we can do is recognize its virtues and give children the time and freedom they need to make it flourish' (Knapp and Knapp 1976: 268).

Today, two of the contemporary cultural trends most threatening traditional play – commercialization of sport and adult control over children's free time – may actually be imploding and, in the process, generating new vitality in children's games. As the powers in organized hockey seek to fix what is wrong with Canada's game, they may in fact address to some extent what is wrong for Canada's children by encouraging free play. The message is translatable throughout our modern world – if there were more 'dreams in action', there would likely be greater hope among the young and, potentially, a spiritual revitalization that would enhance their well-being and empowerment. So armed through play to face life's challenges, more children just might experience greater joy in being alive.

Notes

1 Toronto Public School Board is one example. Kits containing the objects and instructions for such folk games as Jacks and Jump-rope are now widely marketed in North America, further evidence of the decline in their oral transmission among children.

2 As discussed in Caillois (1961: 162–3), Karl Groos (1898) distinguishes 'play as joy in Being from play as motive for culture' in *The Play of Animals*.
3 Behind Finland and New Zealand. According to Statistics Canada figures based on the 1991 census, suicides by young people aged 15–19 doubled to 13.5 per 100,000 between 1979 and 1991. For males in this age range the numbers rose from just over 5 per 100,000 in 1960 to just under 20 per 100,000 in 1990.
4 For the fourth consecutive year in 1998, based on the Human Development Index (HDI).
5 Summer camps might have been included as a fourth milieu but it is beyond the scope of this discussion to make accessible the nature and significance of this phenomenon of Canadian childhood, let alone to explicate the radical trans-formations in game-playing at camps during the period under consideration.
6 Figures available from Information Toronto indicate that the proportion is one in three in Canada's largest city which in 1996 comprised 2.4 million, or 8.3 per cent of all the country's people.
7 As indicated by Sutherland (1986), as well as by my fieldwork in the 1970s on multicultural playgrounds in Toronto, presented in two papers: 'Ethnic bound-ary maintenance among children in a multicultural setting' (American Folklore Society, October 1976) and 'Children and the mosaic: a study of children's games in a multicultural environment' (American Anthropological Association, November 1976), both unpublished owing to subsequent destruction of the data. The papers are on deposit in the Carpenter Collection of the Ontario Folklore-Folklife Archive in the Ontario Folklife Centre at York University, Toronto, Canada.
8 This material is also part of the Carpenter Collection cited above.
9 Statistics Canada data show that there are more frequent suicide attempts by young female Canadians, but more of the attempts by young males are fatal.
10 A member of the team virtually from its establishment, this informant served numerous years as a prominent academic administrator, yet each week had his secretary block out the practice time on Fridays as a 'special committee meeting', which he tried never to miss, as he said, 'No matter what'.

Conclusion: The importance of play for today

Julia C. Bishop and Mavis Curtis

The contributions to this book have been presented in response to adults' widely expressed concerns about the decline in the quality of free play in middle childhood. Each one has touched on aspects of the creativity, continuity and variety of childlore, in terms of forms of play, texts, performance, use of space, skills and interaction with a range of sources, including mass media, children of differing cultural backgrounds, and adults. They have included data on the way in which children view their play, what they say they do when playing, and first-hand observations of children at play, principally, but not exclusively in the setting of the primary school playground. The overwhelming impression from these contributions is that there is a great deal happening in school playgrounds around the world, much of which is vibrant, complex, enjoyable and positive for the children involved.

Each chapter is therefore, implicitly or explicitly, advocating the value of periods of self-directed play among children in today's world. In particular, several chapters warn of the threat to children's play through the intervention of adults and the imposition of adult notions of what children need and will benefit from. Thus, the contributors to this book suggest an approach which emphasizes children's ownership of their culture, the widespread vitality of this culture, and therefore the need for adults to be extremely cautious about intervening in it.

Blatchford has characterized this approach as the 'romantic view' of playground behaviour (1994: 17–19). This view is expressed par excellence in the work of the Opies in such statements as 'in the present day we assume children have lost the ability to entertain themselves, we become concerned, and are liable by our concern, to make what is not true a reality. In the long run nothing extinguishes self-organised play more effectively than does activity to promote it' (1969: 16; cf. Douglas 1931:

67, 85; Knapp and Knapp 1976: 268, quoted by Carpenter, Chapter 9, p. 178). Blatchford contrasts this approach with what he dubs the 'problem view' which stresses the existence of antisocial behaviour, such as bullying, violence and aggression, among children in the playground. Each approach leads to a different response to playground behaviour, non-intervention in the case of the 'romantic view' and various forms of intervention and supervision by adults in the case of the 'problem view'.

We question whether the term 'romantic view' is appropriate in this context, however, since it implies an idealized view of reality. Those who are classed as espousing this view have conducted detailed and extensive first-hand ethnographic studies of children's play pursuits, including not just what children say they do but close observation of what children actually do. The term 'romantic' suggests that they have overlooked or ignored the desultory or antisocial behaviour of children in their research. So often, though, they have found a flourishing play culture despite dire warnings to the contrary (see, for example, Knapp and Knapp 1976: xi; Brinton 1985: 1; Zumwalt 1995: 41; Opie and Opie 1997: 9–10; Arleo, personal communication, 2000). Roberts even began his work as a sceptic, admitting 'I expected to find that the Opies' sparkling account of middle childhood (in both its lore and outdoor play) would prove to be a considerable overstatement, if a proper cross-section of children were examined in a quantitative way. I was wrong' (1980: 140).

It is notable that the findings of these researchers do not ignore aspects of 'problem' behaviour among the children studied. Their work contains accounts of taunts, teasing, name-calling, cruel humour, and so on (for example, Browne 1954; Opie and Opie 1959; Fine 1981; Sluckin 1981; Boyes 1995). A number of contributors to this book document examples of conflict and tension in the playground (for example, Armitage, Chapter 2, Carpenter, Chapter 9). A recent study by Beresin, employing video recording methods, documents in detail outbreaks of aggression in an American school playground:

Consistently, at the end of the recess period, violent interactions were visible on the wide-angle screen. In glimpses from the micro footage, one can clearly see a definite rippling of anger, kicking, punching, and fighting during the transition back to the classroom. Typically within two minutes of the ringing of the bell, an almost palpable tension is trackable. In the macro footage alone, eight out of the nine sample tapes showed distinctly violent conflict in the lining up transition, with six out of the eight violent interactions occurring less than one minute before the bell, and the other two occurring within two minutes of the bell. In more than half of the micro footage, taken of a variety of games, there are incidences, indirectly captured, of real fighting or direct violence. And, in all of these images, with only one exception, the tension occurs within a minute and a half of the ringing of the bell.

(Beresin 1995: 89)

Beresin reports that many teachers at the school found it hard to accept the evidence of the video recordings of positive play from earlier in the playtime period, many having observed nothing but bad behaviour on the playground because they were only familiar with the time after the bell had gone when conflict arose (1995: 90).

There is, therefore, no denial of problematic behaviour in the playground, or of changes in playtime activities, among those of the 'romantic', 'non-interventionist' or 'positive' outlook. What these researchers share, it seems to us, is the exercising of a strong degree of caution in placing the blame for negative behaviour on children themselves. They also tend to reserve judgement on changes in activities as for the better or the worse until strenuous efforts have been made to understand how they relate to children's present lives. Similarly, they are reluctant to intervene in children's free play before its dynamics, its meaning from the children's point of view, and the often overlooked adult factors which affect it detrimentally are fully appreciated. In the words of Armitage, 'as adults our role should be to support [the ways in which children are already organizing their own play] and provide an environment that caters for what children actually play as opposed to what they should or could play, or even what we think they play' (see Chapter 2, p. 56). This applies not just to the physical environment, which is Armitage's main focus here, but also the time allowed for play and the 'emotional space' permitted to children for their own self-directed activities.

The contributors to this volume, aware of the debate concerning the decline in traditional play, present abundant evidence from around the world of the many positive, self-renewing and beneficial features of children's free play. They demonstrate not only the continued transmission of older traditional items but also the transmission of the relevant skills and abilities which enable the creation of new traditions and the updating of existing ones. McDowell (1995: 61) has pointed out that the robustness of children's folklore forces us

to confront the creative potential of every folkloric transaction, the capacity for new forms and items to emerge from traditional competencies. These creative factors are regenerative rather than degenerative, facilitating the continuous emergence of folkloric materials freshly coined in response to the experiences and needs of their hosts. It is this facet of folklore that lends the materials we study their authenticity and vitality, as trenchant markers of individual and community identity.

We suggest that the view of traditional games and play as being in decline is considerably overstated, that stability is observable in many areas of childlore, and that change and innovation are healthy, indeed essential, signs. What is striking about the contributions to this book is the richness and complexity of play activities at the turn of the century, despite the threats and problems relating to them. It is our contention that these activities, though not divorced from earlier play traditions, represent the reality of play for *today*. As Mary and Herbert Knapp observe, 'while children are remarkably conservative . . . they are also very flexible in adapting their lore to present concerns' (1976: 14). Webb also warns that posterity is not a factor in children's play: 'a game will flourish and spread only if it is fun *now*. Children have no sense of preserving a game because it is of historical interest' (1984: 12).

Thus, the research presented in this book suggests the need for adults concerned about children's play to develop a greater awareness of what is happening in contemporary children's play and how this relates to the children's world, especially as the children perceive this, and to update these understandings on a regular basis. Crucially, the evidence of this book suggests that adults can foster play by providing quality time, conducive space and low-key supervision for children's self-directed activities, during which children can satisfy their psychological and physical needs and develop their own social networks; social, cognitive and artistic skills; and imagination and creativity.

Bibliography

Alderson, P. (2000) Children as researchers: the effects of participation rights on research methodology, in A. James and P. Christensen (eds) *Research with Children: Perspectives and Practices.* London: Falmer Press.

Allin, J. and Wesker, A. (1974) *Say Goodbye: You May Never See Them Again.* London: Jonathan Cape.

Ariès, P. (1962) *Centuries of Childhood*, trans. Robert Baldick. Harmondsworth: Penguin (first published in French 1960).

Arleo, A. (1997) Counting-out and the search for universals. *Journal of American Folklore*, 110: 391–407.

Arleo, A. (1998) 'When Suzy was a baby': un tape-mains de la tradition orale enfantine. *Bulletin de la Société de Stylistique Anglaise*, 19: 81–103.

Arleo, A. (1999) On the phonology of nonsense syllables, in S. Ferré and S. Wauquaier-Gravelines (eds) *Actes des IIèmes journées d'études linguistiques: syllabes.* Nantes: Université de Nantes.

Arleo, A., Despringre, A-M., Fribourg, J., Olivier, E. and Panayi, P. (1997) *Chants enfantins d'Europe: systèmes poético-musicaux de jeux chantés (France, Espagne, Chypre, Italie).* Paris: L'Harmattan.

Avedon, E.M. and Sutton-Smith, B. (eds) (1971) *The Study of Games.* New York: John Wiley.

Avis, W.S., Crate, C., Drysdale, P. *et al.* (eds) (1967) *A Dictionary of Canadianisms on Historical Principles.* Toronto: W.J. Gage.

Bakhtin, M. (1968) *Rabelais and his World.* Cambridge, MA: MIT Press.

Barthes, R. (1970) Historical discourse, in M. Lane (ed.) *Structuralism: A Reader.* London: Cape.

Bascom, W.R. (1965) Four functions of folklore, in A. Dundes (ed.) *The Study of Folklore.* Englewood Cliffs, NJ: Prentice Hall.

Bateson, G. (1972) *Steps to an Ecology of Mind.* New York: Ballantine.

Bateson, P. and Martin, P. (1999) *A Design for Life.* London: Jonathan Cape.

Bauman, R. (1984) *Verbal Art as Performance.* Prospect Heights, IL: Waveland Press.

Ben-Amos, D. (1971) Toward a definition of folklore in context. *Journal of American Folklore*, 84: 3–15.

Ben-Amos, D. and Goldstein, K.S. (1975) *Folklore: Performance and Communication*. The Hague: Mouton.

Bennett, M. (1998) A tribute to William and Norah Montgomerie. Unpublished paper presented to The State of Play: Perspectives on Children's Oral Culture Conference, University of Sheffield, 14–17 April.

Beresin, A.R. (1995) Double dutch and double cameras: studying the transmission of culture in an urban school yard, in B. Sutton-Smith, J. Mechling, T.W. Johnson and F.R. McMahon (eds) *Children's Folklore: A Source Book*. New York: Garland.

Berger, J. (1972) *Ways of Seeing*. Harmondsworth: Penguin.

Blacking, J. (1985) Versus gradus ad parnassum musicum: exemplum Africanum, in *Becoming Human Through Music: The Wesleyan Symposium on the Perspectives of Social Anthropology in the Teaching and Learning of Music*. Reston, VA: Music Educators National Conference.

Blacking, J. (1995) *Venda Children's Songs: A Study in Ethnomusicological Analysis*. Chicago: University of Chicago Press.

Blatchford, P. (1989) *Playtime in the Primary School: Problems and Improvements*. Windsor: NFER-Nelson.

Blatchford, P. (1994) Research on children's school playground behaviour in the UK: a review, in P. Blatchford and S. Sharp (eds) *Breaktime and the School: Understanding and Changing Playground Behaviour*. London: Routledge.

Blatchford, P. (1998) *Social Life in School: Pupils' Experience of Breaktime and Recess from 7 to 16 Years*. London: Falmer Press.

Blatchford, P. and Sharp, S. (eds) (1994) *Breaktime and the School: Understanding and Changing Playground Behaviour*. London: Routledge.

Blatchford, P., Creeser, R. and Mooney, A. (1990) Playground games and playtime: the children's view. *Educational Research*, 32(3): 163–74.

Böhme, F.M. (ed.) (1897) *Deutsches Kinderlied und Kinderspiel*. Leipzig: Breitkopf & Härtel.

Bolton, H.C. (1888) *The Counting-Out Rhymes of Children*. London: E. Stock.

Boyes, G. (1990) Alice Bertha Gomme (1852–1938): a reassessment of the work of a folklorist. *Folklore*, 101: 198–208.

Boyes, G. (1995) The legacy of the work of Iona and Peter Opie: the lore and language of today's schoolchildren, in R. Beard (ed.) *Rhyme, Reading and Writing*. London: Hodder & Stoughton Educational.

Brewster, P.G. (1952) Children's games and rhymes, in *The Frank C. Brown Collection of North Carolina Folklore*, vol. 1. Durham, NC: Duke University Press.

Brewster, P.G. (1953) *American Non-Singing Games*. Norman, OK: University of Oklahoma Press.

Brinton, R. (1985) 'The southern French child at play: aspects of his traditional lore', unpublished PhD thesis, University of Bath.

Bronner, S.J. (1988) *American Children's Folklore*. Little Rock, AR: August House.

Browne, R.B. (1954) Children's taunts, teases, and disrespectful sayings from southern California. *Western Folklore*, 13: 190–8.

Bruckert, J. (1998) Regards croisés sur Fanny: aspects vocaux et musicaux, in A. Bustarret (ed.) 'Jeux de cour 25 comptines, tape-mains, rondes et jeux dansés: étude pluridisciplinaire d'une enquête vidéo', unpublished study deposited at Médiathèque Pédagogique de la Cité de la Musique, Paris.

Bruner, J.S., Jolly, A. and Sylva, K. (eds) (1976) *Play: Its Role in Development and Evolution.* Harmondsworth: Penguin.

Brunvand, J.H. (ed.) (1979) *Readings in American Folklore.* New York: Norton.

Buckland, T. (1993) Introduction, in T. Buckland and J. Wood (eds) *Aspects of British Calendar Customs.* Sheffield: Sheffield Academic Press.

Burton, A. (1978) Anthropology of the young. *Anthropology of Education Quarterly,* 9(1): 54–70.

Bustarret, A. (ed.) (1998) 'Jeux de cour 25 comptines, tape-mains, rondes et jeux dansés: étude pluridisciplinaire d'une enquête vidéo', unpublished study deposited at Médiathèque Pédagogique de la Cité de la Musique, Paris.

Bustarret, A. and Hurel, G. (1998) 'Regards croisés sur Fanny: apprentissage et remémoration dans les 7 réalisations', in A. Bustarret (ed.) 'Jeux de cour 25 comptines, tape-mains, rondes et jeux dansés: étude pluridisciplinaire d'une enquête vidéo', unpublished study deposited at Médiathèque Pédagogique de la Cité de la Musique, Paris.

Butt, B. and Small, L. (eds) (1993) *Folk Literature: Voices through Time.* St John's, Newfoundland: Breakwater.

Caillois, R. (1961) *Man, Play, and Games,* trans. Meyer Barash. New York: The Free Press of Glencoe (first published in French 1958).

Carey, S. (1985) *Conceptual Change in Childhood.* Cambridge, MA: MIT Press.

Carpenter, J.M. (1972) The James Madison Carpenter Collection, unpublished collection of traditional ballad and folksong, drama and children's games. Archive of Folk Culture, American Folklife Center, Library of Congress, AFC 1972/001.

Caspi, M. (1986) The personal component in playing interface, in G.C. Cupchik and J. Laszlo (eds) *Emerging Visions of the Aesthetic Process.* Cambridge: Cambridge University Press.

Chauvin, C. (1999) 'Comptines, formulettes et jeux enfantins dans les Alpes occidentales (région Rhône-Alpes, Suisse romande et Val d'Aoste): étude gestuelle, rythmique et verbale', unpublished PhD thesis, Université Stendhal, Grenoble.

Chukovsky, K. (1963) *From Two to Five,* translated and edited by Miriam Morton. Brisbane: Jacaranda Press (first published in Russian 1925).

Collins, J. (1991) *Migrant Hands in a Distant Land,* 2nd edn. Leichhardt, NSW: Pluto Press.

Cox, H. (1969) *The Feast of Fools: a Theological Essay on Festivity and Fantasy.* Cambridge, MA: Harvard University Press.

Craig, W.M. and Pepler, D.J. (1995) Peer processes in bullying and victimization: an observational study. *Exceptionality Education Canada,* 5(3–4): 81–95.

Craig, W.M. and Pepler, D.J. (1997) Observations of bullying and victimization in the school yard. *Canadian Journal of School Psychology,* 13(2): 41–60.

Craig, W.M. and Pepler, D.J. (1998) Observations of aggressive and nonaggressive children on the school playground. *Merrill-Palmer Quarterly,* 44(1): 55–76.

Cubberley, E.P. (1920) *Readings in the History of Education.* Boston, MA: Houghton Mifflin.

Curtis, M. (1998) 'Aspects of children's oral tradition in Keighley, West Yorkshire', unpublished PhD thesis, University of Sheffield.

Daley, V. (1898) [No title] *The Bulletin* (Sydney), 26 February; reprinted in I. Turner (1969) *Cinderella Dressed in Yella.* Melbourne: Heinemann.

Dargan, A. and Zeitlin, S. (1990) *City Play.* New Brunswick: Rutgers University Press.

Department for Education and Employment (1998) *The National Literacy Strategy: Framework for Teaching*. London: DfEE.

Department for Education and Employment/Qualifications and Curriculum Authority (1999) *The National Curriculum: Handbook for Primary Teachers in England, Key Stages 1 and 2*. London: DfEE/QCA.

Doekes, E. (1992) Music and movement in the children-streetculture (2). *De Pyramide*, 46(5): 94–8.

Dorson, R.M. (1968) *The British Folklorists: a History*. London: Routledge & Kegan Paul.

Douglas, N. (1931) *London Street Games*, 2nd edn. London: Chatto & Windus.

Dryden, K. and MacGregor, R. (1989) *Home Game: Hockey and Life in Canada*. Toronto: McClelland & Stewart.

Dundes, A. (1964) On game morphology: a study of the structure of non-verbal folklore. *New York Folklore Quarterly*, 20: 276–88.

Dundes, A. (ed.) (1965) *The Study of Folklore*. Englewood Cliffs, NJ: Prentice Hall.

Dundes, A. (1979) The devolutionary premise in folklore theory, in J.H. Brunvand (ed.) *Readings in American Folklore*. New York: Norton.

Eifermann, R.R. (1971) *Determinants of Children's Game Styles: on Free Play in a 'Disadvantaged' and in an 'Advantaged' School*. Jerusalem: The Israel Academy of Sciences and Humanities.

Einon, D. (1985) *Creative Play*. Melbourne: Penguin.

Eisen, G. (1988) *Children and Play in the Holocaust*. Amherst, MA: University of Massachusetts Press.

Elkind, D. (1988) *The Hurried Child: Growing Up Too Fast Too Soon*. Reading, MA: Addison-Wesley (first published c.1981).

Everitt, P. (1993) Exploring folk culture in the classroom. *Lore and Learning*, 1: 16–24.

Factor, J. (1983) *Far Out Brussel Sprout*. Melbourne: Oxford University Press.

Factor, J. (1988) *Captain Cook Chased a Chook: Children's Folklore in Australia*. Ringwood, Victoria: Penguin.

Factor, J. and Marshall, A. (1992) *Roll over Pavlova!* Rydalmere, NSW: Hodder & Stoughton.

Fine, G.A. (1981) Rude words: insults and narration in preadolescent obscene talk. *Maledicta*, 5: 51–68.

Fine, G.A. (1995). Methodological problems of collecting folklore from children, in B. Sutton-Smith, J. Mechling, T.W. Johnson and F.R. McMahon (eds) *Children's Folklore: A Source Book*. New York: Garland.

Finnegan, R. (1992) *Oral Traditions and the Verbal Arts: a Guide to Research Practices*. London: Routledge.

Flavell, J.H. (1975) *The Development of Role-taking and Communication Skills in Children*. Huntington, NY: Krieger.

Fowke, E. (ed.) (1969) *Sally Go Round the Sun: 300 Songs, Rhymes and Games of Canadian Children*. Toronto: McLelland & Stewart.

Fowke, E. (1988) *Red Rover, Red Rover: Children's Games Played in Canada*. Toronto: Doubleday Canada.

Garthwaite, T. (1976/77) Unpublished manuscript at the Archives of Cultural Tradition, ACT 98–545, National Centre for English Cultural Tradition, University of Sheffield.

Gilbert, M. (1981) *Jewish History Atlas*, 2nd edn. London: Weidenfeld & Nicolson.

Glass, R. (1993) There cannot be such a thing as a national curriculum without folklore. *Lore and Learning*, 1:12–16.

Goldstein, K.S. (1971a) On the application of the concepts of active and inactive traditions to the study of repertory. *Journal of American Folklore*, 84: 62–7.

Goldstein, K.S. (1971b) Strategy in counting out: an ethnographic folklore fieldwork study, in E.M. Avedon and B. Sutton-Smith (eds) *The Study of Games*. New York: John Wiley.

Gomme, A.B. (ed.) (1894) *Children's Singing Games*. London: David Nutt.

Gomme, A.B. ([1894, 1898] 1984) *The Traditional Games of England, Scotland, and Ireland*, vols 1 and 2. London: Thames & Hudson.

Goodwin, M.H. (1985) The serious side of jump rope: conversational practices and social organization in the frame of play. *Journal of American Folklore*, 98: 315–30.

Gougoulis, C. (1992) Portrayals of future identities in children's make-believe: the case of focean girls. Unpublished paper presented to the International Conference for Children's Play/The Association for the Study of Play, 'Play Prepares for the Future Conference', Paris.

Grider, S. (1980) A select bibliography of childlore. *Western Folklore*, 39: 248–65.

Grider, S. (1995) Who are the folklorists of childhood? in B. Sutton-Smith, J. Mechling, T.W. Johnson and F.R. McMahon (eds) *Children's Folklore: a Source Book*. New York: Garland.

Groos, K. (1898) *The Play of Animals*. New York: Appleton.

Grugeon, E. (1988) Children's oral culture: a transitional experience, in M. Maclure, T. Phillips and A. Wilkinson (eds) *Oracy Matters*. Milton Keynes: Open University Press.

Grugeon, E. (1993) Gender implications of children's playground culture, in P. Woods and M. Hammersley (eds) *Gender and Ethnicity in Schools*. Buckingham: Open University Press.

Grugeon, E. (1996) O-U-T spells out: children's play in the 1990s. *Lore and Learning*, 3: 10–12.

Grugeon, E. (1999) The state of play: children's oral culture, literacy and learning. *Reading*, 33(1): 13–16.

Grugeon, E. (2000) Girls' playground language and lore: what sort of texts are these?, in E. Bearne and V. Watson (eds) *Where Texts and Children Meet*. London: Routledge.

Grunfeld, F. (ed.) (1975) *Games of the World*. New York: Holt, Rinehart & Winston.

Gump, P.V. and Sutton-Smith, B. (1971) The 'it' role in children's games, in E.M. Avedon and B. Sutton-Smith (eds) *The Study of Games*. New York: John Wiley.

Hall, H. (1984) 'A study of the relationship between speech and song in the playground rhymes of primary school children', unpublished PhD thesis. Monash University.

Hall, H.S. (1993) Musical and poetic characteristics of children's folklore, in G.B. Davey and G. Seal (eds) *The Oxford Companion to Australian Folklore*. Melbourne: Oxford University Press.

Halpert, H. (1946) 'Folk rhymes of New York City children', unpublished MA thesis. Columbia University.

Halpert, H. (comp.), assisted by Halpert, V.M. (1971) 'Genre classification for individual student collections', unpublished typescript. Memorial University of Newfoundland, St John's, Newfoundland, Canada.

Halpert, H. (1982) Childlore bibliography: a supplement. *Western Folklore*, 41: 205–28.

Harlow, I. (1994) Transcription of 'Susie rhyme'. Recorded in Glencolumbkille, County Donegal, Ireland, in 1992. Letter, 6 May 1994.

Harter, J-L. (1998) Regards croisés sur Fanny: aspects ludiques, in A. Bustarret (ed.) 'Jeux de cour 25 comptines, tape-mains, rondes et jeux dansés: étude pluridisciplinaire d'une enquête vidéo', unpublished study deposited at Média-thèque Pédagogique de la Cité de la Musique, Paris.

Hartup, W.W. (1992) Friendships and their developmental significance, in H. McGurk (ed.) *Childhood Social Development: Contemporary Perspectives*. Hove: Lawrence Erlbaum.

Harwood, E.E. (1992) Girls' handclapping games: a study in oral transmission. *Bulletin of the International Kodály Society*, 17(1): 19–25.

Harwood, E.E. (1993a) Content and context in children's playground songs. *Update*, fall/winter: 4–8.

Harwood, E.E. (1993b) A study of apprenticeship learning in music. *General Music Today*, 6(3): 4–8.

Harwood, E.E. (1994) Miss Lucy meets Dr Pepper: mass media and children's traditional playground song and chant, in H. Lees (ed.) *Musical Connections: Tradition and Change*. Auckland, NZ: International Society for Music Education.

Heft, T. (1943) *Danske Saeder og Skikke [Danish Manners and Traditions]*. Copenhagen: Chr. Erichsens Forlag.

Hinkson, K.T. (1991) *Victorian Singing Games*. Library Publications, no. 9. London: Folklore Society (first published as a series of articles in 1896–7).

Holbrook, D. (1957) *Children's Games*. Bedford: Gordon Fraser.

Hone, W. (1825) *The Every-Day Book; or, The Guide to the Year*. London: W. Hone.

Houston, W. (1998) A game in crisis, *Globe and Mail* (Toronto), 4, 6–11, 13–17 April.

Howard, D. (1938) 'Folk jingles of American children', unpublished Ed.D thesis, New York University.

Howard, D. (1965) Folklore of Australian children. *Keystone Folklore Quarterly*, 10: 99–115.

Howard, D. (1971) Marble games of Australian children, in E.M. Avedon and B. Sutton-Smith (eds) *The Study of Games*. New York: John Wiley.

Hubbard, J.A. (1982) Children's traditional games from Birdsedge: clapping songs and their notation. *Folk Music Journal*, 4(3): 246–64.

Hughes, L.A. (1993) 'You have to do it with style': girls' games and girls' gaming, in T. Hollis, L. Pershing and M.J. Young (eds) *Feminist Theory and the Study of Folklore*. Urbana, IL: University of Illinois Press.

Huizinga, J. ([1938] 1950) *Homo Ludens: A Study of the Play-Element in Culture*. Boston, MA: Beacon.

Isenberg, J.P. and Jalongo, M.R. (1993) *Creative Expression and Play in the Early Childhood Curriculum*. New York: Merrill.

James, A. (1993) *Childhood Identities: Self and Social Relationships in the Experience of the Child*. Edinburgh: Edinburgh University Press.

James, A. and Prout, A. (1997) *Constructing and Reconstructing Childhood: Contemporary Issues in the Sociological Study of Childhood*, 2nd edn. London: Falmer Press.

James, A., Jenks, C. and Prout, A. (eds) (1998) *Theorizing Childhood*. Cambridge: Polity Press.

Jansen, W.H. (1965) The esoteric-exoteric factor in folklore, in A. Dundes (ed.) *The Study of Folklore*. Englewood Cliffs, NJ: Prentice Hall.

Johnson, D. (1998) All work and no play: should schools really skip recess? *International Herald Tribune*, 8 April.

Jones, B. and Hawes, B.L. (1987) *Step It Down: Games, Plays, Songs and Stories from the African-American Heritage*. Athens, GA: Brown Thrasher Books, University of Georgia Press (first published 1972).

Jones, T.V. (1986) 'Chwaraeon-gwerin plant Cymru, 1860–1980 [The folk games of children in Wales, 1860–1980]', unpublished MA thesis, University of Wales.

Jorgensen, M.G. (1980) An analysis of boy-girl relationships portrayed in contemporary jump rope and handclapping rhymes. *Southwest Folklore*, 4(3–4): 63–71.

Kellett, R. (n.d.) 'The heritage of the streets', unpublished manuscript deposited at the Vaughan Williams Memorial Library, Cecil Sharp House, London.

Kelsey, N.G.N. (1981) When they were young girls: a singing game through the century. *Folklore*, 92: 104–9.

Kirshenblatt-Gimblett, B. (ed.) (1976) *Speech Play: Research and Resources for Studying Linguistic Creativity*. Philadelphia, PA: University of Pennsylvania Press.

Kleiber, D. and Roberts, G. (1983) Games and sport involvement in later childhood. *Research Quarterly for Exercise and Sport*, 54(2): 200–3.

Knapp, M. and Knapp, H. (1976) *One Potato, Two Potato: the Folklore of American Children*. New York: W.W. Norton.

Kociumbas, J. (1997) *Australian Childhood: A History*. Sydney: Allen & Unwin.

Lakoff, G. (1987) *Women, Fire, and Dangerous Things: What Categories Reveal about the Mind*. Chicago: University of Chicago Press.

Landau, J.M. (1969) *The Arabs in Israel: a Political Study*. London: Oxford University Press.

Laslett, P. (1971) *The World We Have Lost*. London: Methuen (first published 1965).

Lecourt, E. (1998) Regards croisés sur Fanny: regard clinique, in A. Bustarret (ed.) 'Jeux de cour 25 comptines, tape-mains, rondes et jeux dansés: étude pluridisciplinaire d'une enquête vidéo', unpublished study deposited at Médiathèque Pédagogique de la Cité de la Musique, Paris.

Lévi-Strauss, C. (1966) *The Savage Mind*. Chicago: University of Chicago Press.

Lewis, D. (1978) *The Secret Language of Your Child: How Children Talk Before They Can Speak*. London: Souvenir Press.

Lichman, S. (1997) Knowing ourselves/knowing each other: traditional creativity in the multicultural school setting of Israel. *Lore and Language*, 15 [Special Issue comprising papers from the Folklore 150 Conference, University of Sheffield, July 1996]: forthcoming.

Lichman, S. and Sullivan, K. (2000) Harnessing folklore and traditional creativity to promote better understanding between Jewish and Arab children in Israel, in M. Leicester, S. Modgil and C. Modgil (eds) *Education and Culture and Values*: vol. 6, *Politics, Education, and Citizenship*. London: Falmer Press.

Lovett, E. (1901) The ancient and modern game of Astragals. *Folk-Lore*, 10(3): 280.

McCosh, S. (1976) *Children's Humour: a Joke for Every Occasion*. London: Granada.

McDowell, J.H. (1979) *Children's Riddling*. Bloomington, IN: Indiana University Press.

McDowell, J.H. (1995) The transmission of children's folklore, in B. Sutton-Smith, J. Mechling, T.W. Johnson and F.R. McMahon (eds) *Children's Folklore: A Source Book*. New York: Garland.

McGurk, H. (ed.) (1992) *Childhood Social Development: Contemporary Perspectives*. Hove: Lawrence Erlbaum.

McKinty, J. (1998) Transcription of 'When Suzy was a Baby', collected by Heather Russell at Debney Meadows Primary School, Melbourne, 1984. Email, 20 February.

Maclagan, R.C. (comp.) (1901) *The Games & Diversions of Argyleshire*. London: David Nutt (for the Folklore Society).

Manne, A. (1998) Sweet bird of youth, *The Age*, 31 January.

Marsh, K. (1997) 'Variation and transmission processes in children's singing games in an Australian playground', unpublished PhD thesis, University of Sydney.

Mechling, J. (1986) Children's folklore, in E. Oring (ed.) *Folk Groups and Folklore Genres: An Introduction*. Logan, UT: Utah State University Press.

Merrill-Mirsky, C. (1988) 'Eeny meeny pepsadeeny: ethnicity and gender in children's musical play', unpublished PhD dissertation, University of California, Los Angeles.

Millar, S. ([1968] 1975) *The Psychology of Play*. Harmondsworth: Penguin.

Minks, A. (1999) Growing and grooving to a steady beat: pop music in fifth grader's social lives. *Yearbook for Traditional Music*, 31: 77–101.

Montgomerie, N. and Montgomerie, W. (1985) *Scottish Nursery Rhymes*. Edinburgh: Chambers.

Moore, R.C. (1986) *Childhood's Domain: Play and Place in Child Development*. London: Croom Helm.

Neale, R.E. (1969) *In Praise of Play*. New York: Harper & Row.

Newell, W.W. ([1883] 1963) *Games and Songs of American Children*. New York: Dover.

Nicolaisen, W.F.H. (1995) A gleaner's vision. *Folklore*, 106: 71–6.

Nielsen, E.K. (1994) English translation of two Danish versions of a girls' singing game. Letter, 16 June.

Opie, I. (1993) *The People in the Playground*. Oxford: Oxford University Press.

Opie, I. and Opie, P. (1959) *The Lore and Language of Schoolchildren*. Oxford: Oxford University Press.

Opie, I. and Opie, P. (1969) *Children's Games in Street and Playground*. Oxford: Clarendon Press.

Opie, I. and Opie, P. (1980) Certain laws of folklore, in V.J. Newall (ed.) *Folklore Studies in the Twentieth Century*. Woodbridge: Boydell & Brewer.

Opie, I. and Opie, P. (1985) *The Singing Game*. Oxford: Oxford University Press.

Opie, I. and Opie, P. (1997) *Children's Games with Things*. Oxford: Oxford University Press.

Oring, E. (1986) On the concepts of folklore, in E. Oring (ed.) *Folk Groups and Folklore Genres: an Introduction*. Logan, UT: Utah State University Press.

Packard, V. (1983) *Our Endangered Children: Growing Up in a Changing World*. Cambridge: Cambridge University Press.

Palmer, P. (1986) *The Lively Audience: a Study of Children around the TV Set*. Sydney: Allen & Unwin.

Parrott, S. (1972) Games children play: ethnography of a second-grade recess, in J.P. Spradley and D.W. McCurdy (eds) *The Cultural Experience: Ethnography in Complex Society*. Chicago: Science Research Associates.

Parry-Jones, D. (1964) *Welsh Children's Games and Pastimes*. Denbigh: Gee.

Pellegrini, A.D. (1995) *School Recess and Playground Behaviour: Educational and Developmental Roles*. Albany, NY: State University of New York Press.

Pentikäinen, J. (1976) Repertoire analysis. *Studia Fennica*, 20: 262–72.

Pollock, L.A. (1983) *Forgotten Children: Parent–Child Relations from 1500–1900*. Cambridge: Cambridge University Press.

Postman, N. (1982) *The Disappearance of Childhood*. New York: Delacorte Press.

Riddell, C. (1990) 'Traditional singing games of elementary school children in Los Angeles', unpublished PhD dissertation, University of California, Los Angeles.

Ritchie, J.T.R. (1964) *The Singing Street*. Edinburgh: Oliver & Boyd.

Ritchie, J.T.R. (1965) *Golden City*. Edinburgh: Oliver & Boyd.

Roberts, A. (1980) *Out to Play: the Middle Years of Childhood*. Aberdeen: Aberdeen University Press.

Roberts, J.M. and Enerstvedt, Å. (1986) Categorisations of play activities by Norwegian children, in B. Mergen (ed.) *Cultural Dimensions of Play, Games and Sport* (Association for the Anthropological Study of Play Series, vol. 10). Champaign, IL: Human Kinetics Publishers.

Roberts, J.M. and Sutton-Smith, B. (1971) Child training and game involvement, in E.M. Avedon and B. Sutton-Smith (eds) *The Study of Games*. New York: John Wiley.

Roberts, K. (1982) *Bruegel*, 3rd edn. Oxford: Phaidon.

Robson, C. (1993) Folk arts in the National Curriculum. *Lore and Learning*, 1: 3–6.

Rodriguez, J.-C. (1980) Maman, on a tracé des jeux dans la cour de l'école! *Vers l'éducation nouvelle*, 346: 44–7.

Roemer, D.M. (1995) Riddles, in B. Sutton-Smith, J. Mechling, T.W. Johnson and F.R. McMahon (eds) *Children's Folklore: a Source Book*. New York: Garland.

Rogers, C.R. (1970) Towards a theory of creativity, in P.E. Vernon (ed.) *Creativity: Selected Readings*. Harmondsworth: Penguin.

Romet, C. (1980) The play rhymes of children: a cross-cultural ethnomusicological study, in *Children's Literature: More Than a Story*. Geelong: Deakin University Open Campus Program.

Roseman, M. (1995) Decolonising ethnomusicology: when peripheral voices move in from the margins. Keynote address presented at the University of Melbourne Faculty of Music Centennial Conference, Melbourne, 5–9 June.

Rosen, H.M. (1970) *The Arabs and Jews in Israel: the Reality, the Dilemma, the Promise*. New York: The American Jewish Press.

Roud, S. (1984) Random notes from an Andover playground. *Downs Miscellany*, 2(1): 21–32.

Royce, A.P. (1980) *The Anthropology of Dance*. Bloomington, IN: Indiana University Press.

Rubin, D.C. (1995) *Memory in Oral Traditions: the Cognitive Psychology of Epic, Ballads, and Counting-out Rhymes*. Oxford: Oxford University Press.

Rusk, R.R. (1962) *The Doctrines of the Great Educators*. London: Macmillan.

Russell, H. (1984) Unpublished field notes. Children's Folklore Collection, University of Melbourne Archives.

Russell, H. (1986) *Play and Friendships in a Multi-cultural Playground*. Melbourne: Australian Children's Folklore Publications.

Russell, H. (1990) *Toodaloo Kangaroo*. Sydney: Hodder & Stoughton.

Sanches, M. and Kirshenblatt-Gimblett, B. (1976) Children's traditional speech play and child language, in B. Kirshenblatt-Gimblett (ed.) *Speech Play: Research and Resources for Studying Linguistic Creativity*. Philadelphia, PA: University of Pennsylvania Press.

Sarbin, T.R. (1954) Role theory, in G. Lindzey (ed.) *Handbook of Social Psychology*, vol. 1. Cambridge, MA: Addison-Wesley.

Schafer, R.M. (1970) *When Words Sing*. Toronto: Clark and Cruikshank.

Schulz, B. (1989) Tailors' dummies, in *The Complete Fiction of Bruno Schulz*, trans. C. Wieniewska. New York: Walker (first published in Polish, 1934).

Schwartzman, H.B. (1978) *Transformations: the Anthropology of Children's Play*. New York: Plenum Press.

Seabourne, M. (1971) *The English School: Its Architecture and Organisation 1370–1870*. London: Routledge.

Simpson, J. (1982) Obituary: Peter Mason Opie, M.A. (1918–1982). *Folklore*, 93: 223.

Slaby, A. and Garfinkel, L.F. (1994) *No One Saw My Pain: Why Teenagers Kill Themselves*. New York: Norton.

Sluckin, A. (1981) *Growing Up in the Playground: the Social Development of Children*. London: Routledge & Kegan Paul.

Smilansky, S. (1968) *The Effects of Socio-Dramatic Play on Disdvantaged Pre-School Children*. New York: John Wiley.

Smith, G. (1981) Social bases of tradition: the limitations and implications of 'The seach for origins', in A.E. Green and J.D.A. Widdowson (eds) *Language, Culture and Tradition*. Leeds: Institute of Dialect and Folklife Studies; Sheffield: Centre for English Cultural Tradition and Language.

Smith, P.K. (1994) What children learn from playtime, and what adults can learn from it, in P. Blatchford and S. Sharp (eds) *Breaktime and the School: Understanding and Changing Playground Behaviour*. London: Routledge.

Snow, C.E. (1976) The language of the mother–child relationship, in S. Rogers (ed.) *They Don't Speak Our Language*. London: Edward Arnold.

Somerville, J. (1982) *The Rise and Fall of Childhood*. Beverly Hills, CA: Sage.

Stevenson, R.L. (1882) A gossip on romance. *Longman's Magazine*, 1(1).

Stewart, S. (1979) *Nonsense: Aspects of Intertextuality in Folklore and Literature*. Baltimore, MD: Johns Hopkins University Press.

Stone, L.J. and Church, J. (1957) *Childhood and Adolescence: A Psychology of the Growing Process*. New York: Random House.

Strutt, J. (1830) *The Sports and Pastimes of the People of England*. London: Reeves (first published 1801).

Stutz, E. (1996) Is electronic entertainment hindering children's play and social development?, in T. Gill (ed.) *Electronic Children: How Children Are Responding to the Information Revolution*. London: National Children's Bureau.

Sutherland, N. (1986) 'Everyone seemed happy in those days': the culture of childhood in Vancouver between the 1920s and the 1960s. *History of Education Review*, 15(2): 37–51.

Sutton-Smith, B. (1970) Psychology of childlore: the triviality barrier. *Western Folklore*, 29: 1–8.

Sutton-Smith, B. (1972) *The Folkgames of Children*. Austin, TX: University of Texas Press for the American Folklore Society.

Sutton-Smith, B. (ed.) (1976) *A Children's Games Anthology: Studies in Folklore and Anthropology*. New York: Arno.

Sutton-Smith, B. (1981a) *The Folkstories of Children*. Philadelphia, PA: University of Pennsylvania Press.

Sutton-Smith, B. (1981b) *A History of Children's Play: the New Zealand Playground 1840–1950*. Philadelphia, PA: University of Pennsylvania Press.

Sutton-Smith, B. (1986) *Toys as Culture*. New York: Gardner Press.

Sutton-Smith, B. (1990) School playground as festival. *Children's Environments Quarterly*, 7(2): 3–7.

Sutton-Smith, B., Mechling, J., Johnson, T.W. and McMahon, F.R. (eds) (1995) *Children's Folklore: A Source Book*. New York: Garland.

Thoms, W. [Merton, A.] (1846) Letter, *The Athenaeum*, 982, 12 August: 862–3. (Reprinted in A. Dundes (ed.) *The Study of Folklore*. Englewood Cliffs, NJ: Prentice Hall.)

Thomson, D. (1983) *Children of the Wilderness*. Melbourne: Currey O'Neil.

Thorne, B. (1993) *Gender Play: Girls and Boys in School*. New Brunswick, NJ: Rutgers University Press.

Tobin, B. (1982) *Eenie-Meenie-Des-O-Leenie: the Folklore of the Children of Alps Road Elementary School*. Perth: Western Australian Institute of Technology.

Toelken, B. (1979) *The Dynamics of Folklore*. Boston, MA: Houghton Mifflin.

Tolkien, J.R.R. ([1947] 1975) On fairy-stories, in *Tree and Leaf*. London: Allen & Unwin.

Tucker, N. (1977) *What is a Child?* London: Open Books.

Turner, I. (1969) *Cinderella Dressed in Yella*. Melbourne: Heinemann.

Turner, I., Factor, J. and Lowenstein, W. (1982) (eds) *Cinderella Dressed in Yella*, 2nd edn. Melbourne: Heinemann.

Turner V. (1974) Liminal to liminoid in play, flow and ritual. *Rice University Studies*, 60(3): 53–92.

Turner V. (1977) *The Ritual Process*. Ithaca, NY: Cornell University Press.

Valéry, P. (1958) *The Art of Poetry*, trans. D. Folliot. London: Routledge & Kegan Paul.

Van Peer, W. (1988) Counting out: form and function of children's counting-out rhymes, in M. MacLure, T. Phillips and A. Wilkinson (eds) *Oracy Matters*. Milton Keynes: Open University Press.

Vann, R.T. (1982) The youth of centuries of childhood. *History and Theory*, 21(2): 281–3.

Virtanen, L. (1978) Children's lore. *Studia Fennica*, 22. Helsinki: Suomalisen Kirjallisuuden Seura.

Ward, C. (1990) *The Child in the City*. London: Bedford Square Press.

Webb, D. (1984) Introduction, in A.B. Gomme (ed.) *The Traditional Games of England, Scotland, and Ireland*. London: Thames & Hudson.

Wein, Elizabeth E. (1999) The discipline of play: is there a future for children's lore in academia? *Children's Folklore Review*, 21(2): 5–16.

Widdowson, J.D.A. (1976) The language of the child culture: pattern and tradition in language acquisition and socialisation, in S. Rogers (ed.) *They Don't Speak Our Language*. London: Edward Arnold.

Widdowson, J.D.A. (1979) The linguistic skills of a five-year old: a case study. *First Language*, 2: 151–7.

Widdowson, J.D.A. (1987) English dialects and folklore: a neglected heritage. *Folklore*, 98: 41–52.

Widdowson, J.D.A. (1990) English language and folklore: a national resource. *Folklore*, 101: 209–20.

Widdowson, J.D.A. (1993) Pre-school and peer group traditions in the classroom. *Lore and Learning*, 1: 6–12.

Williams, R. (1983) *Keywords: A Vocabulary of Culture and Society*. London: Fontana.

Winn, M. (1983) *Children without Childhood*. New York: Pantheon Books.

Winnicott, D.W. (1971) *Playing and Reality*. Harmondsworth: Penguin.

Wolfenstein, M. (1954) *Children's Humor: a Psychological Analysis*. Glencoe, IL: The Free Press.

Zumwalt, R. (1976) Plain and fancy: a content analysis of children's jokes dealing with adult sexuality. *Western Folklore*, 35: 258–67.

Zumwalt, R.L. (1995) The complexity of children's folklore, in B. Sutton-Smith, J. Mechling, T.W. Johnson and F.R. McMahon (eds) *Children's Folklore: a Source Book*. New York: Garland.

Audio-visual references

Arleo, A. (1985) Two audio recordings of 'Quand Fanny était un bébé' and 'Quand Delphine était un bébé', Saint-Nazaire, France.

Bustarret, A. (ed.) and Association 'Chants et gestes' (1998) Video recording of five versions of 'Quand Fanny était un bébé', recorded in Créteil, Chatillon sur Seiche, Rennes, Bains de Bretagne and Saint-Remèze, France, in 1991–2. Deposited at Médiathèque pédagogique de la Cité de la Musique, Paris.

Fribourg, J. (1991) Video recording of 'Nos hemos conocido', with transcription in Spanish and French translation, recorded in Madrid in June 1991.

Hawes, B.L. (1969) *Pizza Pizza Daddy-O*. Film and video. University of California Extension Media Center.

Panayi-Tulliez, P. (*c*.1992) Video recording of 'Aliki Vujuklaki', with transcription in Greek and French translation, recorded at Tersefanou school, Cyprus.

Webb, D. (1983) *Children's Singing Games*, 12-inch LP, Saydisc Records, SDL 338.

Games and rhymes index

This index covers the titles of games and first lines of rhymes. For generic names, such as singing games, see main index.

Index

JUST PLAYING?
THE ROLE AND STATUS OF PLAY IN EARLY CHILDHOOD EDUCATION

Janet R. Moyles

Play is a means by which humans and animals explore and learn from a variety of experiences in different situations for diverse purposes. Yet how far is play truly valued by those involved with the education and care of young children? How often is play and choosing play materials reserved as an activity for when children have finished 'work', thus reducing both its impact and its effect on the child's development?

Just Playing explores why we should encourage, promote, value and initiate play in our classrooms, and why teachers should be part of it. Janet Moyles draws on research findings from several countries which provide further evidence for establishing the value of play. She focuses on children between 4 and 8, examining the principles of play in early childhood education, and indicates how these principles can be put into practice. She provides a full justification for including play in the early years curriculum and encourages teachers, through examples of children at play, to review their own thinking on the issues in the light of core curriculum pressures.

This is essential reading for trainee and practising nursery and primary teachers, and nursery nurses; and for all those concerned with the education and development of young children.

Contents
Part 1 – Unravelling the 'mystery' of play? – Play and learning – Part 2 – Play through and with language – Solving problems through play – Play and creativity – Part 3 – Play, curriculum and organization – Play and progress: observing, recording and assessing the value of play – Play and the 'different' child – Play and adult expectations – Play in childhood and adulthood – References – Index.

208pp   0 335 09564 X (Paperback)

THE EXCELLENCE OF PLAY

Janet R. Moyles (ed.)

Child: When I play with my friends we have lots of fun... do lots of things... think about stuff... and... well...
Adult: Do you think you learn anything?
Child: Heaps and heaps – not like about sums and books and things ... um... like... well... like *real* things.

Anyone who has observed play for any length of time will recognize that, for young children, play is a tool for learning. Professionals who understand, acknowledge, and appreciate this can, through provision, interaction and intervention in children's play, ensure progression, differentiation and relevance in the curriculum.

The Excellence of Play gathers together authoritative contributors to provide a wide-ranging and key source text reflecting both up-to-date research and current classroom practice. It tackles how we conceptualize play, how we 'place' it in the classroom, how we relate it to the curriculum, and how we evaluate its role in learning in the early years. It will stimulate and inform debate through its powerful argument that 'a curriculum which sanctions and utilizes play is more likely to provide well-balanced citizens of the future as well as happier children in the present'.

Contents

Introduction – Part 1: The culture of play and childhood – Play and the uses of play – Play in different cultures and different childhoods – Sex-differentiated play experiences and children's choices – Play, the playground and the culture of childhood – Part 2: Play, schooling and responsibilites – Play and legislated curriculum. Back to basics: an alternative view – 'Play is ace!' Developing play in schools and classrooms – Fantasy play: a case for adult intervention – Making play work in the classroom – Part 3: Play and the early years curriculum – Play, literacy and the role of the teacher – Experiential learning in play and art – Bulbs, buzzers and batteries: play and science – Mathematics and play – Part 4: Assessing and evaluating play – Evaluating and improving the quality of play – Observing play in early childhood – Play, the universe and everything! – Afterword – References – Index.

Contributors

Lesley Abbott, Angela Anning, Tony Bertram, David Brown, Tina Bruce, Audrey Curtis, Rose Griffiths, Nigel Hall, Peter Heaslip, Jane Hislam, Victoria Hurst, Neil Kitson, Janet R. Moyles, Christine Pascal, Roy Prentice, Jeni Riley, Jane Savage, Peter K. Smith.

240pp   0 335 19068 5 (Paperback)

TEACHING THROUGH PLAY
TEACHERS' THINKING AND CLASSROOM PRACTICE

Neville Bennett, Liz Wood and Sue Rogers

This book is based on the findings of a research project into Reception Teachers' Theories of Play funded by the Economic & Social Research Council. There is strong ideological and theoretical support for a play-based curriculum in the early years. But evidence suggests that teachers find this difficult to translate into practice. The educational potential of play is not realized.

This study focuses on nine reception class teachers, ranging from novices to experts, in order to discover their theories of play and how these relate to classroom practice. The data reveal new insights into how they strive to incorporate play into the curriculum in contrasting ways and the constraints they encounter in this process.

There is a need to improve the quality of teaching and learning through play. *Teaching Through Play* makes a valuable contribution to this process.

Contents
Play: rhetoric and reality – Teacher thought and action: theory and method – Teachers' theories of play – Theory into practice – Changing theories and practice – Teaching through play: retrospect and prospect – Appendices: Teacher biographies – Interview schedule – Concept map of key ideas – Jennie's interpretations of learning through play – References – Index.

160pp   0 335 19732 9 (Paperback)   0 335 19733 7 (Hardback)